Reparations and Reparatory Justice

Reparations and Reparatory Justice

Past, Present, and Future

Edited by

SUNDIATA KEITA CHA-JUA,

MARY FRANCES BERRY,

AND V. P. FRANKLIN

UNIVERSITY OF ILLINOIS PRESS

Urbana, Chicago, and Springfield

Library of Congress Cataloging-in-Publication Data
Names: Cha-Jua, Sundiata Keita, 1953- editor. | Berry, Mary
    Frances, editor. | Franklin, V. P. (Vincent P.), 1947- editor.
Title: Reparations and reparatory justice : past, present, and
    future / edited by Sundiata Keita Cha-Jua, Mary Frances
    Berry, and V.P. Franklin.
Description: Urbana : University of Illinois Press, [2024] |
    Collection of essays by Danny Glover and 19 others. | Includes
    bibliographical references and index.
Identifiers: LCCN 2023045677 (print) | LCCN 2023045678
    (ebook) | ISBN 9780252045776 (hardcover) | ISBN
    9780252087875 (paperback) | ISBN 9780252056642 (ebook)
Subjects: LCSH: African Americans--Reparations. | African
    Americans--Politics and government. | African Americans-
    -Social conditions. | Reparations for historical injustices. |
    United States--Race relations--History.
Classification: LCC E185.89.R45 R44 2024 (print) | LCC E185.89.
    R45 (ebook) | DDC 323.1196/073--dc23/eng/20231012
LC record available at https://lccn.loc.gov/2023045677
LC ebook record available at https://lccn.loc.gov/2023045678

Contents

Introduction

The topic of reparations for enslavement is not a new subject of advocacy, analysis, debate, or social movement activism. Some scholars, including A. J. Davis, who compiled, "An Historical Timeline of Reparations Payments Made from 1783 through 2020 by the United States Government, States, Cities, Religious Institutions, Colleges and Universities, and Corporations," which follows this introduction, trace reparations demands back to Belinda Sutton who petitioned the Massachusetts General Court in 1783 for a pension for herself and her daughter from the estate of Isaac Royall, her deceased former owner. "Fifty years her faithful hands have been compelled to ignoble servitude of Isaac Royall," Sutton declared, but was "denied the enjoyment of not a morsel of the immense wealth, apart whereof hath been accumulated by her own industry and the whole augment by her servitude." Sutton had to petition the legislature a total of five times before she was awarded even a minimal annual payment, which she only received for one year.[1]

Scholars have unearthed similar petitions and requests for reparations in other parts of North America, South America, and the Caribbean.[2] Yet, when Great Britain abolished slavery in its colonial territories in 1834, for example, it was not the newly emancipated workers who were compensated for their years of unpaid labor. It was the slaveholders who received payment from the British Parliament—£20 million or a 2010 equivalent of $40 billion—for the loss of their human "property." In *Britain's Black Debt: Reparations for Slavery and Native Genocide*, historian Hilary McD. Beckles called it the "final pillage . . . the last grains from the slave-endowed public granary."[3]

It was the same for enslaved workers in the United States following the outbreak of the Civil War. As formerly enslaved people began to make their way into Union areas—Delaware, Maryland, and Washington, DC—President Abraham Lincoln encouraged emancipation legislation and Delaware passed such a bill at the end of 1861. In Washington, DC, however, slaveholders balked when the District of Columbia Emancipation Act was proposed in 1862. They exerted their influence over congressional leaders to include a stipulation that slaveholders would receive compensation for the loss of property to the tune of up to $300 for each emancipated worker. At least one thousand slave owners received payments for three thousand enslaved workers who had been emancipated, but who received no reparations themselves. Under a law passed in 1864, slaveholders in the border states could receive up to $300 compensation for the enslaved people who enlisted in the military, and up to $100 for those who were drafted.[4]

The demand for reparations emerged during enslavement and has recurred in every generation since. However, the reparations movement's roots are located primarily in the philosophy and practices of the newly freed people. And secondarily in the articulations and actions of radical Republican military officers, congressmen, and some Freedmen Bureau agents who encouraged the freedpeople's belief that the "yank government" would confiscate and redistribute the rebels' land to them. In *Black Reconstruction*, Du Bois argued, "Again and again, crudely, but logically, the Negroes expressed their right to the land and the deep importance of that right."[5] The ideas of Bayley Wyatt, a freedman from Yorktown, Virginia, and the social praxis of the Rev. Tunis Campbell, a New Jersey–born Freedmen's Bureau agent, provide evidence for Du Bois's interpretation. Campbell, who governed Ossabaw, Delaware, Colonels, St. Catherine's, and Sapelo islands, illustrates the freedpeople's desire for compensation in land. Campbell divided the land into forty-acre family plots among the freedpeople, established an autonomous government, launched schools, and created a three hundred–man militia to protect the freedpeople from the Ku Klux Klan and other white terrorist groups. Wyatt contended the freedpeople had "*a divine right to the land*" because of the super exploitation of their labor and the physical abuse and mental trauma they endured under the slavery regime. Wyatt was especially adept at connecting enslaved African Americans' cash crop production to the international marketing of those commodities in northern cities such as New York. He correctly claimed Black folk's labor built the South and the North.[6]

In the last few years, support for reparations for labor super exploitation, convict leasing, racial pogroms, and resulting land and property confiscation, lynching, apartheid residential zoning laws, redlining in housing and insurance policies, and police brutalization and killing leveled against African Americans in the United States as well as for enslavement has become a powerful global storm shaking the foundations of Western governments, locally, nationally, and internationally. On October 14, 2013, Caribbean nations sued eleven European nations, among them Britain, France, and Holland, for "the awful lingering effects of the Atlantic Slave Trade."[7] Building on Walter Rodney's thesis of economic underdevelopment, Caribbean Reparations Commission (CARICOM) posits, "France, the Netherlands, Britain all massively benefited through the course of this time. It was built on the backs of the slavery trade."[8] In March of 2014, the presidents of fifteen Caribbean nations endorsed the CARICOM's "Ten Point Program for reparatory justice for indigenous genocide and the enslavement of African and Afro-Caribbean people.[9]

Meanwhile the winds of change blowing in the United States reached the Democratic presidential primary season by 2019. Pushed by the increasingly forceful gusts of the reparations movement, many Democratic presidential candidates—Senators Kamala Harris, Elizabeth Warren, Cory Booker, former Secretary of Housing and Urban Development Julian Castro, among others—advocated for H.R. 40, calling for the formation of a commission to study and make recommendations for the implementation of some type of reparations program for African Americans.[10] By the end of the primary season, that strong breeze compelled the party's nominee, Joseph R. Biden, to shift his position. Previously, Biden had stated, "I don't feel responsible for the sins of my father and grandfather . . . I'll be damned if I feel responsible to pay for what happened 300 years ago." As the nominee, he claimed, if Congress passed a bill calling for the formation of a commission to study and make recommendations for the implementation of some type of reparations program for African Americans, he would sign it.[11] On April 14, 2021, the Judiciary Committee of the U.S. House voted to send HR 40 to the full House.[12]

Mid-July 2020 represented the turning point in the struggle for African American reparations. A series of events made the Judiciary Committee's vote possible. On July 16, California passed Assembly Bill 3121 establishing a "Task Force to Study and Develop Reparation Proposals for African Americans."[13] The Task Force issued its final report on June 1, 2023.

The commissioners found that though California entered the union as a free state in 1850, its early governments supported the "peculiar institution." They found proslavery sentiment was so high in the new state that in 1852 it passed a more stringent fugitive slave act than the one included in the 1850 Compromise, which admitted California into statehood. Indeed, the commission discovered that California mirrored national patterns in racial terrorism, political disfranchisement, residential apartheid, separate and unequal education, and racially discriminatory structural arrangements and institutional policies. To implement its far-reaching recommendations, the

Task Force proposed that California create a cabinet-level agency, the African American Freedmen Affairs Agency and recommended compensation for those victimized by housing, education, and employment discrimination facilitated by the state government.[14]

By July of 2020, nearly a score of U.S. cities in fifteen states had passed pro-reparations resolutions. The three most recent, Evanston, Illinois, Ashville, North Carolina, and Providence, Rhode Island, offer models for a federal process and policy. All three municipalities propose a tripartite process: (1) a search for the Truth, collecting data on the role of the city government (and other institutions) in imposing, perpetuating, and profiting from racial oppression; (2) creation of a Reconciliation process, the education of the public about the municipality's role in generating and maintaining racial disparities; and (3) Reparations, the creation of a commission that would recommend specific remedial programs and allocation of resources to repair the damage done to the African American and Indigenous nations. All three municipalities provide for African American community participation in the decision-making process, though unfortunately largely through appointed committees advisory to the city councils. The documentary film, *The Big Payback* (2023), traces the development of the "Reparations Program" established by the Evanston city council in 2019 through the leadership of Councilwomen Robin Rue Simmons. It profiles Simmons and city officials and community partners who acknowledged that housing discrimination before 1969, as well as those Black residents who received compensation, set at the paltry amount of $25,000, from the reparations program.

The most exciting element in the municipal reparations process is a proposal for mass democratic participation by Cook County Circuit Court Judge Lionel Jean Batiste, a commissioner on the National African American Reparations Commission. A former Evanston Council member, Batiste proposed a Black community–led "Reparations Stakeholder Authority." This body would likely consist of local "historically significant" African American institutions and organizations. While the emphasis on historically significant could pose some limitations, such as excluding newly formed groups and younger activists engaged in the George Floyd protests, it also ensures the participation of anchor African American institutions and organizations that have fought for freedom, justice, and equality, self-determination, or social transformation for decades.[15]

This book contributes to the continuing examination of the international Black Reparations movement. It chronicles the historical development of the movement for reparations for African people, locally, nationally, and globally. *Reparations and Reparatory Justice* locates the contemporary struggle for African American reparations in the sociohistorical context of the global African demand for reparations, particularly the Caribbean nation-states, CARICOM, and the "2001 Durban I World Conference against Racism, Racial Discrimination, Xenophobia, and Related Intolerance," held in Durban, South Africa, in September 2001. Thus, this volume is sensitive to and supportive of the reparations demands by people of African descent on the African continent and throughout the African Diaspora in the Caribbean; North, Central, and South America; Europe; Australia; and the islands of the sea; as well as of a wide array of U.S. ethnicities/nationalities and racial and social groups. Moreover, we find no contradiction in demanding reparations from the United States government, capitalist enterprises, and social institutions, including religious and educational, for historic and ongoing oppression, dispossession, discrimination, criminalization, brutalization, and genocide.

Black reparations demands have inspired many social and political activists to organize to repair past and on-going damage by governments and national and multinational corporations. The demand is being made for "climate reparations" from the petrochemical industry and other businesses exploiting and despoiling the natural environment for inordinate profit. In the name of reparatory justice, the case for "gay reparations" has been made, and there are activists organizing and calling for "healthcare reparations" for American citizens living without access to proper ongoing healthcare.[16]

We present speeches, essays, and research articles on grassroots, national, and international approaches, and policies for the development of reparations plans and programs. Our contributors fill huge gaps in the current discussions of reparations for slavery, legal racial discrimination during the nearly one hundred years of segregation/apartheid, and contemporary structural racism, which constitute the foundations of the extreme disparities in wealth and income and quality of life that currently exist between Black and non-Black individuals, families, and households in the United States.

Reparations and Reparatory Justice traces the history of the African American reparation's movement from the period of enslavement into Donald Trump's anti-Black fascistic presidential regime. Several essays supply a primer in the history of the African American reparations movement and an introduction to the philosophical, political, economic, legal, and ethical issues surrounding the question of Black reparations. The contributors to this volume provide background information on reparations organizations, campaigns, and past movements inside and outside the United States. Historian and legal scholar Mary Frances Berry illuminates the largely unknown case of Callie House and the Ex-Slave Mutual Relief Bounty and Pension Association's (ESMRBPA) suit against the United States Treasury Department.

House and the ESMRBPA sued to have the $68,073,388.99 cotton taxes confiscated by the Union between 1862 and 1868 distributed among the aged former slaves.[17] Another contributor, political scientist Charles Henry, takes a personal approach. Henry challenges the limitations of traditional African American reparations narratives by expanding the class of people eligible for reparations to include descendants of Blacks born beyond slavery's shadow. Grounding his argument on the experiences of his ancestors, Henry argues the descendants of "quasi-free Blacks," like the progeny of the freedpeople, should be afforded reparations.[18]

Reparations and Reparatory Justice posits "reparatory justice" as a composite of processes and policies that seeks to repair the harm done to Black folk, as a people. We contend reparations must consist of American governmental units—federal, state, and municipal—corporations and other U.S. institutions such as colleges and universities apologizing and atoning for the exploitation and oppression of the African American people, other colonized ethnicities/nationalities, and other oppressed social groups. We insist these entities accept responsibility for causing and benefitting from the suffering of Black folk and work in consultation with African American selected self-determined apparatuses to initiate remedies that rehabilitate, compensate, and commemorate African Americans and other historically victimized groups.[19]

Specifically, our contributors call for the restoration of Black people's human and civil rights and material and psychological well-being. Chuck Collins, Dedrick Asante-Muhammad, and V. P. Franklin advocate for specific compensatory programs, although the idea is central to all our commentators. Collins and Asante-Muhammad promote material programs such as direct cash payments, first-time home buyers' programs, and tuition-free higher education, while Franklin conceives of the "Reparations Superfund" as a means to eliminate student loan debt and issues in the field of education. Whereas much emphasis has been put on the need to remove Confederate and other racist memorials, several of our authors call for novel ways to commemorate the African American sociohistorical experience, including endowments for cultural institutions and the reconstruction of public-school instruction to infuse knowledge about the Black experience into the curricula.

This project advances new and innovative interpretations that push us to rethink the extent and complexity of the effects of enslavement, post-slavery labor super exploitation, apartheid social relations, economic discrimination, police and white vigilante brutalization and murder, somatic and cultural degradation, and denial of their resulting psychological traumas. One contributor, economist James Stewart, expands the discussion of reparations by tracing the connection between "nutritional deprivation" during enslavement and "inheritable diseases or conditions that are implicated in contemporary racial morbidity and mortality differences."[20] In much the same way economists and historians have connected contemporary African American impoverishment and economic inequality, and low homeownership rates in particular to historic racial oppression, by which we mean—labor super exploitation, economic discrimination, in consumption and taxation, racial pogroms, and ethnic cleansing—Stewart links health disparities to slave-era malnourishment. Another contributor, Brian Jones wades into the race v. class debate over reparations between Ta-Nehisi Coates and Senator Bernie Sanders via political scientist Cedric Johnson.[21] Jones challenges the narrow traditional socialist opposition to African American reparations as reflected in Sanders's initial rejection of the idea in favor of a universal redistribution program. Moreover, like this book's editors, Jones supports reparations to Indigenous nations, the descendants of Mexicano/as incorporated into the United States through the Treaty of Guadalupe Hidalgo, Chinese and European immigrant workers, and other oppressed social groups in the United States (see V. P. Franklin, "Reparatory Justice Campaigns in the Twenty-First Century" in this volume). This both/and approach toward reparations and universal redistributive programs recovers Dr. Martin Luther King Jr.'s joint strategy (see Sundiata Keita Cha-Jua's essay in this volume).

Reparations and Reparatory Justice is groundbreaking in other ways as well. Writing for Scholars for Social Justice (SSJ), Adom Getachew acknowledges the central role of the state in generating and perpetuating racial oppression, but insists universities also have a long history of creating, propagating, and maintaining racial inequities. Getachew and SSJ reflect a growing focus on universities and colleges. Meanwhile, Franklin decries the ravages done particularly to Black youth by the repressive institutions of the carceral state. He details the inhumane crimes committed against incarcerated Black men, women, and youth across gender and identity and demands the creation of a "Reparations Superfund" to rehabilitate lives and repair the damage by providing alternatives to mass racialized incarceration, especially for African American youth. And contrary to most African American reparationists, who emphasize economics, Sundiata Keita Cha-Jua views reparations as primarily a political project. He posits the struggle for reparations' major role is to maximize African American autonomy. He calls for the creation of a self-governing apparatus with attendant independent institutions that can serve as the base for building dual power and constructing a self-determined future.

As we creatively imagine a future in which African Americans can determine their own destiny, it is necessary to excavate the history of the struggle for reparations. While that history for African Americans goes back into the eighteenth century and predates the consolidation of the United States as a federal republic, it became a social movement during and in the wake of the overthrow of Reconstruction. There is much for contemporary advocates to learn from past struggles, from the movement's successes and failures and from periods of high tide and low or of struggle.

A Short History of Reparations Movements in the United States

Starting in the late nineteenth century, reparations groups were formed in the southern United States to pursue pensions for aging formerly enslaved workers. Callie House, leader of the ESMRBPA, worked hard to obtain pension funds from the federal government for formerly enslaved African Americans. Berry's "Taking the United States to Court," included in this volume, describes the efforts of House and others to obtain pensions through the taxes on cotton grown in the Confederate states. House was subsequently targeted by state and federal officials, falsely accused of criminal activity, and imprisoned.[22] In the early 1960s, Queen Mother Audley Moore led the efforts to form the Reparations Committee for the Descendants of American Slaves (RCDAS). In December 1962, the group issued a pamphlet entitled *Why Reparations? Reparations Is the Battle Cry for the Social and Economic Freedom of 26 Million Descendants of American Slaves*. RCDAS was unsuccessful in its calls for the federal government to provide "economic redress for the wrongs of slavery and Jim Crow."[23]

In 1969, James Forman issued the "Black Manifesto," which the National Black Economic Development Conference (NBEDC) adopted. In it Forman argued that wealthy, predominantly white Protestant and Roman Catholic denominations and churches had accumulated great wealth from the slave trade and the enslavement of Africans and African Americans and should pay reparations. While there is little evidence that Forman or the NBEDC received funds from these religious institutions, it has been determined that some NDEBC-affiliated Black caucuses, local Black Power, and religious organizations within Methodist, Episcopal, Presbyterian, and other Protestant denominations did receive financial support for African Americans' economic development and educational projects in the 1970s.[24]

The National Coalition of Blacks for Reparations in America (N'COBRA) was founded in July 1987. The new group was a "mass-based coalition of organizations and individuals organized for the sole purpose of obtaining reparations for African descendants in the United States." In 1988, the U.S. Congress passed the Civil Liberties Act, which granted reparations payments to Japanese Americans who were removed from their homes on the West

Coast and interned in concentration camps during World War II. Following up on this development, N'COBRA became one of the major supporters of Detroit Congressman John Conyers's House Bill H.R. 40, introduced in 1989, calling for the formation of a commission to study and make recommendations for reparations programs for African Americans. Since that time, Conyers introduced the bill every year he was in Congress. Texas Representative Sheila Jackson Lee joined Conyers as a co-sponsor and since his resignation and death has steered the bill out of committee.[25]

One of the more recent reparations cases involved the state of North Carolina and the compensation paid to *some* of the over 7,600 women who were forcibly sterilized by state agencies between 1929 and 1976. After years of deliberation, North Carolina legislators in 2013 appropriated $10 million to pay up to $50,000 in reparations to each woman who was involuntarily sterilized at the behest of state officials. However, the flaws in allowing the victimizers to determine the terms and amount of compensation were soon revealed. Women were disqualified if they were unable to provide documentation of their sterilization; they were disqualified if they did not sign up for the program by a certain date; and many asked: was $50,000 enough to compensate the women for their loss? This situation demonstrates the need for the establishment of an independent agency such as a "Reparations Superfund" to determine and carry out the distribution of funds received from corporations or governments as reparations payments.[26]

The current upsurge in the African American reparations movement and scholarship on it reflects trends that transcend the continental boundaries of the United States. The contemporary African American reparations movement is the product of local, national, and international socioeconomic and political transformations that has accelerated income and wealth inequality, especially for BIPOC (Black Indigenous and People of Color) ethnicities/nationalities and has eviscerated liberal democratic norms throughout the West. These are the conditions that produced the storm. However, in addition to a declining socioeconomic and political situation, when Representative Jackson Lee introduced a revised and updated version of H.R. 40 in the U.S. Congress in 2018, the new bill [see 2018 H.R. 40 Bill in this volume] was also pushed forward by African Americans' participation in a web of Pan-African networks. The United Nations–sponsored the World Conference against Racism I (WCAR I), the formation of the Caribbean Reparations Commission and its Ten Point Action Plan, and the United Nations' declaration of 2015–2024 as the "International Decade for People of African Descent" all helped shape an international climate conducive to the emergence of a rising tide of struggle for reparations by African Americans.

Global Reparations Movements

As previously stated, diasporic and Pan-African networks seeded the storm that became the contemporary Caribbean, African American, and African reparation movements. In preparation for WCAR I, several African scholars, social activists, and leaders met on Gorée Island in Senegal that June under the auspices of the Inter-African Union for Human Rights. In the official statement of the *Goree Initiative,* as it came to be known, the contributors concluded that "the principal foundations of slavery, the Slave Trade and colonialism are essentially based on supremacist claims which automatically incite the exploitation of man by man." It went on to declare that African Americans in the United States are "the prime victims of marginalization and discriminatory practice" by law enforcement and penal systems. The report cited the "grave and massive crimes committed against the continent" and argued that "the principle of just and fair reparation for the Slave Trade and enslavement of Africans" is the "usual result" when these crimes and injustices are recognized.[27]

Colin Powell and Condoleezza Rice led the U.S. delegation to WCAR I. They were guided by a May 2001 U.S. State Department directive that it would entertain no discussion of "international compensatory measures," or reparations. The European Union and other industrialized nations followed the Americans' lead in opposing any discussion of reparations at WCAR I. The Caribbean nations, however, boldly called for consideration of reparations as the first step in the politics of "truth and reconciliation," but Nigeria, Senegal, the European Union, and the United States opposed their proposal. Thus, the issue of reparations was effectively buried, and the final WCAR I declaration meekly stated that "slavery and the slave trade are crimes against humanity and *should* always have been so."[28]

The leaders of CARICOM were undaunted. Considering the genocide of the Indigenous population and the enslavement and exploitation of African people, they decided to pursue reparations from the former colonial powers primarily as a strategy for economic development. At a meeting in July 2013, the CARICOM leaders agreed to establish a national reparations committee in each member state and a regional CARICOM Reparations Commission (CRC). Antigua and Barbuda Prime Minister Baldwin Spencer called reparations an "integral element in the Community's development strategy."[29] Subsequently, the CRC issued a Ten Point Action Plan for using reparations to advance the economic and cultural conditions of poor and working-class people in the Caribbean nations.[30] Should the European nations that had colonies in the Caribbean refuse to act on these formal requests, CARICOM plans to take the matter to the International Court of Justice.[31]

In December 2014, the Barbadian historian Sir Hilary Beckles, chair of the CARICOM Reparations Commission, addressed the UN General Assembly to mark the launch of the International Decade for People of African Descent. Beckles described how it had taken "all of the twentieth century for African descendants to convert their legal freedom into citizenship and institutional leadership" and how their progress had been "continually threatened by force rooted in slavery's enduring legacies" (see Beckles's speech in this volume).

Members of the CARICOM Reparations Commission came to New York City in April 2015 for a joint "Reparations Summit" with the newly established National African American Reparations Commission (NAARC), convened by Dr. Ron Daniels, president of the Institute for the Black World 21st Century. The two groups agreed to work in concert in the promulgation of Ten Point Plans, outlining the specific strategies, goals, and objectives for the *collective* economic advancement for people of African descent in the United States and the Caribbean using reparations funds. (See Jesse Jackson's speech and Ron Daniels's statement in this volume.)

To gather information for its "Ten Point Plan," NAARC held reparations "Town Hall Meetings" in Atlanta and New Orleans in 2016 and 2017. Actor and human rights advocate Danny Glover spoke at both events and argued that reparations is "An Issue Whose Time Has Come" (see Danny Glover speech in this volume). From these meetings came resolutions to pursue class action lawsuits aimed at institutions that have damaged African Americans. These include government bodies and private entities, such as the banks that pushed subprime mortgage loans on middle- and working-class African American home purchasers that contributed to the Great Recession.

Much of the current discussion around this issue was catalyzed by the publication of Ta-Nehisi Coates's article "The Case for Reparations," in the June 2014 issue of *The Atlantic*. It sparked a vigorous national debate and led to the expression of support for reparations by historians, social scientists, public intellectuals, and presidential hopefuls.[32] It should be noted that his important article addressed many of the same topics explored in the 2012 issue of *The Journal of African American History*, edited by V. P. Franklin, and published by the Association for the Study of African American Life and History (ASALH).[33]

Juxtaposing Coates's widely acclaimed essay with Franklin's edited academic journal article invites a conversation about the power relationship between specialist scholars, celebrities, and public intellectuals. It's important that the groundbreaking work of scholars who excavate issues like reparations are not ignored after prominent commentators bring previously buried issues to public consciousness. We believe our volume addresses the most pertinent aspect of this question by bringing together in a single volume an intellectually, ideologically, and methodologically diverse group of authors who span academia, celebrity, and the Black liberation movement. We contend the relationship between celebrities, public intellectuals, and specialist academics though filled with tension is essentially complementary. From our vantage point, we view the popularity of Danny Glover, Jesse Jackson, and Earl Ofari Hutchinson as helping to attract a broader audience to the work of the academic specialists included in our volume.

Celebrities, public intellectuals, and academic specialists largely use different methodologies and approaches. The inclusion of a diverse body of authors offers the public an opportunity to observe the strengths and weaknesses of each approach. Our celebrity or popular leaders' (Jesse Jackson, for example) contributions largely reflect direct personal experience and the oral tradition of the African American community. Many of Jackson's ideas are drawn from what historian George Rude called an "'inherent' traditional element." Jackson's speech also depicts what Anthony Bogues refers to as the *redemptive prophetic* tradition. That is, he incorporates aspects from what Rude terms the "derived tradition," which borrows from others and evidences a genesis in more systematic ideologies, religious or political. Jackson's talk is steeped in religious symbolism and logic. Except for the religious aspects, Glover's speech grows out of the same popular subsoil as Jackson's. He too speaks in a colloquial voice, recalls and interprets incidents from personal experience, and valorizes the African American oral tradition. However, Glover pulls more thoroughly from Rude's "derived tradition" than does Jackson. In Bogues's conceptual frame, Glover's talk is also rooted in the *heretical tradition*. Glover references radical Black intellectuals Franz Fanon and Langston Hughes. He constructs his argument from an alternative radical Black tradition that challenges mainstream American thought. Both Jackson and Glover approach the question of reparations through the medium of storytelling and analogy. Both seek to concretize reparations for their audience by demonstrating a personal connection through an ancestor, in their cases a grandmother who was either enslaved or among the first freed generation. This narrative strategy shatters the "too long ago" argument, but it only alludes to questions of how to calculate payment for exploitation, abuse, and trauma. Unlike our academic specialists, neither Jackson nor Glover engage issues concerning the form of remuneration and distribution of reparations.[34]

On the other hand, our academic specialists (Berry and James Stewart, for example) build their arguments on a broad body of historical evidence and statistical data. Charles Henry constructs a unique historical narrative, not from oral tradition but from an unpublished family history, which he supplements with primary sources and a deep engagement with the secondary literature. It is entirely through a derived or heretical tradition. Our scholars also locate their ideas about reparations in more structured ideologies (socialism for Brian Jones; revolutionary Black nationalism for Sundiata Cha-Jua). By including popular intellectuals alongside specialist academics, we highlight the different but complementary use of sources, modes of presentation, and analysis.

It's also important for us to stress that the celebrities included in our volume (Glover, for example) are not simply social commentators but longtime activists with ties to social movements. Both Jackson's and Glover's speeches were delivered to movement organizations, specifically at the NAARC summit and the New Orleans townhall meeting.

These Black Liberation movement activists elevated reparations to public awareness. Even before reparations became a topic of contemporary concern, scholars pursued it as a contemporary and historical topic of research. They produced documentary collections, studies, and essays that further cemented the importance of reparations in the mind of the public. As this process unfolded, reparations caught the awareness of some celebrities who by their endorsement attracted an even broader public to the issue. We believe this cycle ultimately creates further interest in academics' production of research articles, books, and presentations to mass audiences and the media.

In this volume we explore the ideological and practical goal of "reparatory justice" to repair the damage to individuals, communities, cultures, and the environment in the pursuit of profits by national and multinational capitalist corporations as well as governments. Accordingly, reparatory justice campaigns should be aimed at repairing the damage to former coal miners by silicosis disease; to the thousands of victims of the opioid epidemic; to homeowners forced into foreclosure after being targeted by the banks for subprime mortgages, especially African Americans and other people of color; to low-wage earners lured into taking pay-day loans and the other usurious practices of banks and financial institutions. Reparatory justice is the moral principle; reparations payments and memorialization initiatives are the form of restitution and compensation.

There is every reason to believe that the reparations movement spawned by the enslavement and victimization of African-descended people would generate reparatory justice campaigns by other oppressed groups. In the first half of the nineteenth century, the movement to end the enslavement of African American workers, in which Black and white women played a major role, also spurred the emergence of the women's rights movement in the 1840s and 1850s. Many women came to view the patriarchal and sexist restrictions placed on their lives as like those enslaved African American workers faced. In other words, the women's rights movement emerged out of the struggles to gain freedom for enslaved Black workers.[35]

In the twentieth century, the campaigns associated with the Civil Rights Movement not only ended American apartheid and marginalization in the polity for African Americans and other darker peoples, but also contributed greatly to the emergence of the third iteration of the Women's Liberation Movement.[36] And the Civil Rights and Black Power movements of the 1960s and 1970s led to calls for Student Rights, Red Power, Chicano Power, Gay Liberation, and Environmental Justice.[37] Given this historical precedent, the reparations movement among African Americans will likely advance campaigns for reparatory justice for other social, cultural, and economic groups.

Each oppressed group must determine its own road to reparatory justice based on their historical experiences and current socioeconomic conditions. There is an urgent need to remedy the extreme economic inequality resulting from under-regulated financialized global racial capitalism.

The African American movement for reparations and the scholarship on it has grown immensely during the moment in which the racial wealth gap exploded. It is no coincidence that the reparations movement and its scholarship has increased and matured during a time in which income and wealth inequality and ravages to the environment have escalated and the socioeconomic conditions of racialized communities have decidedly deteriorated. Reparations like the wider Black Liberation movement experiences upturns during moments of economic downturn and retreat from racial justice. "The movement's resurgences seem tied to periods of regression, to those moments in which the Black Liberation wave is being rolled back, the 1850s, 1890s, the late 1970s, and the late 1990s, for example" and since the killing of Michael Brown in 2014 and the election of Donald Trump.[38]

The "Black Lives Matter" slogan burst into public consciousness during the protests over Ferguson, Missouri, police officer Darren Wilson's killing of Brown on August 9, 2014.[39] That powerful watchword mobilized tens of thousands of Black millennials and Generation Zers into action. The potency of the "Black Lives Matter" slogan derives from a simple truth: in the U.S., Black lives matter least. Life expectancy is one quality of life measure that reflects the undervaluation of Black life in the U.S. Longevity among Black people has increased significantly and the gap between African and white Americans has shrunk tremendously since 1900. Nevertheless, disparities persist. Since 2019, Black life expectancy has declined, and the racial gap increased. Between 2019 and the first six months of 2020, Black life expectancy declined by 2.7 years, from 74.7 to 72 years, which increased the Black-white life expectancy gap from 4.1 to 6 years.[40]

The turnaround in life expectancy reflects the society's historic devaluing of Black life and is symptomatic of the broader reversal in African American's situation. Black youth's contemporary upsurge is a product of the historic patterns of anti-Black racial oppression, the most recent regression in African Americans' socioeconomic conditions and the U.S.'s retreat from racial justice. It also reflects the historical pattern of regressive social conditions and political repression stimulating progressive Black social movement responses. These truths gained even more dynamism after Minneapolis police officer Derek Chauvin's murder of George Floyd on May 25, 2020. The protests following the deaths of Floyd, Breonna Taylor, Ahmaud Arbery, and other victims of police violence transformed a new generation of African American youth's struggle into a worldwide multiracial uprising.

Like every generation of African Americans, Gen Xers and young millennial activists soon began to demand reparations. The #Black Lives Matter Global Network Foundation (BLGNF), the organization started by Alicia Garza, Patrice Cullors, and Opal Tometi, issued its first call for reparations, to commemorate the Tulsa Race Massacre of 1921, on June 3, 2021. However, the demand for reparations was integral at the formation of the Movement 4 Black Lives (M4BL) of which the BLGNF is a member organization. A coalition of fifty Black organizations, the M4BL's *A Vision for Black Lives: Policy Demands for Black Power, Freedom, and Justice* ranks reparations as the second of its six policy demands. M4BL takes a comprehensive historical and cultural perspective on reparations, calling for reparations for "past and continuing harms." *A Vision for Black Lives* and subsequent M4BL statements address reparations in five areas, offering a political education toolkit and a framework for political action (see Movement for Black Lives Reparations Platform in this volume). M4BL's five areas—open admission and free access to technical and higher education, plus loan forgiveness; a livable income for divestment from Black communities; transformation of educational curricula and cultural memorials; reparations for the effects of environmental racism; and legislation acknowledging the impact of slavery—resemble aspects of the National African American Reparations Commission's 10-Point Plan. The similarities between the two documents suggest reparations constitute the site of intergenerational convergence, where remnants of sixties radical Black organizers and contemporary millennial activists come together around a liberatory agenda.[41]

Published Works on Reparations

There is a necessary lag between a movement swell and scholarship on that movement. The increased monographic and anthological literature of the new millennium is largely a response to the formation of N'COBRA, Congressman Conyer's introduction of H.R. 40, the Durban or World Conference against Racism, and Daedria Farmer-Paellman's pioneering suit against Aetna, Fleet-Boston Financial Corporation, and the CSX Corporation. Historically, literature on the African American reparations movement was produced by movement activists. In contrast, much of the contemporary literature has come from scholars, albeit Black scholar activists such as Mary Frances Berry, Raymond A. Winbush, and Ronald W. Walters.

Even still, this change in authorship brought its own contradiction. At precisely the moment in which the movement for African American reparations was becoming more popular, the writings on the movement trended toward academia, not the general audience. Consequently, of the literature published in the early years of the twenty-first century, only Randall Robinson's *The Debt: What America Owes to Blacks* (2001) sought and captured a broad popular audience. The books published before and after 2001 have *all* been aimed at an academic audience. That was the case with Boris Bittker's *The Case for Black Reparations* (2003), though first published in 1973. The same was true of the Roy L. Brooks edited volume *When Sorry Isn't Enough: The Controversies over Apologies and Reparations for Human Injustice*, published in 1999. All the books published since 2001 have been aimed at the academic market: Joe R. Feagin and Kimberley Ducey, *Racist America: Roots, Current Realities, and Future Reparations* (2001); Raymond A. Winbush, ed., *Should America Pay? Slavery and the Raging Debate over Reparations* (2003); Ronald P. Sulzberger and Mary Turck, eds., *Reparations for Slavery: A Reader* (2004); Mary Frances Berry, *My Face Is Black Is True: Callie House and the Struggle for Ex-Slave Reparations* (2005); Charles Henry, *Long Overdue: The Politics of Racial Reparations* (2007); Michael T. Martin and Marilyn Yacinto, eds., *Redress for Historical Injustices: On Reparations for Slavery, Jim Crow, and Their Injustices* (2007); Alfred L. Brophy, *Reparations: Pro and Con* (2008); Ronald W. Walters, *The Price for Racial Reconciliation* (2008); and Hilary McD. Beckles, *Britain's Black Debt: Reparations for Caribbean Slavery and Native Genocide* (2013).

The works that have appeared since 2017 have also aimed primarily at an academic audience. These books include Ana Lucia Araujo, *Reparations for Slavery and the Slave Trade* (2017); Roy L. Brooks, *Atonement and Forgiveness:*

A New Model for Black Reparations (2019); and Katherine Franke, *Repair: Redeeming the Promise of Abolition* (2019). We have structured *Reparations and Reparatory Justice* to appeal to both a popular and an academic audience by providing accessible speeches, essays, and research articles. *Reparations and Reparatory Justice* discusses the historical background and proffers current information on reparations issues not just in the United States, but globally. This book offers popular and scholarly analyses of reparations claims past and present, as well as insightful and important statements by prominent and well-known public figures and social commentators on the issue of reparations in the twenty-first century.

Reparations and Reparatory Justice

The authors of *Reparations and Reparatory Justice* consist of well-known Black Liberation movement activists, recognized scholars, and elected officials. Our book is a collection of pathbreaking analyses by individuals who are on the frontlines in the struggle for reparations. Whereas many of the works published since the 1990s anthologize previously published work, *Reparations and Reparatory Justice* consists overwhelmingly of new and significantly revised work.

This book is divided into two sections: (1) Speeches and Documents and (2) Research Articles and Essays. The speeches and documents section consists of short statements and documents by a diverse group of prominent activists, public intellectuals, and elected officials such as the Rev. Jesse Jackson, Danny Glover, Sir Hilary McD. Beckles, Texas Representative Sheila Jackson Lee, and racial justice organizations such as the National Coalition for Black Reparations in America (N'COBRA), National African American Reparations Commission, and Scholars for Social Justice. The speeches by Jackson and Glover were delivered at a major reparations summit. In the case of Jackson Lee her contribution is from her statement introducing a revised H.R. 40 before the House of Representatives during the U.S. Congress. And Beckles's talk was presented at the United Nations for the launching of the UN's "International Decade for People of African Descent."

"Part I—Reparations: Speeches and Documents" includes Ron Daniels's firsthand account of the preparations for the "National/International Conference on Reparations" held in New York City in April 2015. The historic event brought together hundreds of social activists from the United States, the Caribbean, South America, and Europe to chart the course for reparations campaigns globally. Daniels argues strongly for reparations as assistance in communal development, rather than individual cash payments. His speech sowed the soil for the development of an African American 10-Point Reparations program.

The speeches by Jesse Jackson Sr. and Danny Glover put forward resolutions and collective demands for reparations. Using allegory and personal stories, Jackson highlights the role of force in creating the racial wealth gap as he convincingly contends, "To not believe in reparations is to believe in ethnic cleansing as valid." Through a discussion of his grandmother, Mary Brown, and the still extant slave auction-market in Louisville, Georgia, Glover makes a direct connection between living African Americans and enslavement. Beckles catalogues the numerous crimes against humanity committed by the slave trade and enslavement. He offers a global framework, though British colonialism and its exploitation of the Caribbean is his primary concern. Notably, he emphasizes the ways in which African minds and cultures enriched the West as well as the exploitation of "enchained" African-descendant hands, backs, arms, and feet.[42]

Jackson's and Glover's personal narratives highlight the contemporality of past anti-Black racial oppression. Earl Ofari Hutchinson and N'COBRA offer frames from which to interpret the current rise of the reparations movement. Regarding the United States, popular commentator Hutchinson identifies the U.S. state and economic institutions such as banks, and shipping and insurance companies as responsible for enslavement. He further discusses the main reasons why reparations movements continue to arise. He especially emphasizes the continuities in racial discrimination and inequalities for African-descended people into the twenty-first century. Whereas Hutchinson emphasizes the United States, Kamm Howard locates reparations in a global perspective. He defines the current moment of upsurge as the "Post Durban Era." In that sense he mirrors Beckles global Pan-African concerns. For him, the Durban Conference unleashed the pent-up anger and aspirations of Black people worldwide and established the sociohistorical context in which Caribbean leaders could pursue reparations from former European colonial powers and U.S. presidential candidates in 2020 were persuaded to support African Americans' reparations demands.

Hutchinson directed our attention toward U.S. economic institutions and the exploitation of African people's labor; V. P. Franklin and Adom Getachew, however, focus on educational institutions. Franklin also offers a highly innovative approach to reparations and African American reparations. Whereas Getachew and SSJ focus on mainstream higher educational institutions, Franklin takes aim at for-profit institutions and prisons. He emphasizes how federal policies fueled the student loan debt crisis by permitting federally backed student loans to pay for 90 percent of the "diploma mills" annual income. To repair the abuses perpetuated by these institutions, Franklin calls for a "Reparations Superfund." This pool of monies would come from the public, private, and for-profit educational and technical institutions, and corporations that have specifically damaged African American youth, such as testing services, Big Pharma, and the petrochemical companies. While Franklin focuses on for-profit educational institutions, the pharmaceutical and fossil fuel industries, Getachew, on behalf of the recently formed SSJ, emphasizes the institution of higher education. They highlight several ways in which universities and colleges contributed to the socioeconomic subordination of Black people and Indigenous nations. Many colleges and universities benefited from slavery or the slave trade. Other educational institutions engaged in the production of enslaved labor, financial support from fortunes made from slavery or the slave trade, production and dissemination of disinformation rationalizing racial oppression, and the exclusion and incorporation of policies and practices that undermined Black upward mobility.

Also included in Part I is the bill to establish the "Commission to Study and Make Proposals to Develop Reparations Proposals for African Americans." Jackson Lee stresses that the question of reparations includes but transcends issues of economic inequality embedded in slavery and subsequent systems of racial oppression. For the Congresswoman, "the legacy of slavery lingers heavily in this nation," thus her central questions are ethical and concern issues of memorialization. In her words, the primary issue is "whether and how this nation can come to grips with the legacy of slavery that still infects current society" (see Sheila Jackson Lee essay in this volume).

Jackson Lee and the high-profile movement activists and scholars presented in Part I reflect the mainstreaming of reparations in the African American "nation within an empire" and serve to underscore the urgency of this new moment in the struggle for reparations. These short punchy speeches and essays set the table for the longer more research-oriented pieces that appear in the second part of this book. "Part II—Reparations: Articles and Essays" provides new analyses and research on reparations, documenting the various campaigns and movements developed in the past and present.

Interrogating the exchange between Jourdon Anderson and his former slaveowner, Colonel Patrick Anderson, in "Industrial Slavery and Dietary Deprivation," James B. Stewart intrudes the question of labor exploitation in urban industry, rather than in plantation agriculture. Stewart uses their discussion posit the need for a different calculus for industrial slave labor super exploitation than that used to quantify reparations claims for agricultural labor exploitation.[43] Building on Robert S. Starobin's arguments, Stewart establishes that the enslaved in industrial and plantation enterprises shared the same standard of living but that the enslaved employed in capitalist industrial companies were more apt to experience malnourishment because the conditions of industrial labor were worse and required a greater expenditure of energy. Stewart's central question for reparations claims is the degree to which "nutritional deprivation" caused long-term health problems for the descendants of enslaved laborers.

In reconstructing the story of the 1915 lawsuit filed by Callie House and the National Ex-Slave Mutual Relief, Bounty and Pension Association against the Treasury Department, Mary Frances Berry excavates the perils of fighting for African America reparations. In chronicling the first reparations suit against the U.S. government, Berry exposes the difficulties of bringing a case before the court, but also the extent to which the government's repressive apparatuses will be deployed to destroy the litigants. For Chuck Collins and Dedrick Asante-Muhammad, reparations are the means to eliminate the racial wealth gap. They point out that at the current rate it would take 228 years or nine and a half generations before African Americans would achieve parity with white Americans. Consequently, "What Reparations Could Actually Look Like" focuses on the thorny questions of who pays and how reparations payments could be used to transform the lives of African-descended people in the areas of education, housing, and cultural production. They also offer recommendations for memorialization.

Brian Jones makes "The Socialist Case for Reparations." He emphasizes that socialists and social democrats, such as Vermont Senator Bernie Sanders, should support reparations for African-descended people and others as part of the larger struggle to redistribute the wealth in the United States from the top 1 percent to middle- and working-class citizens whose incomes have stagnated over the last forty years. Cutting to the heart of the matter, Jones contends Coates erred in assuming "socialists necessarily adopt a reductionist, 'class first' politics." And while he distinguishes Sander's universalism from Obama's, he also argues social democrats like Sanders and socialists should support Black reparations because it raises troubling questions, which are dangerous to the ruling class. In contrast to Sanders and Cedric Johnson, an African American political scientist, but in accordance with Rev. Martin Luther King, Jones argues for the fusion of reparations for African Americans and a universal program to redistribute "wealth and power."[44] In "Reparations: Democrats, Universalism, and the African American Struggle for Autonomy," Sundiata Cha-Jua traverses some of the territory Jones navigated. He too contrasts universalist redistributive programs with African American reparations, but additionally he compares Black peoples' approach to reparations with that of Indigenous nations.

Like Jones, Cha-Jua favors King's joint approach of fusing both a universal redistributive program with a particular program of reparations for African Americans. Echoing Matthew Fletcher, an Indigenous professor of law, Cha-Jua further contends African American reparationists have much to learn from American Indians. Despite the severe limitations of settler colonialism, native nations' exercise of "dual sovereignty" offers Indigenous peoples substantive areas of self-determination, which Black people do not have. Cha-Jua believes the goal of reparations should be the exercise of dual power and the acquisition of autonomy.

In "Family Roots of Reparations in the Era of Trump," Charles P. Henry describes his family's background and traces it to the antebellum quasi-free Black communities in Ohio. He shows that the descendants of quasi-free African Americans who were also plagued by racial discrimination and economic exploitation in the South, North, and Midwest also deserve reparations. In "Reparatory Justice Campaigns in the Twenty-First Century," V. P. Franklin focuses on reparatory justice struggles currently underway launched by N'COBRA, NAARC, and other groups for African Americans; and by the state attorneys general in lawsuits against the pharmaceutical companies that profited enormously from the "opioid epidemic." Franklin argues that similar campaigns for reparatory justice should be mounted in the twenty-first century against the standardized testing industry, the huge student loan debt, and the land-grant colleges built on and supported by lands taken from the Indigenous peoples. Franklin and the other contributors to this volume all agree that reparations and reparatory justice campaigns will become the major social justice movement in the twenty-first century.

Reparations and Reparatory Justice presents a broad interpretation of Black reparations across time, space, ideology, and framework for distribution. Our diverse group of authors offer essays and research articles that span from the eighteenth century when Belinda Sutton filed her petition for compensation for her "ignoble servitude" to Isaac Royall before the Massachusetts General Court in 1783 to the Democratic Party's top-tier presidential candidate's endorsement of H.R. 40 in 2020. Our authors largely address reparations for African Americans but in addition to Beckles's speech before the United Nations General Assembly addressing reparations for the CARICOM nations, Ron Daniels and others speak to the demand for reparations for global Africa. *Reparations and Reparatory Justice* presents often neglected perspectives of revolutionary nationalists and socialists, such as the essays by Sundiata Keita Cha-Jua and Brian P. Jones and the document by the New Afrikan Peoples Organization/Malcolm X Grassroots Movement. And our collection examines several proposals for repair, restitution, and compensation. While most of our writers support the inclusion of individual payments, contributors like

V. P. Franklin, Chuck Collins, and Dedrick Asante-Muhammad forcefully argue for collective institution-building compensation as necessary to repair the harm done to Black people as a collective entity.

Notes

1. "Belinda's Petition"; www.royallhouse.org/beinda-suttons-1783-petition-fulltext/; Raymond Winbush, *Belinda's Petition: A Concise History of Reparations for the Transatlantic Slave Trade* (New York: Ex Libris, 2009).

2. Ana Lucia Araujo, *Reparations for Slavery and the Slave Trade* (London: Bloomsbury Academic, 2017); and *Shadows of the Slave Past: Memory, Heritage, and Slavery* (New York: Routledge, 2014).

3. Hilary McD. Beckles, *Britain's Black Debt: Reparations for Caribbean Slavery and Native Genocide* (Kingston, Jamaica: University of the West Indies Press, 2013), quote on 143.

4. Stanley Harrold, *Subversives: Antislavery Community in Washington, DC, 1828–1865* (Baton Rouge: Louisiana State University, 2003); and Kate Masur, *An Example for All the Land: Emancipation and the Struggle over Equality in Washington, DC* (Chapel Hill: University of North Carolina Press, 2010). See for example John W. Blassingame, "The Recruitment of Negro Troops in Missouri During the Civil War," *Missouri Historical Review* 58 (April 1964): 326–38.

5. W. E. B. Du Bois, *Black Reconstruction in America, 1860–1880* (New York: The Free Press, 1992; rprt. 1935), 368.

6. Bayley Wyatt, "Report of a Speech by a Virginia Freedman," Freedmen & Southern Society Project, http://www.freedmen.umd.edu/Wyat.html; T.G. Campbell, *Sufferings of the Rev. T.G. Campbell and his Family in Georgia* (Washington: Enterprise Publishing, 1877; reprt. 2016), 7–8; Russell Duncan, *Freedom's Shore: Tunis Campbell and the Georgia Freedmen* (Athens: University of Georgia Press, 1986), 67–88; Walter Johnson, *Rivers of Dark Dreams: Slavery and Empire in the Cotton Kingdom* (Cambridge, MA: The Belknap Press of Harvard University Press, 2013), 257–62; Richard Follett, Sven Beckert, Peter Coclamis and Barbara Hahn (eds.), *The American South and Its Global Commodities* (Baltimore: Johns Hopkins University, 2016).

7. Tom Lenard and Simon Tomilson, "14 Caribbean Nations Sue Britain, Holland, and France for Slavery Reparations that could Cost Hundreds of Billions of Pounds," *The Daily Mail*, 10 October 2013, https://www.dailymail.co.uk/news/article-2451891/14-Caribbean-nations-sue-Britain-Holland-France-slavery-reparations.html.

8. See Walter Rodney, *How Europe Underdeveloped Africa* (Washington: Howard University Press, 1982; reprt. 1972), 13–29. Kelcey Haddon Leggett, "All Eyes on Slavery Reparations Case by Caribbean Nations" *Panoramas: Scholarly Platform*, October 20, 2016, https://www.panoramas.pitt.edu/news-and-politics/all-eyes-slavery-reparations-case-caribbean-nations.

9. The Caribbean Reparations Commission, "Ten Point Action Plan," Caribbean Reparations Commission, https://caricomreparations.org.

10. Connor Friedersdorf, "What Do 2020 Candidates Mean When They Say 'Reparations'?" *The Atlantic* June 5, 2019, https://www.theatlantic.com/ideas/archive/2019/06/reparations-definition-2020-candidates/590863/; P.R. Lockhart, "The 2020 Democratic Primary Debate over Reparations Explained," *Vox*, June 19, 2019, 9:37 am EDT, https://www.vox.com/policy-and-politics/2019/3/11/18246741/ reparations-democrats-2020-inequality-warren-harris-castro.

11. Stephanie Saul, "Biden Was Asked About Segregation and His Answer Included a Record Player," *The New York Times,* September 12, 2019, https://www.nytimes.com/2019/09/12/us/politics/biden-record-player.html.

12. Nicholas Fandos, "House Panels Advances Bill to Study Reparations in Historic Vote, *New York Times,* April 14, 2021, updated May 31, 2021, https://www.nytimes.com/2021/04/14/ us/ politics/reparations-slavery-house.html.

13. Shirley Weber, Assembly Bill 3121, California Legislature, https://leginfo.legislature.ca.gov/faces/ billTextClient.xhtml?bill_id=201920200AB3121.

14. California Reparations Task Force, California Task Force to Study and Develop Reparation Proposals for African Americans: Final Report (Sacramento: State of California, June 2023).

15. Larry Gavin, "Preparing A Historical Basis for Reparations," *Evanston Roundtable,* Tuesday, July 14, 2020, 2:09 PM; Joel Burgess, *Ashville Citizen Times,* "In Historic Move, North Carolina City Approves Reparations for Black Residents," *USA Today,* 1:22 pm EDT, July 15, 2020, https://apple.news/ Au_9N690eR12atQFOEhhSOA; Neil Vigor, "North Carolina City Approves Reparations for Black Residents," *The New York Times,* July 16, 2020, https://www.nytimes.com/2020/07/16/us/reparations-asheville-nc.html; Ashville City Government, "Resolution Supporting Community Reparations for Black Ashville," http://pulse.ncpolicywatch.org/wp-content/uploads/2020/07/468705276-New-B-Reso-Supporting-Community-Reparations-for-Black-Asheville.pdf; Golocal/Prov Political Team, "Providence Councilwoman on Reparations for Black Community: Don't Over Promise & Under Deliver," Wednesday, July 15, 2020, https://www.golocalprov.com/politics/providence-councilwoman-harris-on-reparations-for-black-community-dont-over; Steve Alhquist, "Providence announces Truth, Reconciliation, and Reparations process," *UPRISE RI,* https://upriseri.com/2020-07-15-truth-reconciliation-reparations/.

16. Manaan Donghoe and Andre M. Perry, "The Case for Climate Reparations in the United States," Brookings Institute, March 2023: brookings.edu/articles/the-case-for-climate-reparations-in-the-united-states/; Mary Bassett, "Reparations as a Public Health Priority," *New England Journal of Medicine* 2020: 383: 2101-2103; Omar G. Encarnacion, *The Case for Gay Reparations* (New York: Oxford University Press, 2021).

17. Mary Frances Berry, *My Face Is Black Is True: Callie House and the Struggle for Ex-Slave Reparations* (New York: Knopf, 2005), 88–89.

18. John Hope Franklin and Alfred Moses, *From Slavery to Freedom: A History of African Americans Eighth Edition* (Boston: McGraw-Hill, 2000), 167. See Charles Henry essay this volume.

19. *The Case for Gay Reparations*, 6.

20. Stewart, "Industrial Slavery and Dietary Deprivation," in this volume.

21. Brian Jones, "The Socialist Case for Reparations," *Jacobin*, March 1, 2016, https:// www.jacobinmag.com/2016/03/reparations-ta-nehisi-coates-cedric-johnson -bernie-sanders. See Ta-Nehisi Coates, "Why Precisely Is Bernie Sanders Against Reparations?," *The Atlantic*, January 19, 2016, https:// www.theatlantic.com/politics/ archive/2016/01/bernie-sanders-reparations/424602/; Ta-Nehisi Coates, "Bernie Sanders and the Liberal Imagination," *The Atlantic*, January 24, 2016, https://www.the atlantic.com/politics/ archive/2016/01/bernie-sanders-liberal-imagination/425022/; Cedric Johnson, "An Open Letter to Ta-Nehisi Coates and the Liberals Who Love Him," *Jacobin*, February 3, 2016, https://www.jacobinmag.com/2016/02/ta-nehisi-coates -case-for-reparations-bernie-sanders-racism/; Cedric Johnson, "Reparations Isn't a Political Demand," *Jacobin*, March 7, 2016, https://www.jacobinmag.com/2016/03/ cedric-johnson-brian-jones-ta-nehisi-coates-reparations.

22. Mary Frances Berry, *My Face Is Black Is True: Callie House and the Ex-Slave Movement for Reparations* (New York: Knopf, 2005); and "Taking the United States to Court: Callie House and the 1915 Cotton Tax Reparations Litigation," *Journal of African American History (JAAH)* 103 (Winter-Spring 2018): 91–104; see also, James M. Davidson, "Encountering the Ex-Slave Reparations Movement from the Grave: The National Industrial Council and the National Liberty Party, 1901–1907," *JAAH* 97 (Winter-Spring 2012): 13–38.

23. Ashley Farmer, "Reframing African American Women's Grassroots Organiz- ing: Audley Moore and the Universal Association of Ethiopian Women, 1957–1963," *JAAH* 101 (Winter-Spring 2016): quote on p. 90.

24. As a teenager, Sundiata Keita Cha-Jua was employed as a community (youth) organizer by the Decatur, Illinois, Black Central Coordinating Committee in 1969 and 1970 with the funds supplied by the Illinois Conference of Churches (ICC). Religious denominations generally contributed to interdenominational organizations such as the Interreligious Foundation for Community Organization (IFCO) or statewide entities like the ICC. The Cairo, Illinois, Black United Front received $500,000 as well as significant in-kind resources such as staff support between 1969 and 1974. See Kerry Pimblott, *Faith in Black Power: Religion, Race, and Resistance in Cairo, Illinois* (Lexington: University Press of Kentucky, 2017), 152, 161–71. Elaine Allen Lechtreck, "'We Are Demanding $500 Million in Reparations': The Black Manifesto, Mainline Religious Denominations, and Black Economic Development," *JAAH* 97 (Winter- Spring 2012): 39–71.

25. Adjoa A. Aiyetoro, "The National Coalition of Blacks for Reparations in Amer- ica (N'COBRA): Its Creation and Contributions to the Reparations Movement," in *Who Should Pay? Slavery and the Raging Debate on Reparations*, ed. Raymond A. Winbush (New York: Amistad, HarperCollins, 2003), 209–25.

26. Valerie Bauerlein, "North Carolina to Compensate Sterilization Victims," *Wall Street Journal*, July 26, 2013; Madeleine Davis, "North Carolina Passes Bill Granting Reparations to Victims of Forced Sterilization, But Is it Enough?" Jezebel: Feminist

News Website, May 31, 2012; Jim Morrill, "North Carolina Eugenics Victims Shut Out of Settlement by Law's Wording," *Charlotte Observer*, December 5, 2014.

27. Beckles, *Britain's Black Debt*, 278.

28. Ibid.

29. See www.caricomreparations.org.

30. CARICOM Reparations Commission, "10-Point Reparation Plan," accessed August 22, 2017, http://caricomreparations.org/caricom/caricoms-10-point-reparation -plan/.

31. Ibid., see also, V. P. Franklin, "Commentary—Reparations as an Economic Development Strategy: The CARICOM Reparations Commission," *JAAH* 98 (Summer 2014): 363–66.

32. Ta-Nehisi Coates, "The Case for Reparations," *The Atlantic*, June 2014.

33. V. P. Franklin, "Introduction: African Americans and Movements for Reparations: Past, Present, and Future," *JAAH* 97 (Winter-Spring 2012): 1–14; see also Nicola Frith and Joyce Hope Scott, "Introduction: National and International Perspectives on Movements for Reparations," *JAAH* 103 (Winter-Spring 2018): 1–17.

34. George Rude, *Ideology and Popular Protest* (1995; reprint 1980); Anthony Bogues in *Black Heretics/Black Prophets: Radical Political Intellectuals* (2003).

35. Eleanor Flexner, *Century of Struggle: The History of the Women's Rights Movement in the United States* (Cambridge, MA: Harvard University Press, 1975); Gerda Lerner, *The Grimke Sisters of South Carolina: Pioneers of Women's Rights and Abolition* (1964; reprinted Chapel Hill: University of North Carolina Press, 2004); Catherine Birney, *The Grimke Sisters: The First Women Advocates of Abolition and Women's Rights* (1970; reprinted Palo Alto, CA: Create Space Publishing, 2013); and Sally McMillan, *Seneca Falls and the Origins of the Women's Rights Movement* (New York: Oxford University Press, 2008).

36. Sara Evans, *Personal Politics: The Roots of Women's Liberation in the Civil Rights Movement and New Left* (New York: Knopf, 1979); and *Born for Liberty: A History of Women in America* (New York, the Free Press, 1989); Faith S. Holseart, et al., ed., *Hands on the Freedom Plow: Personal Accounts by Women in SNCC* (Urbana: University of Illinois Press, 2010).

37. Dennis Banks, *Ojibwa Warrior: Dennis Banks and the Rise of the American Indian Movement* (Norman: Univ. of Oklahoma Press, 2005); Troy Johnson, *American Indian Occupation of Alcatraz Island: Red Power and Self-Determination* (Omaha: University of Nebraska Press, 2008); F. Arturo Rosales, *Chicano: The History of the Mexican American Civil Rights Movement* (Houston: Arte Publico Press, 1996); Paul Chaat Smith and Robert Allen Warrior, *Like a Hurricane: The Indian Movement from Alcatraz to Wounded Knee* (New York: The New Press, 1997); Peter Matthiessen, *Sal Si Puedes: Cesar Chavez and the New American Revolution* (Berkeley: University of California Press, 2000).George Mariscal, *Brown-Eyed Children of the Sun: Lessons from the Chicano Movement, 1965–1975* (Albuquerque: University of New Mexico Press, 2005); Robert Cohen and Reginald Zelnik, eds., *The Free Speech Movement: Reflections on Berkeley in the 1960s* (Berkeley: University of California Press, 2002);

Gael Graham, *Young Activists: American High School Students in the Age of Protest* (DeKalb: Northern Illinois University Press, 2006); Robbie Liberman, *Prairie Power: Voices of the 1960s Midwestern Student Protests* (Columbia: University of Missouri Press, 2004); David Carter, *Stonewall: The Riots That Started the Gay Revolution* (New York: St. Martin's Press, 2004); Craig A. Rimmerman, *From Identity to Politics: The Lesbian and Gay Movements in the United States* (Philadelphia, PA: Temple University Press, 2002); and *The Lesbian and Gay Movements: Assimilation or Liberation?* (Philadelphia, PA: Westview Press, 2008); Martin Duberman, *Stonewall* (New York: Dutton, 1992); Lillian Faderman, *The Gay Revolution: The Story of the Struggle* (New York: Simon and Shuster, 2014); Kirkpatrick Sale, *The Green Revolution: The American Environmental Movement, 1962–1992* (New York: Hill and Wang, 1993); and Dorceta Taylor, *The Environment and the People in American Cities, 1600s to 1900s: Disorder, Inequality, and Social Change* (Durham, NC: Duke University Press, 2009).

38. Sundiata Keita Cha-Jua, "Robert L. Allen, 'Past Due': The African American quest for Reparations: A Contemporary Observation," *The Black Scholar* 44, No. 3 (Winter 2014), 29.

39. After the killing of Trayvon Martin in 2012, Alicia Garza, Patrice Cullors, and Opal Tometi created the #Black Lives Matter slogan. It exploded into public consciousness in August 2016, after the killing of Michael Brown. See Alicia Garza, "A Herstory of the #BLACKLIVESMATTER MOVEMENT," *PROUDFLESH: NEW AFRIKAN JOURNAL OF CULTURE, POLITICS & CONSCIOUSNESS* ISSUE NO. 10, 2014; Keeanga-Yamahtta Taylor, *From# BlackLivesMatter to Black Liberation* (Chicago: Haymarket Books, 2016), 151; Barbara Ransby, *Making All Black Lives Matter* (Berkeley: University of California Press, 2018), 5–6, 75.

40. Elizabeth Arias, Betzaida Tejada-Vera, and Farida Ahmad, "Provisional life expectancy estimates for January through June 2020" (2021).

41. Black Lives Matter, "Why Reparations?," June 3, 2021, https://blacklivesmatter.com/why-reparations/; Movement 4 Black Lives, *A Vision for Black Lives*, "Reparations," https://m4bl.org/policy-platforms/reparations/; National African American Reparations Commission, "Reparations Plan," https://reparationscomm.org/reparations-plan/.

42. Walter Johnson, *River of Dark Dreams: Slavery and Empire in the Cotton Kingdom* (Harvard University Press, 2013); Edward E. Baptist, *The Half Has Never Been Told: Slavery and the Making of American Capitalism* (New York: Basic Books, 2014); Sven Beckert, *Empire of Cotton: A Global History* (New York: Alfred A. Knopf, 2014); Zach Sell, *Trouble of the World: Slavery and Empire in the Age of Capital* (Chapel Hill: University of North Carolina Press, 2021).

43. For a problematization of the relationship between plantation slavery, capitalism, and colonialism see Sell, *Trouble of the World*, 2, 6–9, 72–84, 192–220.

44. Martin Luther King Jr., *Why We Can't Wait* (New York: Signet Classics, 2000; rprt. 1963), 170; Martin Luther King Jr., *Where Do We Go from Here: Chaos or Community?* (Boston: Beacon Press, 1986; rprt. 1968), 126.

A Historical Timeline of Reparations Payments Made from 1783 through 2020 by the United States Government, States, Cities, Religious Institutions, Colleges and Universities, and Corporations

ALLEN J. DAVIS

"Reparations are a program of acknowledgement, redress, and closure for a grievous injustice."

—William A. Darity, Jr. and A. Kirsten Mullen, *From Here to Equality, Reparations for Black Americans in the 21st Century* (2).

1700–1899

1783: *Belinda Sutton* (also Royal or Royall) was born in modern-day Ghana in 1713 and sold into slavery as a child to Isaac Royall in Massachusetts. After 50 years of enslavement, she was made a freedwoman when Royall fled to Nova Scotia. Sutton petitioned the commonwealth of Massachusetts for a pension. In 1783 she was awarded a pension of 15 pounds, 12 shillings, to be paid from the estate of Isaac Royall.

1865: On January 12, during the Civil War, General William T. Sherman and US Secretary of War Edwin M. Stanton met with 20 Black leaders in Savannah, Georgia. Four days later, General Sherman issued *Special Field Order No. 15* stating that Black people would receive *an army mule and not more than forty acres* on the coastal plains of South Carolina and Georgia. By June, roughly 40,000 Blacks had settled on four hundred thousand acres of land before Confederate landowners, aided by the new Andrew Johnson administration, started taking back "their" land.

1866: *Southern Homestead Act*: Made nearly 46 million acres of public land available for low-cost purchase in the states of Alabama, Arkansas, Florida, Louisiana, and Mississippi. It granted freed people 6 months or until January 1, 1867, to purchase land without competition from white Southerners and Northern investors. Due to their impoverishment, the machinations of Southern bureaucrats, and the violence of whites, freed people were only able to file 6,500 land claims of which about 1,000 were awarded. The act was repealed in June 1876.

1878: In 1853, *Henrietta Wood* a free Black woman living and laboring as a domestic worker in Cincinnati was lured across the Ohio River and into the slave state of Kentucky by a white man named Zebulon Ward. Ward then sold her to slave traders, who took her to Texas, where she remained enslaved through the Civil War. Wood eventually returned to Cincinnati, and in 1870 sued Ward for $20,000 in damages and lost wages. In 1878, an all-white jury decided in Wood's favor and ordered Ward to pay $2,500, perhaps the largest sum ever awarded by a court in the United States in restitution for slavery.

1900–1949

1924*: With the *Pueblo Lands Act of 1924*, Congress authorized the establishment of the Pueblo Lands Board to adjudicate land title disputes, along with a payment of $1,300,000 to the Pueblo nation for the land they lost (although the Pueblo disputed the amount).

1927: The Shoshones were paid over $6 million for land illegally seized from them. However, that sum was only half the appraised value of the land.

1934*: Congress passed the *Indian Reorganization Act* authorizing $2 million a year in appropriations for the acquisition of land for Indians (except for the state of Oklahoma and the territory of Alaska until 1936). Congress made appropriations until 1941. In total $5.5 million was appropriated for 400,000 acres of land. Further legislation added another 875,000 acres. In total, one million acres of grazing land and nearly one million acres for homesteading were returned to Indian nations.

1944: California Attorney General Earl Warren *sued the federal government in the Court of Claims* on behalf of California's Indian Nations after the United States failed to ratify solemn treaties with various indigenous nations. The plaintiffs were eventually awarded $17 million, but after "costs" were deducted by the federal government, they received only $5 million.

1946*: Congress created the *Indian Claims Commission* to hear fraud and treaty violation claims against the United States government. The Commission was adjourned in 1978 with all pending cases transferred to the United States Court of Claims. By this time the Commission had adjudicated 546 claims and awarded more than $818 million in judgments.

1950–1969

1950*: The *Navajo-Hopi Rehabilitation Act* appropriated $88,570,000 over 10 years for a program to benefit the Navajo and Hopi. It included soil conservation, education, business and industry development on reservation, and assistance in finding employment off-reservation.

1956: The Pawnee nation was awarded more than $1 million in a suit brought before the Indian Claims Commission for land taken from them in Iowa, Kansas, and Missouri.

1962: Georgia restored many Cherokee landmarks, a newspaper plant, and other buildings in New Echota. It also repealed its repressive anti–Native American laws of 1830.

1968: In the United States Court of Claims case *Tlingit and Haida Indians of Alaska v. United States*, the plaintiff tribes won a judgment of $7.5 million as just compensation for land taken by the United States government between 1891 and 1925.

1969: *The Black Manifesto* was one of the first calls for reparations in the modern era. Authored by *James Forman*, former Executive Director of SNCC (Student Nonviolent Coordinating Committee) and the League of Black Revolutionary Workers, the manifesto was presented at the National Black Economic Development Conference in Detroit. The manifesto demanded $500 million in reparations from predominantly white religious institutions for their role in perpetuating slavery and post-slavery racial oppression. About $215,000 (other sources say $500,000) was raised from the Episcopal and Methodist churches through rancorous deliberations that ultimately tore the coalition apart. The money was used to establish organizations such as a Black-owned bank, television networks, and the *Black Economic Research Center*.

1970–1989

1970: Richard Nixon signed into law House Resolution 471 restoring Blue Lake and the surrounding area to the Taos Pueblo (New Mexico). The land had been taken by presidential order in 1906.

1971*: Around $1 billion + 44 million acres of land were appropriated in the *Alaska Native Claims Settlement Act*.

1974: The federal government reached a $10 million out-of-court settlement with victims of the Tuskegee Experiment, their surviving wives, and descendants. About 400 Black men living in Macon County, Alabama, were deceived by the US Public Health Service (PHS) into participating in a study of "bad blood" that was actually a *study of untreated syphilis* in which they were denied available treatments.

1980: $81 million to the Klamath Nation of Oregon.

1980: $105 million to the Sioux of South Dakota for seizure of their land.

1985: $12.3 million to Seminoles of Florida.

1985: $31 million to Chippewas of Wisconsin.

1986: $32 million per 1836 Treaty to Ottawas of Michigan.

1988: President Ronald Reagan signed the Civil Liberties Act of 1988 providing $1.2 billion ($20,000 a person) and an apology to each of the approximately 60,000 living Japanese Americans who had been interned during World War II. An additional $12,000 and an apology were given to 450 Unangan (Aleut) Nation for their internment during WWII, and a $6.4 million trust fund was created for their communities.

1989*: Congressman John Conyers, D-Michigan introduced bill H.R. 3745 which aimed to create a *Commission to Study Reparation Proposals for African Americans*. The commission would study the impact of slavery and its "lingering effects," including racial discrimination, on Black people, from 1619 to the present and recommend "appropriate remedies," including compensation for eligible claimants.

1990–2009

1993*†: US Congress passed a *joint resolution acknowledging and apologizing* to Native Hawaiians for the United States' illegal overthrow of the sovereign Hawaiian nation.

1994: The state of Florida approved $2.1 million for the living survivors of a 1923 racial pogrom that resulted in multiple deaths and the decimation of the Black community in the town of Rosewood.

1995†: The Southern Baptists apologized to African American church members for the denomination's endorsement of slavery.

1997†: President Bill Clinton apologized to the survivors of the US Public Health Services' sponsored Tuskegee Experiment, the untreated syphilis tests of Black men in Tuskegee, Alabama.

1998*: President Clinton signed into law the *Sand Creek Massacre National Historic Study Site Act*, which officially acknowledges an 1864 slaughter of a peaceful Cheyenne village located in the territory of Colorado by seven hundred US soldiers. Hundreds, largely women and children, were massacred. The act established a federally funded Historic Site at Sand Creek in 2007.

1999: A *class action lawsuit* by Black farmers against the United States Department of Agriculture was settled by a consent decree in which the plaintiffs were awarded nearly $1 billion in payments. The lawsuit alleged systematic racial discrimination in the allocation of farm loans from 1981 to 1996. A further $1.2 billion was appropriated by Congress for the second part of the settlement (*The Pigford Cases*). Even then, it was not until 2013 that some plaintiffs in *Pigford v. Glickman* began receiving monetary awards and further financial help for Black farmers has since been stalled.

2001: The Oklahoma legislature passed, and Governor Frank Keating signed, a bill to pay reparations for the destruction of the Greenwood, Oklahoma, community known popularly as "Black Wall Street" in 1921. Compensation was to be paid in the form of low-income student scholarships in Tulsa; an economic development authority for Greenwood; a memorial; and the awarding of medals to the 118 known living survivors of the destruction of Greenwood.

2002[†]: Governor Mark Warner of Virginia issued a formal apology for the state's decision to forcibly sterilize more than 8,000 of its residents under the Virginia's Eugenical Sterilization Act of 1924.

2005[*†]: The US Senate approved, by voice vote, S.R. 39 which called for the lawmakers to apologize to lynching victims, survivors, and their descendants (several of whom watched from the gallery) for the Senate's failure to pass anti-lynching legislation.

2005: Five decades after Prince Edward County and other locales shut down their public schools in support of apartheid/segregation the state of Virginia apologized and offered reparations in the form of scholarships. John Kluge, a billionaire media investor, donated $1 million which the state matched to provide up to $5,500 to any state resident who was denied a proper education during the state's "Massive Resistance" campaign against desegregation.

2005: Banking corporation JPMorgan Chase issued an apology for their historical ties to the slave trade. The corporation set up Smart Start Louisiana, a $5 million scholarship fund for Black students to attend college.

2007–2008[†]: State legislatures in Virginia, Maryland, North Carolina, Alabama, New Jersey, and Florida passed measures apologizing for slavery and apartheid/segregation.

2008/2009[*†]: US *House Resolution 194* and *Senate Concurrent Resolution 26* made formal apology to the African American community for "centuries of brutal dehumanization and injustices." Plus, the resolutions admitted that "African Americans continue to suffer from the complex interplay between slavery and Jim Crow long after both systems were formally abolished through enormous damage and loss, both tangible and intangible, including the loss of human dignity."

2010–present

2014: The state of North Carolina set aside $10 million for reparations payments to living survivors of its eugenics program, which forcibly sterilized approximately 7,600 people.

2015: The City of Chicago signed into law an *ordinance* granting cash payments, free college education, and a range of social services to 57 living survivors of police torture (Burge Reparations). Explicitly defining the compensatory measures totaling $5.5 million as reparations, the ordinance includes a formal apology from Mayor Rahm Emanuel and a mandate to teach the broader public about the torture through a memorial and public-school curriculum.

2016: Georgetown University acknowledged the school profited from the sale of enslaved persons and "reconciled" its past by *naming two buildings* after African Americans and offering preferred admission to any descendant of the enslaved people who worked at the university.

2016: The state of Virginia, one of more than 30 states that practiced forced sterilizations, followed North Carolina's lead and since 2016 has been *awarding $25,000 to each survivor.*

2016: The US government reached a settlement of $492 million with 17 Native American tribes to resolve lawsuits alleging the federal government mismanaged tribal land, resources, and money.

2018: The Supreme Court, in a 4–4 deadlock, *let stand a lower court's order* that the state of Washington make billions of dollars' worth of repairs to roads, where the state had built culverts below road channels and structures in a way that prevented salmon from swimming through and reaching their spawning grounds. These practices damaged the state's salmon habitats and contributed to population decline. The case involved the *Stevens Treaties*, a series of agreements in 1854–55, in which Indian nations in Washington State ceded millions of acres of land in exchange for "the right to take fish." Implicit in the treaties, courts ruled, was a guarantee that there would be enough fish for them to harvest.

2019*: Senator Cory Booker, D-New Jersey, introduced bill S. 1083 (*H.R. 40 Commission to Study and Develop Reparation Proposals for African Americans Act*) in the Senate. It is a concurrent to HR 40 which was introduced into the House by Rep. Sheila Jackson Lee of Texas. Both would provide for a commission to study and report on the impact of slavery and discrimination against African Americans and deliver a verdict on different proposals for reparations.

2019: In a nonbinding student-led referendum, undergraduate students at Georgetown University voted to add a new fee of $27.20 per student per semester to their tuition bill with proceeds going to support education and health programs for the 4,000 known living descendants of enslaved Black people who toiled at the university.

2019: The Virginia Theological Seminary earmarked $1.7 million to pay reparations to descendants of enslaved African Americans who worked on their campus.

2019: Princeton Theological Seminary announced a $27 million commitment for various initiatives to recognize how it benefited from the enslavement of Black people.

2019: Georgetown University announced that it would raise about $400,000 a year to benefit descendants of the 272 enslaved people who were sold to aid the college 200 years ago, and the funds will be used to support community projects.

2019: The City Council of Evanston, Illinois, voted to allocate the first $10 million in tax revenue from the sale of recreational marijuana (which became legal in the state on January 1, 2020) to fund reparations initiatives that address the gaps in wealth and opportunity of its Black residents.

2020[†]: The University of Mississippi has apologized to dozens of African Americans who were arrested in 1970 for protesting racial inequality and Confederate imagery on campus.

2020: The Museum of Fine Arts in Boston reached an agreement with the Massachusetts Attorney General's Office to implement policies and procedures and initiate a $500,000 fund to address diversity issues. The agreement follows an incident of racial discrimination toward Black students visiting the museum in May 2019.

2020[†]: The town of Asheville, North Carolina, voted to provide reparations to its Black residents in the form of a public apology and investments in Black communities.

Reparations Paid by Other Countries

1952: Germany paid $822 million to Holocaust survivors in the German Jewish Settlement.

1984: Argentine President Raúl Alfonsín created the Comisión Nacional sobre la Desaparición de Personas (*National Commission on the Disappearance of Persons*) to investigate the whereabouts of desaparecidos ("the disappeared") who were abducted or killed by the military during the previous dictatorship. The Commission issued a report (*Nunca Más*) that led to prosecution of those involved, reparations paid to families of the victims in the form of pensions, and new standards implemented to provide accountability for human rights violations.

1988: Canada returned 250,000 sq. miles of land to First Nations and Inuit peoples.

1988: Canada agreed to pay $230 million to Japanese Canadians who were interned and had their property seized during World War II.

1990: Austria enacted legislation to pay $25 million to Holocaust survivors.

2014: France: More than 700 claims have been filed under an agreement between the United States and France in which French officials have agreed to pay out $60 million for the deportations carried out by the French National Railway Company (SNCF), France's railway system. In exchange, the US government agreed to ask courts to dismiss lawsuits against SNCF or the French government.

2015: The Japanese government approved $8.3 million to provide old-age care to Korean "Comfort Women" survivors plus issue a new apology.

2016: France: The US State Department has paid or approved 90 claims for a total of $11 million in reparations by France to former WWII prisoners who were carried to Nazi Death Camps in French trains—the first French reparations paid to Holocaust survivors in the United States.

Works Cited

The 1854–1855 Western Washington Treaties. (2011, March 1). *Native American Netroots.* http://nativeamericannetroots.net/diary/881.

AG's Office and Museum of Fine Arts reach historic agreement to support diversity and inclusivity (2020, May 5). Museum of Fine Arts, Boston. https://www.mfa.org/press-release/historic-agreement-to-support-diversity-and-inclusivity.

Alaska Native Claims Settlement Act. (2020, June 11). In Wikipedia. https://en.wikipedia.org/w/index.php?title=Alaska_Native_Claims_Settlement_Act&oldid=962062119.

---

*Congressional actions
†Apologies from government institutions and other organizations

Apologizing for the enslavement and racial segregation of African Americans. H.Res.194, 110th Cong. (2007). https://www.congress.gov/bill/110th-congress/house-resolution/194.

Belinda Royall. (2020, May 17). In Wikipedia. https://en.wikipedia.org/w/index.php?title=Belinda_Royall&oldid=957229717.

Benton-Lewis, D. (1996). *Black reparations now!: 40 acres, $50 dollars, and a mule, + interest.* Rockville, MD: Black Reparations Press.

Blythe, A. (2017, March 17). Families of NC eugenics victims no longer alive still have shot at compensation. *The News & Observer.* https://www.newsobserver.com/news/politics-government/state-politics/article139219933.html.

Booker announces introduction of bill to form commission for study of reparation proposals for African Americans. (n.d.). Senator Cory Booker. Retrieved June 25, 2020, from https://www.booker.senate.gov/news/press/booker-announces-introduction-of-bill-to-form-commission-for-study-of-reparation-proposals-for-african-americans.

Branigin, A. (2019, September 24). WWJD: Princeton Theological Seminary announces $27 million reparations plan. T*he Root.* https://www.theroot.com/wwjd-princeton-theological-seminary-announces-27-mill-1839304752.

Branigin, A. (2020, July 15). A liberal North Carolina town has unanimously voted to give its Black residents reparations. *The Root.* https://www.theroot.com/a-liberal-north-carolina-town-has-unanimously-voted-to-1844389058.

Branigin, W. (2002, May 3). Va. Apologizes to the victims of sterilizations. *Washington Post.* https://www.washingtonpost.com/archive/local/2002/05/03/va-apologizes-to-the-victims-of-sterilizations/9cbfe2ad-950c-47f8-a186-c68e4d1e362e/.

Burge Reparations information. (2017, February 9). City of Chicago. https://web.archive.org/web/20170209184557/https://www.cityofchicago.org/city/en/depts/dol/supp_info/burge-reparations-information.html.

Burns, J. F. (1988, September 6). Canada to give Indigenous people an Arctic area the size of Texas. *The New York Times.* https://www.nytimes.com/1988/09/06/world/canada-to-give-indigenous-people-an-arctic-area-the-size-of-texas.html.

Burns, J. F. (1988, September 23). Ottawa will pay compensation to uprooted Japanese Canadians. *The New York Times.* https://www.nytimes.com/1988/09/23/world/ottawa-will-pay-compensation-to-uprooted-japanese-canadians.html.

Castillo, E. D. (n.d.). *Short overview of California Indian history.* Native American Heritage Commission. Retrieved June 25, 2020, from http://nahc.ca.gov/resources/california-indian-history/.

Civil Liberties Act of 1988. (2020, April 14). In *Wikipedia.* https://en.wikipedia.org/w/index.php?title=Civil_Liberties_Act_of_1988&oldid=950881809.

Coates, T.-N. (2014, June). The case for reparations. *The Atlantic.* https://www.theatlantic.com/magazine/archive/2014/06/the-case-for-reparations/361631/.

Coates, T.-N. (2017). *We were eight years in power: An American Tragedy.* New York, NY: One World, 176.

Commission to Study Reparation Proposals for African Americans Act, H.R.3745, 101st Cong. (1989). https://www.congress.gov/bill/101st-congress/house-bill/3745

CONADEP. (1984). *Nunca más. http://www.desaparecidos.org/nuncamas/web/english/library/nevagain/nevagain_001.htm*. A concurrent resolution apologizing for the enslavement and racial segregation of African Americans, S.Con. Res.26, 111th Cong. (2009). https://www.congress.gov/bill/111th-congress/senate -concurrent-resolution/26.

Corlett, J. A. (2003). *Race, racism, & reparations*. Ithaca, NY: Cornell University Press.

Cowles, C. D., Moodey, J. S., Ainsworth, F. C., Kirkley, J. W., Perry, L. J., Davis, G. B., Lazelle, H. M., & Scott, R. N. (1880). *The War of the Rebellion: A compilation of the official records of the Union and Confederate armies*. Washington, DC: Government Printing Office. https://catalog.hathitrust.org/Record/000625514.

Darity, W. A., Jr., & Mullen, A. K. (2020). *From here to equality: Reparations for black Americans in the twenty-first century*. Chapel Hill, NC: The University of North Carolina Press.

Darling, D. (2005, June 21). Spending spree. *Herald and News*. https://www.heraldand news.com/news/top_stories/spending-spree/article_08f68a22-1e83-51b8-bfae -coee266fob3f.html.

Debo, A. (1984). *A history of the Indians of the United States* (Revised ed.). Norman, OK: University of Oklahoma Press.

Eligon, J. (2018, June 11). "This ruling gives us hope": Supreme Court sides with tribe in salmon case. *The New York Times*. https://www.nytimes.com/2018/06/11/us/ washington-salmon-culverts-supreme-court.html.

Engel, R. (1990, February 13). Austria to pay $25 million more in support of Holocaust survivors. *JTA Daily News Bulletin, 68*(30), 3. https://www.jta.org/1990/02/13/ archive/austria-to-pay-25-million-more-in-support-of-holocaust-survivors.

Forman, J. (1969). *Black Manifesto*. https://episcopalarchives.org/church-awakens/ files/original/c20bd83547dd3cf92e788041d7fddfa2.pdf.

Forty acres and a mule. (2020, June 17). In *Wikipedia*. https://en.wikipedia.org/w/ index.php?title=Forty_acres_and_a_mule&oldid=963075337.

Georgetown to rename building for Isaac Hawkins, one of 272 enslaved in 1838 sale. (2017, April 13). Georgetown University. https://www.georgetown.edu/news/ georgetown-to-rename-building-for-isaac-hawkins-one-of-272-enslaved-in -1838-sale/.

Glenza, J. (2016, January 3). Rosewood massacre a harrowing tale of racism and the road toward reparations. *The Guardian*. http://www.theguardian.com/us -news/2016/jan/03/rosewood-florida-massacre-racial-violence-reparations.

Hanson, J. (2015, March 5). Virginia votes compensation for victims of its eugenic sterilization program. *Biopolitical Times*. https://www.geneticsandsociety.org/biopolitical -times/virginia-votes-compensation-victims-its-eugenic-sterilization-program.

Hassan, A. (2019, April 12). Georgetown students agree to create reparations fund. *The New York Times.* https://www.nytimes.com/2019/04/12/us/georgetown-reparations.html.

Henrietta Wood. (2020, June 14). In *Wikipedia.* https://en.wikipedia.org/w/index.php?title=Henrietta_Wood&oldid=962584919.

Henry, C. P. (2007). *Long overdue: The politics of racial reparations.* New York, NY: NYU Press.

Hersher, R. (2016, September 27). U.S. government to pay $492 million to 17 American Indian tribes. *NPR.* https://www.npr.org/sections/thetwo-way/2016/09/27/495627997/u-s-government-to-pay-492-million-to-17-american-indian-tribes.

H.R. 40 Commission to Study and Develop Reparation Proposals for African-Americans Act, S.1083, 116th Cong. (2019). https://www.congress.gov/bill/116th-congress/senate-bill/1083.

Indian Claims Commission. (2020, May 14). In *Wikipedia.* https://en.wikipedia.org/w/index.php?title=Indian_Claims_Commission&oldid=956687858.

Indian Reorganization Act. (2020, June 17). In *Wikipedia.* https://en.wikipedia.org/w/index.php?title=Indian_Reorganization_Act&oldid=963042093.

Janofsky, M. (2005, July 31). A new hope for dreams suspended by segregation. *The New York Times.* https://www.nytimes.com/2005/07/31/education/a-new-hope-for-dreams-suspended-by-segregation.html.

Jim Forman delivers Black Manifesto at Riverside Church. (n.d.). *SNCC Digital Gateway.* Retrieved June 25, 2020, from https://snccdigital.org/events/jim-forman-delivers-black-manifesto-at-riverside-church/.

A joint resolution to acknowledge the 100th anniversary of the January 17, 1893, overthrow of the Kingdom of Hawaii, and to offer an apology to Native Hawaiians on behalf of the United States for the overthrow of the Kingdom of Hawaii, S.J.Res.19, 103rd Cong. (1993). https://www.congress.gov/bill/103rd-congress/senate-joint-resolution/19.

JP Morgan Chase creates "Smart Start Louisiana." (n.d.). *Howard University News Service.* Retrieved June 25, 2020, from *http://hunewsservice.com/news/jp-morgan-chase-creates-smart-start-louisiana/*JPMorgan: Predecessors linked to slavery. (2005, January 21). *NBC News.* http://www.nbcnews.com/id/6851727/ns/business-us_business/t/jpmorgan-predecessors-linked-slavery/.

Kenny, R. W. (1944). *History and proposed settlement, claims of California Indians.* California State Printing Office. https://www.scribd.com/document/444168305/Robert-Kenny-History-and-Proposed-Settlement-Claims-of-California-Indians-1944.

Kunichoff, Y., & Macaraeg, S. (2017, Spring). Black and blue Chicago finds a new way to heal. *YES Magazine.*

McDaniel, W. C. (2019, September 4). The former slave who sued for reparations and won. *The New York Times.* https://www.nytimes.com/2019/09/04/opinion/henrietta-wood-reparations-slavery.html.

Meadows, J. (2019, November 27). Future weed revenue will fund Evanston's new reparations program. *Patch.* https://patch.com/illinois/evanston/evanston-recreational-cannabis-tax-fund-referendum-program.

Meyers, C. C. (2008). Sherman's Special Field Orders, No. 15. In *The Empire State of the South: Georgia History in Documents and Essays.* Macon, GA: Mercer University Press.

Mustard, D. B. (2003). *Racial justice in America: A reference handbook.* Goleta, CA: ABC-CLIO.

National Coalition of Blacks for Reparations in America. Retrieved June 19, 2020, from https://www.ncobraonline.org/.

National Commission on the Disappearance of Persons. (2020, May 7). In *Wikipedia.* https://en.wikipedia.org/w/index.php?title=National_Commission_on_the_Disappearance_of_Persons&oldid=955393491.

Navajo-Hopi Rehabilitation Act, Pub. L. No. 81–474 (1950). https://www.law.cornell.edu/topn/navajo-hopi_rehabilitation_act

Neiman, S. (2019). *Learning from the Germans: Race and the memory of evil.* New York, NY: Farrar, Straus and Giroux.

Neuman, S. (2013, July 25). North Carolina set to compensate forced sterilization victims. *NPR.* https://www.npr.org/sections/thetwo-way/2013/07/25/205547272/north-carolina-set-to-compensate-forced-sterilization-victims.

Ole Miss apologizes to black protesters arrested in 1970. (2020, February 26). *US News & World Report.* https://www.usnews.com/news/us/articles/2020-02-26/ole-miss-apologizes-to-black-protesters-arrested-in-1970.

Order by the Commander of the Military Division of the Mississippi, January 16, 1865. (1865, January 16). Freedmen & Southern Society Project. http://www.freedmen.umd.edu/sfo15.htm.

Pigford v. Glickman. (2019, November 23). In *Wikipedia.* https://en.wikipedia.org/w/index.php?title=Pigford_v. Glickman&oldid=927638368.

The Pigford cases: USDA settlement of discrimination suits by black farmers (No. RS20430). (2013). Congressional Research Service. https://www.everycrsreport.com/reports/RS20430.html.

The Pueblo Lands Act (1924). (2018, January 12). In *Wikipedia.* https://en.wikipedia.org/w/index.php?title=Aboriginal_title_in_New_Mexico&oldid=820050953.

Sand Creek Massacre National Historic Site. (2020, April 4). National Park Service. https://www.nps.gov/sand/learn/historyculture/stories.htm.

Sang-Hun, C. (2015, December 28). Japan and South Korea settle dispute over wartime "comfort women." *The New York Times.* https://www.nytimes.com/2015/12/29/world/asia/comfort-women-south-korea-japan.html

Sharif, D. (2019, September 10). Virginia Theological Seminary sets up $1.7 million fund to pay reparations. *The Root.* https://www.theroot.com/virginia-theological-seminary-with-deep-roots-in-slave-1838025884.

Shaver, K. (2016, September 15). U.S. begins paying out reparations from France to Holocaust survivors and their heirs. *Washington Post.* https://www.washington

post.com/local/trafficandcommuting/us-begins-paying-out-french-reparations
-to-holocaust-survivors-and-their-heirs/2016/09/15/87b1de56-7abb-11e6-bd86
-b7bbd53d2b5d_story.html.

Southern Homestead Act of 1866. (2019, December 2). In *Wikipedia*. https://
en.wikipedia.org/w/index.php?title=Southern_Homestead_Act_of_1866
&oldid=928906905.

Swarns, R. L. (2019, October 30). Is Georgetown's $400,000-a-year plan to aid slave
descendants enough? *The New York Times*. https://www.nytimes.com/2019/10/30/
us/georgetown-slavery-reparations.html

Tlingit and Haida Indians of Alaska v. United States, 389 F. 2d 778 (Ct. Cl. 1968).
https://scholar.google.com/scholar_case?case=11176116812815682061.

Tuskegee study presidential apology. (1997, May 16). Centers for Disease Control and
Prevention. https://www.cdc.gov/tuskegee/clintonp.htm.

Tuskegee syphilis experiment. (2020, June 16). In *Wikipedia*. https://en.wikipedia
.org/w/index.php?title=Tuskegee_syphilis_experiment&oldid=962816558.

Tuskegee timeline. (2020, March 2). Centers for Disease Control and Prevention.
https://www.cdc.gov/tuskegee/timeline.htm.

United States. Bureau of Indian Affairs. (1966). *Indians of California*. Washington,
DC: Government Printing Office. https://catalog.hathitrust.org/Record/000247631

United States v. Sioux Nation of Indians. (2019, September 18). In *Wikipedia*.
https://en.wikipedia.org/w/index.php?title=United_States_v. Sioux_Nation_of
_Indians&oldid=916434838.

U.S. pays restitution; apologizes to Unangan (Aleut) for WWII Internment. (n.d.).
National Library of Medicine. Retrieved June 19, 2020, from https://www.nlm.
nih.gov/nativevoices/timeline/635.html.

van Buren, M. (2010, September 18). Taos Pueblo celebrates 40th anniversary of
Blue Lake's return. *The Taos News*. https://www.santafenewmexican.com/news/
local_news/taos-pueblo-celebrates-40th-anniversary-of-blue-lakes-return/
article_244ed433-d0a4-5747-b099-672bd17c41ff.html.

Victims of Eugenics Sterilization Compensation Program. (n.d.). Virginia Department of Behavioral Health and Developmental Services. Retrieved June 25, 2020,
from http://www.dbhds.virginia.gov/developmental-services/victimsofeugenics.

Washington v. United States, 584 U.S. __ (2018). https://www.scotusblog.com/case
-files/cases/washington-v-united-states/.

West Germany signs 822 million-dollar reparations pacts with Israel govt. And Jewish Material Claims Conference. (1952, September 11). *JTA Daily News Bulletin*.
https://www.jta.org/1952/09/11/archive/west-germany-signs-822-million-dollar
-reparations-pacts-with-israel-govt-and-jewish-material-claims.

PART I

Reparations

Speeches and Documents

1

The National/International Summit

Seizing the Moment to Galvanize the U.S. and Global Reparations Movement

RON DANIELS

Queen Mother Audley Moore was an indefatigable teacher, advocate, and organizer for reparations, the fundamental idea that Africans in America are due compensation to repair the physical, cultural, spiritual, and mental damages inflicted by the holocaust of enslavement. She called herself a "brain surgeon" dedicated to operating on the minds of constipated Negroes to create consciousness of the urgent need for reparations. I was a patient of this great "surgeon." Queen Mother Moore introduced me to the concept of reparations and became my mentor on this issue. As the Institute of the Black World 21st Century (IBW) prepares to convene a potentially historic National/International Summit, April 9–12, 2015, in New York City. I believe our "warrior woman" ancestor was looking down with pride and enthusiasm as reparations advocates from the United States and the Pan-African world gather to galvanize and intensify the global reparations movement.

Reparations to repair the damages of enslavement has been a persistent demand within the multifaceted Black Freedom Struggle in the United States. The movement ebbs and flows, being intense at certain moments in our history and subdued at others. Despite the fact that there is a "State of Emergency" in America's "dark ghettos," the pride associated with the election of the first African American President did not make this the most fertile period for the Reparations Movement. However, two events provided the impetus for a new moment of intense interest and advocacy for reparations in the months and years ahead.

First, the courageous decision by the heads of state in the Caribbean to demand reparations from the former European colonists for Native Genocide and African enslavement and the formation of a CARICOM Reparations

Commission has captured the imagination of reparations activists in the United States and the Pan African world. It is one thing for scholars and activists to advocate for reparations—it is quite another for the leaders of nations who are still in the neo-colonial clutches of the former colonial powers to make such a bold demand. By doing so, they risk economic and political retaliation. No doubt the dismal condition of the masses of their people and the pressure from civil society organizations influenced their decision, but there is no belittling the fact that the demand for reparations was/is a gutsy decision!

Second, the brilliant essay "The Case for Reparations" by Ta-Nehisi Coates, published in the *Atlantic* magazine, has electrified a new generation of Black people who were largely unfamiliar with reparations or unconvinced of its validity and value as a goal. While a dedicated core of true believers has kept the issue of reparations alive, for the movement to grow it must be embraced by a new generation of potential advocates who, like Brother Coates, can be broadened to form a critical mass, a formidable force to advance the demand for reparations. That moment may be at hand. Indeed, Queen Mother Moore would be excited to learn that a National African American Reparations Commission (NAARC) has been established in her memory! [visit the website www.ibw21.org for list of Members] Inspired by the CARICOM Reparations Commission and designed to function as a parallel body, NAARC's primary mission is to develop a preliminary Reparations Program/Agenda as part of an education and advocacy process to expand the Reparations Movement in the United States. Ultimately, NAARC will develop a final Reparations Program/ Agenda as an outgrowth of input from a series of regional community-based hearings and town hall meetings across the country.

This moment presents a major opportunity for discussions on how the Reparations Movement in the United States should proceed. The Coates article tapped into what appears to be a growing sentiment that reparations are due Africans in America not only for enslavement but for the damages done to our people during the era of de jure (in law) and de facto (in fact) segregation. Coates's research on housing patterns in Chicago clearly demonstrates the intergenerational wealth deficit created by discriminatory housing policies and practices. Michelle Alexander has also added her voice to reparations advocates who believe compensation is due for the massive damages to Black families and communities as a result of the "New Jim Crow," mass incarceration. Damages from environmental racism are also a matter which some advocates contend should be on the table. These considerations expand the scope of the reparations demands.

There is also a need to discuss the collective versus individual payment of reparations. This often comes up as a question when arguing the case for reparations. While one could make an argument for both, I am hopeful that a consensus will emerge in favor of collective developmental assistance. The chronic wealth gap and state of emergency in America's major cities are a direct consequence of generations of exploitation and oppression which should be addressed in terms of compensation that will be used to end the underdevelopment of the national Black community. Individuals in the Black community would benefit from increased opportunities resulting from developmental assistance for the group/collective.

Consistent with the concept of collective developmental assistance, it would also be useful to develop a consensus for a reparations Trust fund or similar structure to administer the various types of compensation that might be received from the federal government, state and local governments, corporations/businesses, and institutions like universities implicated in enslavement or other damaging policies and practices inflicted in other eras. Such a Trust Fund would be governed by a Board comprised of a cross-section of credible Black leaders and organizations that would receive various forms of compensation and allocate resources in accordance with a strategic development plan. As an aside, I have a particular interest in demanding that federal lands be transferred to a Trust Fund with the same kind of sovereignty and rights eventually granted Native Americans for the criminal dispossession of their lands.

As the case for reparations for Africans in American is advanced, we need a coherent message about key issues and questions that are often raised by our people like the ones cited above. Hopefully, as NAARC engages in its deliberations, it can be helpful in formulating and advancing recommendations on these vital issues and questions. I continue to believe that HR-40, the Reparations Study Bill, introduced by Congressman John Conyers Jr. every year from 1989 until he retired in 2017, can be a valuable organizing tool to generate discussion and action on this vital issue.

The National/International Reparations Summit was not only be a moment to galvanize the U.S. Reparations Movement, it served to galvanize an emerging global Reparations Movement. A key goal of the Summit was to explore avenues for systemic information-sharing and mutual support as a means of strengthening the global Reparations Movement. As such, it provided an opportunity for a dialogue/interface between NAARC and the CARICOM Reparations Commission (CRC) and advocates from the Caribbean, Central and South America, Canada, and Europe (21 countries). Without question, the CRC was closely examined as the model and has given a major boost to the U.S. and global Reparations Movements. At the end of the deliberations, a mechanism was put in place to sustain the momentum of this incredible moment in history. Let the word go out across the Pan African World, the global Reparations Movement is on the rise and Queen Mother Moore would be pleased!

2

Providing a Landmark and Frame of Reference for Reparatory Justice

REV. JESSE JACKSON SR.

My friend and brother, Dr. Ron Daniels, president of the Institute for the Black World, 21st Century, deserves so much credit for bringing us all together for the National/International Summit; he's so full of hope and determination; such a great mind, and someone full of raw courage. Don't take Ron Daniels for granted. People like Ron don't come in bunches like grapes. They are rare like pearls.

Ron Daniels gave me this assignment tonight of sharing some words, some observations of inspiration. It's been very difficult because I've engaged in many conversations with African American brothers and sisters—and the whites as well—about the idea of reparations and what comes to their mind when the discussion comes up.

I want to just share two verses of scripture, if I was going to preach, and I'm not, but I could. One could not ignore the ancient landmarks our mothers and fathers have set. The Proverb starts at the beginning with the origin of things; it's about the previous generation. It was said to provide a frame of reference. The scripture is from Deuteronomy: 15:12–15:

> And if thy brother, a Hebrew man, or a Hebrew woman, be sold unto thee, and serve thee six years, then in the seventh year thou shalt let him go free from thee. And when thou sendest him out free from thee, thou shalt not let him go away empty. . . . Thou shalt furnish him liberally out of thy flock, and out of thy floor, and out of thy winepress. . . .
>
> Wherewith the Lord thy God had blessed thee, thou shalt give unto him. And thou shalt remember that thou was a bondman in the land of Egypt, and the Lord thy God redeemed thee: therefore I command thee this thing today.

I want to talk a minute about America in denial. What makes this such a difficult discussion is that one thing Black people and white people have in common: neither wants to discuss reparations—for different reasons. White people want to deny it and Black people don't think it's possible, so neither wants to discuss it.

There is a fear of discussing reparations—even discussing. I was talking with some people the day of the conference here in New York. I said, "You gonna be with Ron Daniels tonight at that reparations conference? Man, what's that all about?" The denial is a way of—in the name of civil rights— putting down the idea of the undiscussable repair for damage done: a fear of even research on reparations. John Conyers in his bill is only asking for research—not an examination of the evil—just research. Fear of discussion and denial of the status of the topic. Ain't no such thing, however, as a pain so great that should not be repaired.[1]

To not believe in reparations is to believe in ethnic cleansing. To not believe in reparations is to believe in ethnic cleansing as valid. We must see the measure of our oppression and set it for others, for various reparations movements around the world that we have respected and that we are related to. There will be no TV coverage of this conference tonight or tomorrow because this is off the list of discussable issues: the issue of reparations.

If you received no money for your work, to shift your psychology from creditor to debtor is difficult. There is a sense that we should feel lucky to be here, that somebody civilized and liberated us. Fact of the matter is we are the creditors, not the debtors. But since we have been "brain dead" on the subject, it's hard to break through. And the more educated we are, oftentimes the more ignorant we are of it. That's why there's a limited number of PhDs and college graduates calling for reparations because many times the more educated you are in the system, the more your brain is cooked.

Someone asked Duke Ellington one time—"Ellington, how can you play so many different compositions?" He said, "I never went to college to learn that I couldn't." So one has to be free of the system's capacity to snatch away your mind—denying you the right to think about the idea of freedom.

When I was a little boy growing up in South Carolina in the country, our family became middle class around 1956. We moved up to the housing projects—had an indoor toilet, hot- and cold-running water, a refrigerator, bathtub, and had a "color" television, by putting that piece of colored plastic across the screen (some of you remember the "color" television). And then we got a 1949 Hudson—in 1957. We were flying high. But on a Sunday afternoon we couldn't go to the city park and swim or ride the horses, or even sit in the park to eat. We couldn't go to the skating rink; we couldn't go to any of the downtown restaurants and movies on Sunday—that was for Saturday afternoon, and only upstairs. So on Sunday, we would go out and ride in our new car. We'd go and buy five gallons of Spur Gas for a dollar and get some coupons. Some S&H green stamps. I know most of you don't know anything about getting "green stamps."[2]

And so we would go on our run; we would go to different places—where Dad grew up or where my mom grew up. Grandma said, "This weekend I want you to go out to my old home ground. I want you to follow me. It's over near Easley."[3] We knew where that was, so we got there and we turned—I remember we turned left—and we're going down this long road. So Dad turns around and said, "Grandma, where are we going?" She said, "Just follow what I say." And we kept going up and down these hills and then she said, "I think we're getting closer." We saw nothing but open fields and corn.

And we got to the corn, she said, "Right here! Right here! This is the store where we used to come in and do our sharecropping. This is where we always pay, but would never pay enough. But this is it, where we used to come and got a lot of our grub." She said, "Turn right." And we went over about three miles and without any signs on the land for direction, she said, "I think it's right here." She said to my brother and me, "Get out of the car. And for you, when y'all stop laughing, and pull those weeds back—I think I see a rock." We saw nothing at first, but we finally saw a rock. She said, "I got it!" "Got what?"

She said, "Well, this is the rock. This is the rock. Don't go that way, because it's kind of mushy down there, and that's where the water ends and there're snakes always down there. Don't go there." And she said, "And past where the mushy water is, don't go there because that's where we got baptized. That old church that burned down was over there and behind there is grandpa and grandma's—who were slaves—graveyard." Once she found the landmark—though she could neither read nor write and couldn't see well—once she saw the landmark, everything else made sense.

If we operate without a landmark, without a frame of reference, much of life does not make sense. You might as well just say that slavery time was just something in passing. But it was 246 years of legal slavery. One of the headquarters of the slavocracy was Montgomery, Alabama; and Wall Street was, in fact, the trading place. Wall Street was as deeply involved, if not more so, than parts of the South.[4] We planted and picked the cotton in the South, and they sold it in New York. It was the global trade in cotton that drove the industry of slavery.[5] But the fact is the United States was the last train on the slave trade. We think we're the first because we've been Americanized. But the fact is it came to Brazil and the Caribbean before it got here; and therefore some enslaved Africans started earlier than 1619 and got out earlier than we did and fought fights like they did in Haiti and got out. But within the American framework, it was 246 years in slavery.[6]

This is not a new subject about repair for damage done. Reparation is not a new subject. After 246 years there was the Civil War where we fought to save the Union and to end slavery. The problem was we left the former slave masters in charge of implementing the emancipation. And so we got the right to vote in 1870, but it was taken away and not implemented again until 1965, ninety-five years later; and that's because when the federal officials removed the troops, they removed the capacity to protect the newly promised freedom that we were supposed to have.

The big mistake made was when the troops left, the former slave masters were left in charge of the system. In 1965, we made the same mistake: we left the segregationists in charge of it, and they got in there. I was pained two weeks ago [March 2015] when we went into Selma. What was a celebration should have been a big demonstration because the 1965 Voting Rights Act has been nullified by the 2013 Voting Rights Act. In 1965, Blacks could not vote and white women could not serve on juries, eighteen-year-olds could not vote, you couldn't vote bilingually, you couldn't vote on college campuses. We won that, and sections four and five of the Voting Rights Act protected the right to vote.

This Supreme Court decision was led by Clarence Thomas. I say *led* by him because the court voted five-to-four to remove section four, to remove the oversight, and Clarence Thomas said they should remove sections four *and* five—he said it wasn't extreme enough. He tried to take us back to 1896.[7] He took us back almost to pre-1954 because now from Virginia to Texas they are going back to gerrymandering again. And so, we can vote, but it's diminished because we're locked out by the state legislatures. We have almost no power. Now on that stage at the commemoration of the 50th anniversary of the Selma to Montgomery march sat Governor Robert J. Bentley who collected $120 million from the Department of Education, and spent all of it on prison facilities, and was not tried for misappropriation of money. This occurred in a state where the governor turned down billions of dollars in Medicaid funds; a state where 240,000 folks have lost the right to vote because they've been to prison—180,000 are African American. He sat there in Selma in honor on an occasion of celebration when we should have been demonstrating against Governor Bentley. He is in George Wallace's lineage and legacy. Yet our lack of appreciation of our history makes us ignore the significant impact of ethnic cleansing on our minds. Folks who have taken this situation seriously have sought some measure of reparatory justice.

Notes

1. Detroit Congressman John Conyers introduced HR 40 for the first time in 1989 and reintroduced it in Congress every session after that. It called for the formation of a commission to study and make recommendations for the distribution of reparations to the descendants of the enslaved workers in the United States.

2. "S & H Green Stamps" were "trading stamps" distributed by the Sperry and Hutchinson Company by grocery stores with purchases and once a book of stamps was filled, it could be traded for new household appliances and other goods.

3. Easley, South Carolina, is in Pickens County in the northwest corner of the state near North Carolina.

4. Calvin Schermerhorn, *The Business of Slavery and the Rise of American Capitalism, 1815–1860* (New Haven: Yale University Press, 2014).

5. See Sven Berkert, *The Empire of Cotton: A Global History* (New York: Random House, 2014).

6. Robert E. Conrad, *Children of God's Fire: A Documentary History of Black Slavery in Brazil* (University Park: Penn State University Press, 2000); Hilary McD. Beckles and Verene Shepherd, *Liberties Lost: The Indigenous and Caribbean Slave Systems* (London: Cambridge University Press, 2004); C.L.R James, *Black Jacobins: Toussaint L'Ouveture and the San Domingo Revolution* (1938; reprinted New York: Vintage Press, 1989); Laurent Dubois, *Avengers of the New World: The Story of the Haitian Revolution* (Cambridge, MA: Belknap Press, 2005).

7. In 1896, the Supreme Court sanctioned the "separate but equal" doctrine in the *Plessy v. Ferguson* decision.

3

Reparations

An Issue Whose Time Has Come

DANNY GLOVER

At the outset I must admit the thing about getting older is that there are little moments that crystallize in your mind about how you got to where you are. For me being a paper boy was an important part of that. Every morning I got up to deliver my papers at 4:30 in the morning; and I still have a habit of getting up at 4:30 in the morning. I would look through the paper at fourteen or fifteen years old, eager to find out what was happening in Mississippi with the Congress of Racial Equality (CORE) or with the Student Nonviolent Coordinating Committee (SNCC), eager to read the papers before I delivered them. There are those small things that a child finds—a child growing into an adult and maturing—a way of connecting with the world and finding ways—new ways—in that connection of validating self as well. And I'm thankful for that.

I am—to use Dr. Julianne Malveaux's words—just so proud and also so humbled to be here with you. As I stand here and look upon this esteemed audience of alumni of the university here—Southern University of New Orleans—I also see the faces of many men and women who've played an extraordinary role in pushing us forward in ideas and creating this space for this incredible discussion about reparations and reparatory justice. And we all become a part of the movement, and we've all deemed it necessary. Believing not only that its time has come but also that it came long before this particular moment.

When I think about this moment, I'm reflecting on Mary Brown. I had the distinct opportunity of meeting Mary Brown when I was between six months and three and a half years old. She died when I was four years old.

She was my maternal grandfather's mother. She was born in 1853. So I'm old enough—born in 1946—to have some sort of reference point to begin my life. And Mary Brown was that reference point.

Though born and raised in San Francisco, I spent those early years of nurturing on that farm in Georgia, near Augusta, in little Jefferson County, in rural Louisville, Georgia, and I'm always reminded of that wiry woman whom I saw. It's lodged and continues to be lodged in every memory that I have. It becomes, at some point in time, the reason why I get up in the morning: to know that she laid this foundation and this groundwork for not only my grandfather, one of those extraordinary farmers—he owned 150 acres, which I still have in rural Georgia—and also, for my mother, in a sense, who graduated from Paine College in 1942, and did not pick cotton in September as most other children did. She went to school in September. This change shifted my life and the whole paradigm of my personal narrative.

I think about that and let it marinate for a moment. Knowing that it's important—and sometimes we have to reflect on the history of what has happened to us. I didn't know, as a child growing up, when I would walk in downtown Louisville that the slave auction-market was still there. And it has had various other kinds of uses over a long period of time. But Louisville, Georgia, soon after the ratification of the Constitution in 1789, became, really, the epicenter for the expansion of slavery. When 350 million acres of land were sold to New York land speculators in 1796, no one knew that later that land would become part of Mississippi and Alabama. In what was called the "Yazoo Land Fraud," in which the Supreme Court upheld the initial sale, the Georgia state legislature in 1802 ceded the land to the federal government that ultimately opened it up for settlement in 1814.[1]

The emergence of two important events—the Yazoo Land Fraud and the victory of the enslaved Africans in Haiti over Napoleon's army in 1803 leading to the Louisiana Purchase—fueled the amazing expansion of slavery. We tend to think of slavery as one point in time, as a singular moment—when we view the antebellum encampments and plantations and similar things—but it was an expansion that brought to this country the first step toward the Industrial Revolution. Cotton made the United States by 1845 one of the richest countries economically in the world—on the backs of our enslaved forbearers. And the various ways in which that economic reality was orchestrated, namely through the murderous brutality and other abuses we associate with slavery, also produced an emotional scar. And when I think about my grandmother, Mary Brown, born in 1853 and "emancipated" by 1863, she had to live the rest of her life with that memory—as well as the memory of Jim

Crow after slavery. And some ask, "Why do we talk about that? What do we need?" We need desperately to have reparations at the head of any economic agenda that we discuss in this region, this country, and in the world.

I'd like to say something about Draymond Green, who plays for the Golden State Warriors Basketball Team and in 2017 was the NBA Defensive Player of the Year. Draymond Green said something recently in reference to Mark Cuban, the wealthy businessman and owner of the Dallas Mavericks Basketball Team. Green declared, "Mark Cuban doesn't know how I feel about Charlottesville; it's impossible to know what that makes me feel."[2] Draymond Green is a modern man—a man who has used his skills and talents as a basketball player to become very vocal publicly as well. "Mark Cuban doesn't know what I feel when a black man, a young black boy, is shot down and murdered on the street by police," Green observed. "He doesn't know. He can't relate to it and all we think about." If we think back in our life and use that to talk about what we really feel inside, how we feel and how we move forward—beyond how we feel—to take action in our life every day, we can answer the call for reparations.

I want to applaud my friend, Jesus [Chucho] Garcia, who is in attendance here—my great friend from Venezuela. We have worked with him extensively and with the Venezuelan-Afro-descendant organizations in Venezuela. And my young sister Esther [Ojulari], we were proud to be with her when she organized a conference in Cali around Afro-descendants in Colombia last year [2016]. These voices are very important and critical, and they are voices of the young people. So this is not Dr. Ron Daniels, president of the Institute of the Black World 21st Century, and the older guys like me talking about reparations. I'm talking about young people—younger scholars such as Sir Hilary Beckles, the renowned historian and chair of the CARICOM Reparations Commission. These are scholars who put together the "Ten-Point Program" and talked about the issues that are relevant for economic development in the region.[3] And each one of those things that we identify—whether it is in Colombia or in the Caribbean—is related to the conditions created by slavery and colonialism in the aftermath of slavery, and continue to, in some sense, destabilize our communities and the sense of who we are. These are the things that we have to talk about.

Dr. Ron Daniels, my brother, has provided the opportunity for me to be with you here in 2017 in New Orleans once again. I was here, I recall, before Hurricane Katrina in 2005, when we were discussing "The Algebra Project" and quality education as a civil right.[4] Not "sharecropper education," but *quality* education right here in New Orleans. And certainly when we talk about New Orleans, we have to acknowledge that it was the location of the first Black teachers' organization in the Deep South, which worked for better pay and working conditions for African American teachers.[5] New Orleans is not only the home of the things that we know about—blues, jazz, and other types of music—but also a place where people are known for getting up and taking action before and after the devastation of Hurricane Katrina.[6]

We can talk about what is fascinating: what Donald Trump is doing every day, each moment; but we don't need to devote time to that. We know what we have to do. We know that we have to get beyond that. In the face of Donald Trump, who is a symptom of the disenfranchisement of people of color, particularly African Americans, we have to do our work, and given participants in this conference, we have the will.

In the words of my dear sister, Mireille Fanon, whose father inspired us over the last sixty years—at least for me, when I first read *Wretched of the Earth* in 1967 and changed my life—let's use our power. Let's energize ourselves, knowing that we have to build not simply what we need today, but what we will need tomorrow; and that what we do; when we get up at 4:30 in the morning and deliver our paper routes we're going to change and transform this, our country—I say *our* country, meaning our communities—transform *our* communities. Thank you for, once again, allowing me to be in your presence. You know it is a pleasing honor, a privilege to be here, as we continue our noble battle.

Notes

1. George R. Lamplugh, *Politics on the Periphery: Factions and Parties in Georgia, 1783–1806* (Newark: University of Delaware Press, 1986); and *Rancorous Enmities and Blind Partialities: Factions and Parties in Georgia, 1807–1845* (Lanham, MD: University Press of America, 2015).

2. Green is referencing the march and rally of white nationalists in Charlottesville, Virginia, on August 12, 2017, during which those protesting the event were rammed by a car driven by James Alex Fields, injuring 28 and killing 32-year-old Heather Hayer.

3. For information on the CARICOM Reparations Commission and the Ten Point Plan, see www.caricomreparationscommission/ten-point-plan/.

4. For information on the Algebra Project, see Robert P. Moses and Charles F. Cobb, *Radical Equations: Math Literacy and Civil Rights* (Boston, MA: Beacon Press, 2001).

5. Donald P. Devore and Joseph Logsdon, *Crescent City Schools: Public Education in New Orleans, 1841–1991* (Lafayette: University of Louisiana, 1991); and Donald P. Devore, *Defying Jim Crow: African American Community Development and the*

Struggle for Racial Equality, 1900–1960 (Baton Rouge: Louisiana State University Press, 2015).

6. For an examination of the three centuries of the Black experience in New Orleans, see Molly N. Mitchell and Connie O. Atkinson, eds., "New Orleans at 300: The African American Experience, 1718–2018," *Journal of African American History* 103 (Fall 2018): 491–701.

4

Ten Reasons Why the Pesky Issue of Reparations Won't Go Away

EARL OFARI HUTCHINSON

National polls have consistently showed that an overwhelming majority of whites oppose reparations for African Americans for slavery and the near century of Jim Crow racial suffering afterward. The same polls show that a majority of African Americans support reparations. Oppose or support it, the fierce debate over reparations keeps cropping up, with some top Democratic presidential contenders in 2020 paying lip service to it. The question is why this issue simply won't go away? Here are ten reasons why.

1. The U.S. government, not long-dead Southern planters, bear the blame for slavery. It encoded it in the Constitution in article one. This designated a Black slave as three-fifths of a person for tax and political representation purposes. It protected and nourished it in article four by mandating that all escaped slaves found anywhere in the nation be returned to their masters. In the Dred Scott decision in 1857, the U.S. Supreme Court reaffirmed that slaves remained slaves no matter where they were taken in the United States.

2. Major institutions profited from slavery. Banks, shipping companies, and investment houses made enormous profits from financing slave purchases, investments in Southern land and products, and the transport, and sale of enslaved workers. Insurance companies made big profits from insuring slaves as property.

3. Slavery ended in 1865 but the legacy of slavery still remains. Countless reports and studies have found that Black people are still the major economic and social victims of racial discrimina-

tion. They are far more likely to live in underserved segregated neighborhoods, be refused business and housing loans, be denied promotions in corporations, and attend cash-starved, failing public schools than whites.

4. There's a direct cost for slavery's legacy. Former Federal Reserve Board Chairman Andrew Brimmer estimated that discrimination cost the Black community $10 billion yearly through the black-white wage gap, denial of capital access, inadequate public services, and and other government benefits. This has been called the "black tax."

5. The U.S. government has shelled out billions since the 1960s to pay for resettlement, job training, education, and health programs for refugees fleeing Communist repression in Vietnam. There was no national outcry when the U.S. government made special indemnity payments and provided land and social service benefits to Japanese Americans interned during World War II, Native Americans for the theft of lands and mineral rights, and Philippine veterans who fought with the American army during World War II. Politicians and most of the public enthusiastically backed these payments as the morally and legally right thing to do.

6. The reparations issue will not fuel more hatred of Blacks. Most Americans admit that slavery was a morally monstrous system that wreaked severe pain and suffering on enslaved people. Many major city councils have passed resolutions supporting a federal commission to study reparations. It certainly became a platform debate issue within the Democratic National Committee before the 2020 convention.

7. No legislation has been proposed that mandates taxpayers pay billions to Black people. A bill by former Michigan Democrat John Conyers languished in Congress for two decades. It called for a commission to study the effects of slavery. The estimated cost was less than $10 million. Texas Democratic Representative Sheila Jackson Lee reintroduced the bill in 2018.

8. There is a precedent for paying Black persons for past legal and moral wrongs. In 1997, Clinton apologized and the U.S. government paid $10 million to the Black survivors and family members victimized by the syphilis experiment conducted in the 1930s by the U.S. Public Health Service. In 1994, the Florida legislature agreed to make payments to the survivors and relatives of those

who lost their lives and property when a white mob destroyed the all-Black town of Rosewood in 1923. The carnage was tacitly condoned by public officials and law enforcement officers. The Oklahoma state legislature, however, has refused to consider reparations payments to the survivors and their descendants of the destruction of Black neighborhoods in Tulsa by white mobs in 1921.

9. Mega-rich Black people such as Oprah Winfrey would not receive a penny in reparations. Any tax money to redress Black suffering would go into a fund to bolster funding for AIDS/HIV education and prevention, underfinanced inner-city public schools, to expand job skills and training, drug and alcohol counseling and rehabilitation, computer access and literacy training programs, and to improve public services for the estimated one in four Black people still trapped in poverty.

10. In the early days of his White House tenure, former President Barack Obama did not support reparations. In the waning days of his tenure, he had second thoughts. He consequently said that society had a "moral obligation" to close the racial wealth gap and that there should be a massive investment in programs to do just that. He didn't exactly call it reparations. But he came close.

It was a gingerly and polite way of putting it. But Obama did recognize that America owed a debt to Black America for past and present sins. It still does. That's why the pesky issue of reparations won't go away.

5

Reparations to Fund Alternatives to Mass Incarceration of African American Youth

V. P. FRANKLIN

> This is for the kids who die,
> Black and white,
> For kids will die certainly.
> The old and rich will live on awhile,
> As always,
> Eating blood and gold,
> Letting kids die.
>
> —Langston Hughes

Africans and people of African descent have been targeted historically by those who profit from the construction and maintenance of the U.S. penal system. Carceral practices reflect the larger capitalist system and political economy, but they often operate outside the demands of "the market." From the antebellum period, towns and states contracted out the running of the state penitentiaries and other public penal institutions to the private contractors, and from that time, those who benefitted from those contracts lobbied and corrupted legislators to make sure there was a steady flow of inmates who then could be contracted out to work as laborers in various business enterprises. Already oppressed by unjust enslavement, Africans and African Americans were *not* the prime targets of U.S. penal institutions in the early 19th century. However, emancipation shifted the status of most African Americans who were now no longer someone's property, making them fair game for private contractors with friends in high places. The postbellum convict lease system, portrayed in bone-chilling detail in Douglass Blackmon's book and recent documentary film *Slavery by Another Name*, targeted African Americans and created great wealth with contracts for convict laborers.

Since the 1980s and the greatly expanded privatization of state penal facilities, we have had a proliferation of mandatory sentencing laws, an exponential increase in the prison population, and the targeting of African American children and adults and other people of color disproportionately to ensure the profits of the private prison industry. The menace that these private contractors have brought into the lives of children of color disproportionately is recounted in detail in William Ecenbarger's *Kids for Cash: Two Judges, Thousands of Children, and a $2.8 Million Kickback Scheme* (2012). The judges were on the payroll for PA Child Care, the private contractor, and they made sure a steady flow of "juvenile inmates" filled the company's detention facilities. The children were targeted and Ecenbarger explains how their unfair treatment left indelible scars on their bodies and minds.

When the imprisoned child or adult, aware of the targeting and unfairness, makes a move to resist, this only increases the likelihood of ending up in solitary confinement. The U.S. practice of imprisoning large segments of the population and then keeping those prisoners in solitary confinement for long periods of time has been condemned nationally and internationally. "The United States has come under sharp criticism at home and abroad for relying on solitary confinement in its prisons more than any other democratic nation in the world." In a *New York Times* March 24, 2013, article on "Immigrants Held in Solitary Confinement," Ian Urbina and Catherine Rentz described the conditions for detainees in private-run immigration centers. "In solitary" they are "routinely kept alone for 22 to 23 hours per day, sometimes in windowless 6-foot-by-3-foot cells," where "access to phones and lawyers is far more restricted."

It is the psychological damage that occurs in solitary confinement that leads to violence and attempts at suicide. "Solitary confinement is widely viewed as the most dangerous way to detain people," wrote Urbana and Rentz, "and roughly half of prison suicides occur when people are segregated in this way.... Paranoia, depression, memory loss, and self-mutilation are not uncommon." Human Rights Watch (HRW) and the American Civil Liberties Union (ACLU) issued a report in October 2012, *Growing Up Locked Down*, calling attention to the probable damage to juveniles spending long terms in solitary confinement. It "causes serious psychological and physical harm to young people, including heightened risk of suicide." The report quotes a Florida teenager. "The only thing left to do is go crazy ... Screaming, throwing stuff around—I feel like I am alone, like no one cares about me." Ian Kysel, the report's author, admitted that "officials may need to use limited periods of segregation and isolation to protect young people from other inmates," but what he found across the entire country were "the extremely stark conditions of solitary confinement . . . isolation for 22–24 hours a day, often for weeks or months, [which] harm young people in ways that are different than if they were adults." The HRW/ ACLU report calls for the banning of the lengthy solitary confinement of juvenile detainees.

Journalists have noted that in the numerous incidents of armed violence involving young people they investigate, the shooters seemed to be engaging in "suicidal behavior." The life-threatening gunplay of urban gang bangers, drug pushers, and the violent confrontations over "dumb stuff" often appear suicidal. However, if those who are engaging in these violent shootouts had already experienced prison life, could the self-destructive actions be related to time spent in solitary confinement?

We must also ask: What can we do to change conditions so bad for our children and young people in U.S. cities and towns that they are killing themselves and each other at alarming rates? The increased availability of guns contributes to the epidemic in violence, but what are the alternatives to the physical and psychological dangers of prison and solitary confinement? Predatory capitalists in the prison industry and gun manufacturing have succeeded in constructing a very lucrative pipeline for our youth, but what can be done to disrupt it?

We now know that up to 80 percent of those incarcerated are school dropouts, and thus those interventions that make staying in school more meaningful and important are the ones to be supported. Despite the testing mania created by conservative politicians and school officials, there are successful dropout prevention programs that have not yet been ruined by the increased emphasis on "test preparation." There are successful dropout prevention programs in the form of school-community collaborations, alternative schools, work-study vocational training programs, mentoring and supplemental education projects, and many others. Unfortunately, oftentimes the cost per pupil enrolled in these specialized interventions is greater than the average for the school district, and school officials are unwilling or unable fiscally to provide the increased funding needed to bring the specialized program to their systems. The educational disadvantages African Americans experience in general, and the youth in particular are the reasons why reparations demands have been made on the state and federal government. The establishment of the "Reparations Superfund" has been advocated as a potential source of supplemental funding to school districts seeking to implement successful dropout prevention programs.

But what about our children and young people who have been incarcerated and subjected to solitary confinement and are 50 percent more likely to return to prison unless there is some positive intervention? These former detainees are our children as well and we need to provide alternatives to returning to the streets and prison. The Reparations Superfund should be used to support youth-directed community redevelopment projects where they would learn the trades to restore and repair the houses and other buildings in their own neighborhoods. Arts, music, and sports education, areas known for their success in motivating students and instilling skill and discipline, would be supported through local and national reparations funds. Visual and performing arts and sports programs, aimed at contributing to the quality of life for people in their own neighborhoods, would be targeted for financial support.

The children and young people have to be taught much more than how to prepare to take standardized tests. Alternative educational programs, aimed at mastery of content and methods in a wide range of fields and professions, would allow many young people to fulfill their potential. The longer we wait to establish reparation funds, the more time our children and young people will spend in solitary confinement.

6

H.R. 40

The Commission to Study and Develop Reparations Proposals for African Americans in the United States

SHEILA JACKSON LEE

The impact of slavery and its vestiges continues to affect African Americans and indeed all Americans in communities throughout our nation. This is why I am pleased to introduce H.R. 40, the Commission to Study and Develop Reparations Proposals for African Americans Act. This legislation is intended to examine the institution of slavery in the colonies and the United States from 1619 to the present, and further recommend appropriate remedies. Since the initial introduction of this legislation, its proponents have made substantial progress in elevating the discussion of reparations and reparatory justice at the national level and joining the mainstream international debate on the issues. Though some have tried to deflect the importance of these conversations by focusing on individual monetary compensation, the real issue is whether and how this nation can come to grips with the legacy of slavery that still infects current society. Through legislation, resolutions, news, and litigation, we are moving closer to making more strides in the movement toward reparations.

Today there are more people at the table—more activists, more scholars, more CEO's, more state and local officials, and more Members of Congress. However, despite this progress and the election of the first American president of African descent, the legacy of slavery lingers heavily in this nation. While we have focused on the social effects of slavery and segregation, its continuing economic implications remain largely ignored by mainstream analysis. These economic issues are the root cause of many critical issues in the African American community today, such as education, healthcare, and criminal justice policy, including policing practices. The call for reparations represents a commitment to entering a constructive dialogue on the role of slavery and racism in shaping present-day conditions in our community and American society.

I believe that H.R. 40 is a crucial piece of legislation because it goes beyond exploring the economic implications of slavery and segregation. It is a holistic bill in the sense that it seeks to establish a commission to also examine the moral and social implications of slavery. In short, the commission aims to study the impact of slavery and continuing discrimination against African Americans, resulting directly and indirectly from slavery to segregation to the desegregation process and the present day. The commission would also make recommendations concerning any form of apology and compensation to begin the long-delayed process of atonement for slavery. With the over-criminalization and policing of Black bodies, a reoccurring issue in African American communities, I believe this conversation is both relevant and crucial to restoring trust in governmental institutions in many communities. As in years past, I welcome open and constructive discourse on H.R. 40 and the creation of this commission in the 116th Congress. Though the times and circumstance may change, the principal problem of slavery continues to weigh heavily on this country. A federal commission can help us reach into this dark past and bring us into a brighter future.

117th CONGRESS
1st Session
    H. R. 40

> To address the fundamental injustice, cruelty, brutality, and
> inhumanity of slavery in the United States and the 13 American
> colonies between 1619 and 1865 and to establish a commission
> to study and consider a national apology and proposal for
> reparations for the institution of slavery, its subsequent de jure
> and de facto racial and economic discrimination against African
> Americans, and the impact of these forces on living African
> Americans, to make recommendations to the Congress on
> appropriate remedies, and for other purposes.

IN THE HOUSE OF REPRESENTATIVES

JANUARY 4, 2021

Ms. Jackson Lee (for herself, Ms. Plaskett, Mr. Rush, Mr. Espaillat, Mrs. Watson Coleman, Ms. Norton, Ms. Castor of Florida, Ms. Lee of California, Mr. Khanna, Mrs. Beatty, Mr. McNerney, Mr. Norcross, Mr. Ruppersberger, Ms. Eshoo, Mr. Cooper, Mr. Connolly, Ms. Meng, Mr. Raskin, Mr. Welch, Mrs. Trahan, Ms. Pressley, Ms. Clarke of New York, Mr. Jeffries, Mr. Sarbanes, Mr. Bishop of Georgia, Ms. DeGette, Mr. Kildee, Ms. Bonamici, Mr. Green of Texas, Ms. Moore of Wisconsin, Mrs. Dingell, Ms. Adams, Ms. Williams of Georgia, Mr. Beyer, Ms. Clark of Massachusetts, Mr. Crow, Mr. Suozzi, Mr. Cicilline, Mr. Nadler, Mr. McGovern, Ms. DelBene, Mr. Lynch, Mr. Jones, Mr. Blumenauer, Mr. Keating, Mr. Neguse, Ms. Blunt Rochester, Mr. Evans, Ms. Speier, Ms. McCollum, Ms. Jayapal, Mr. Meeks, Ms. Strickland, Ms. Scanlon, Ms. Velazquez, Mr. Deutch, Mr. Cohen, Mr. Payne, Mr. Morelle, Ms. Wilson of Florida, Mrs. Demings, Mr. Bera, Mr. Takano, Mr. Brendan F. Boyle of Pennsylvania, Ms. Schakowsky, Mrs. Lawrence, Ms. Titus, Mr. Lieu, Mr. Mfume, Mr. Carson, Ms. Fudge, Mr. David Scott of Georgia, Ms. Barragan, Mr. Quigley, Mr. Danny K. Davis of Illinois, Mr. Vargas, Mr. Larson of Connecticut, Mr. Thompson of Mississippi, Mr. Brown, Ms. Wasserman Schultz, Mr. Lowenthal, Mr. Kilmer, Mr. Neal, Mr. Pallone, Ms. Sewell, Ms. Matsui, Mr. Lawson of Florida, Mr. Thompson of California, Mr. Yarmuth, Mr. Costa, Mr. Horsford, Ms. Pingree, Mr. Soto, Ms. Dean, Mrs. Hayes, Mr. Casten, Mr. DeSaulnier, Mr. Pocan, Mr. Gomez, Mr. Veasey, Miss Rice of New York, Ms. Lofgren, Mr. Johnson of Georgia, Ms. Kaptur, Ms. Omar, Ms. Bass, Mr. Peters, Ms. Garcia of Texas, Ms. Escobar, Mr. Swalwell, Mr. Butterfield, Ms. Kelly of Illinois, Mr. Bowman, Ms. Ocasio-Cortez, Ms. Tlaib, Ms. Chu, Mr. Panetta, Mr. Foster, and Ms. Bush) introduced the following bill, which was referred to the Committee on the Judiciary.

A BILL

To address the fundamental injustice, cruelty, brutality, and inhumanity of slavery in the United States and the 13 American colonies between 1619 and 1865 and to establish a commission to study and consider a national apology and proposal for reparations for the institution of slavery, its subsequent de jure and de facto racial and economic discrimination against African Americans, and the impact of these forces on living African Americans, to make recommendations to the Congress on appropriate remedies, and for other purposes.

Be it enacted by the Senate and House of Representatives of the United States of America in Congress assembled,

SECTION 1. SHORT TITLE.

This Act may be cited as the "Commission to Study and Develop Reparation Proposals for African Americans Act."

SEC. 2. FINDINGS AND PURPOSE.

(a) Findings.—The Congress finds that—

(1) approximately 4,000,000 Africans and their descendants were enslaved in the United States and colonies that became the United States from 1619 to 1865;

(2) the institution of slavery was constitutionally and statutorily sanctioned by the Government of the United States from 1789 through 1865;

(3) the slavery that flourished in the United States constituted an immoral and inhumane deprivation of Africans' life, liberty, African citizenship rights, and cultural heritage, and denied them the fruits of their own labor;

(4) a preponderance of scholarly, legal, community evidentiary documentation and popular culture markers constitute the basis for inquiry into the ongoing effects of the institution of slavery and its legacy of persistent systemic structures of discrimination on living African Americans and society in the United States;

(5) following the abolition of slavery the United States Government, at the Federal, State, and local level, continued to perpetuate, condone, and often profit from practices that continued to brutalize and disadvantage African Americans, including sharecropping, convict leasing, Jim Crow, redlining, unequal education, and disproportionate treatment at the hands of the criminal justice system; and

(6) as a result of the historic and continued discrimination, African Americans continue to suffer debilitating economic, educational, and health hardships including

but not limited to having nearly 1,000,000 Black people incarcerated; an unemployment rate more than twice the current White unemployment rate; and an average of less than $1/16$ of the wealth of White families, a disparity which has worsened, not improved over time.

(b) Purpose.—The purpose of this Act is to establish a commission to study and develop Reparation proposals for African Americans as a result of—

(1) the institution of slavery, including both the Trans-Atlantic and the domestic "trade" which existed from 1565 in colonial Florida and from 1619 through 1865 within the other colonies that became the United States, and which included the Federal and State governments which constitutionally and statutorily supported the institution of slavery;

(2) the de jure and de facto discrimination against freed slaves and their descendants from the end of the Civil War to the present, including economic, political, educational, and social discrimination;

(3) the lingering negative effects of the institution of slavery and the discrimination described in paragraphs (1) and (2) on living African Americans and on society in the United States;

(4) the manner in which textual and digital instructional resources and technologies are being used to deny the inhumanity of slavery and the crime against humanity of people of African descent in the United States;

(5) the role of Northern complicity in the Southern based institution of slavery;

(6) the direct benefits to societal institutions, public and private, including higher education, corporations, religious and associational;

(7) and thus, recommend appropriate ways to educate the American public of the Commission's findings;

(8) and thus, recommend appropriate remedies in consideration of the Commission's findings on the matters described in paragraphs (1), (2), (3), (4), (5), and (6); and

(9) submit to the Congress the results of such examination, together with such recommendations.

SEC. 3. ESTABLISHMENT AND DUTIES.

(a) Establishment.—There is established the Commission to Study and Develop Reparation Proposals for African Americans (hereinafter in this Act referred to as the Commission).

(b) Duties.—The Commission shall perform the following duties:

   (1) Identify, compile, and synthesize the relevant corpus of evidentiary documentation of the institution of slavery which existed within the United States and the colonies that became the United States from 1619 through 1865. The Commission's documentation and examination shall include but not be limited to the facts related to—

   (A) the capture and procurement of Africans;

   (B) the transport of Africans to the United States and the colonies that became the United States for the purpose of enslavement, including their treatment during transport;

   (C) the sale and acquisition of Africans as chattel property in interstate and intrastate commerce;

   (D) the treatment of African slaves in the colonies and the United States, including the deprivation of their freedom, exploitation of their labor, and destruction of their culture, language, religion, and families; and

   (E) the extensive denial of humanity, sexual abuse, and the chattelization of persons.

   (2) The role which the Federal and State governments of the United States supported the institution of slavery in constitutional and statutory provisions, including the extent to which such governments prevented, opposed, or restricted efforts of formerly enslaved Africans and their descendants to repatriate to their homeland.

   (3) The Federal and State laws that discriminated against formerly enslaved Africans and their descendants who were deemed United States citizens from 1868 to the present.

   (4) The other forms of discrimination in the public and private sectors against freed African slaves and their descendants who were deemed United States citizens from 1868 to the present, including redlining, educational funding discrepancies, and predatory financial practices.

(5) The lingering negative effects of the institution of slavery and the matters described in paragraphs (1), (2), (3), (4), (5), and (6) on living African Americans and on society in the United States.

(6) Recommend appropriate ways to educate the American public of the Commission's findings.

(7) Recommend appropriate remedies in consideration of the Commission's findings on the matters described in paragraphs (1), (2), (3), (4), (5), and (6). In making such recommendations, the Commission shall address among other issues, the following questions:

(A) How such recommendations comport with international standards of remedy for wrongs and injuries caused by the State, that include full reparations and special measures, as understood by various relevant international protocols, laws, and findings.

(B) How the Government of the United States will offer a formal apology on behalf of the people of the United States for the perpetration of gross human rights violations and crimes against humanity on African slaves and their descendants.

(C) How Federal laws and policies that continue to disproportionately and negatively affect African Americans as a group, and those that perpetuate the lingering effects, materially and psycho-social, can be eliminated.

(D) How the injuries resulting from matters described in paragraphs (1), (2), (3), (4), (5), and (6) can be reversed and provide appropriate policies, programs, projects, and recommendations for the purpose of reversing the injuries.

(E) How, in consideration of the Commission's findings, any form of compensation to the descendants of enslaved African is calculated.

(F) What form of compensation should be awarded, through what instrumentalities, and who should be eligible for such compensation.

(G) How, in consideration of the Commission's findings, any other forms of rehabilitation or restitution to

African descendants is warranted and what the form
and scope of those measures should take.

(c) Report to Congress.—The Commission shall submit a written
report of its findings and recommendations to the Congress not
later than the date which is one year after the date of the first
meeting of the Commission held pursuant to section 4(c).

SEC. 4. MEMBERSHIP.

(a) Number and Appointment.—

    (1) The Commission shall be composed of 13 members, who
shall be appointed within 90 days after the date of enactment of this Act, as follows:

        (A) Three members shall be appointed by the President.

        (B) Three members shall be appointed by the Speaker of
the House of Representatives.

        (C) One member shall be appointed by the President pro
tempore of the Senate.

        (D) Six members shall be selected from the major civil so-
ciety and reparations organizations that have historically championed the cause of reparatory justice.

    (2) All members of the Commission shall be persons who
are especially qualified to serve on the Commission by
virtue of their education, training, activism, or experience,
particularly in the field of African American studies and
reparatory justice.

(b) Terms.—The term of office for members shall be for the life of
the Commission. A vacancy in the Commission shall not affect
the powers of the Commission and shall be filled in the same
manner in which the original appointment was made.

(c) First Meeting.—The President shall call the first meeting of the
Commission within 120 days after the date of the enactment of
this Act or within 30 days after the date on which legislation is
enacted making appropriations to carry out this Act, whichever
date is later.

(d) Quorum.—Seven members of the Commission shall constitute
a quorum, but a lesser number may hold hearings.

(e) Chair and Vice Chair.—The Commission shall elect a Chair and
Vice Chair from among its members. The term of office of each
shall be for the life of the Commission.

(f) Compensation.—(1) Except as provided in paragraph (2), each member of the Commission shall receive compensation at the daily equivalent of the annual rate of basic pay payable for GS-18 of the General Schedule under section 5332 of title 5, United States Code, for each day, including travel time, during which he or she is engaged in the actual performance of duties vested in the Commission.

    (2) A member of the Commission who is a full-time officer or employee of the United States or a Member of Congress shall receive no additional pay, allowances, or benefits by reason of his or her service to the Commission.

    (3) All members of the Commission shall be reimbursed for travel, subsistence, and other necessary expenses incurred by them in the performance of their duties to the extent authorized by chapter 57 of title 5, United States Code.

SEC. 5. POWERS OF THE COMMISSION.

(a) Hearings and Sessions.—The Commission may, for the purpose of carrying out the provisions of this Act, hold such hearings and sit and act at such times and at such places in the United States, and request the attendance and testimony of such witnesses and the production of such books, records, correspondence, memoranda, papers, and documents, as the Commission considers appropriate. The Commission may invoke the aid of an appropriate United States district court to require, by subpoena or otherwise, such attendance, testimony, or production.

(b) Powers of Subcommittees and Members.—Any subcommittee or member of the Commission may, if authorized by the Commission, take any action which the Commission is authorized to take by this section.

(c) Obtaining Official Data.—The Commission may acquire directly from the head of any department, agency, or instrumentality of the executive branch of the Government, available information which the Commission considers useful in the discharge of its duties. All departments, agencies, and instrumentalities of the executive branch of the Government shall cooperate with the Commission with respect to such information and shall furnish all information requested by the Commission to the extent permitted by law.

SEC. 6. ADMINISTRATIVE PROVISIONS.

(a) Staff.—The Commission may, without regard to section 5311(b) of title 5, United States Code, appoint and fix the compensation of such personnel as the Commission considers appropriate.

(b) Applicability of Certain Civil Service Laws.—The staff of the Commission may be appointed without regard to the provisions of title 5, United States Code, governing appointments in the competitive service, and without regard to the provisions of chapter 51 and subchapter III of chapter 53 of such title relating to classification and General Schedule pay rates, except that the compensation of any employee of the Commission may not exceed a rate equal to the annual rate of basic pay payable for GS-18 of the General Schedule under section 5332 of title 5, United States Code.

(c) Experts and Consultants.—The Commission may procure the services of experts and consultants in accordance with the provisions of section 3109(b) of title 5, United States Code, but at rates for individuals not to exceed the daily equivalent of the highest rate payable under section 5332 of such title.

(d) Administrative Support Services.—The Commission may enter into agreements with the Administrator of General Services for procurement of financial and administrative services necessary for the discharge of the duties of the Commission. Payment for such services shall be made by reimbursement from funds of the Commission in such amounts as may be agreed upon by the Chairman of the Commission and the Administrator.

(e) Contracts.—The Commission may—

(1) procure supplies, services, and property by contract in accordance with applicable laws and regulations and to the extent or in such amounts as are provided in appropriations Acts; and

(2) enter into contracts with departments, agencies, and instrumentalities of the Federal Government, State agencies, and private firms, institutions, and agencies, for the conduct of research or surveys, the preparation of reports, and other activities necessary for the discharge of the duties of the Commission, to the extent or in such amounts as are provided in appropriations Acts.

SEC. 7. TERMINATION.

The Commission shall terminate 90 days after the date on which the Commission submits its report to the Congress under section 3(c).

SEC. 8. AUTHORIZATION OF APPROPRIATIONS.

To carry out the provisions of this Act, there are authorized to be appropriated $12,000,000.

7

Reparations Means Full Repair

For 400 Years of Terror and Crimes against Humanity

KAMM HOWARD FOR N'COBRA

The year 2019 marked the 400th anniversary of the arrival of the first kidnapped Africans on the shores of the Virginia Colony in 1619. This was one beginning of the period of enslavement of Africans and their descendants in North America. The National Coalition of Blacks for Reparations in America declared the theme for this anniversary: 400 Years of Terror: A Debt Still Owed.

From the very beginning, terror and psychic trauma were the reality for "those stolen Africans."[1] Not only was the "Middle Passage" a terrifying experience of its own, but history tells us the ships that brought these Africans to the Virginia Colony were not the ships they initially embarked on. Nor was it just thirty-six Africans on that initial voyage—they numbered 350.

In route to its destination of Vera Cruz, Mexico, the original ship, the *San Juan Bautista,* with its full cargo, was attacked in the Gulf of Mexico by two pirate ships, the *White Lion* and the *Treasurer.* At the end of the attack, the *White Lion* delivered from its pirated cargo "20 and odd Africans," and the *Treasurer,* a "half dozen" from an original forty Africans it seized, before it sailed on to Bermuda.[2]

How did these sixty or so Africans survive, since the *San Juan Batista* was destroyed in the attack? Were they pulled from the sea? Were they forced aboard by gunpoint or at the end of a sword? Did they choose the nearest vessel to the one that was sinking and offering certain death? More importantly, what happened to the nearly 300 other Africans who were on the *San Juan Bautista*? Were they still chained together in death as they were in the frightening last months of their lives through the horrific Middle Passage? Thus began the travail of Africans' existence in what has become the United States of America. It has been a terror of unjust enslavement and racial oppression that has yet to cease and has yet to be redressed. This scene would be followed by 246 years of brutal enslavement of Africans and their descendants—treatment so inhumane that Black leader Frederick Douglass said its behavior "would disgrace a nation of savages."[3]

The period of enslavement, culminating in secession and civil war, was followed by a hundred years of legal apartheid, "Jim Crow segregation," backed by the tremendous force of unjust laws and deadly violence. After the bloody conflict, former Confederate Army soldiers, officers, and their offspring created highly organized terrorist groups to reestablish white control over Black labor.[4] Their reach extended all the way to the White House. These groups, including the Ku Klux Klan, the Knights of the White Camellia, and other vigilante "night riders," were responsible for thousands of murders and assassinations, unjust imprisonment of tens of thousands, continued theft of labor and millions of acres of land acquired by African Americans in the post-emancipation era, and at least 4,743 recorded lynchings.[5] This, in addition to the destruction of Black towns and communities and "racial cleansing" and mob violence in predominantly white areas, fueled the mass migrations out of terror-filled regions in the South. Today many descendants of those white oppressors defiantly fly the Confederate flag. After Jim Crow legally ended in 1964 with the passage of the Civil Rights Act, the violent intimidation and overt discrimination against the Black communities and citizens continued.

While organized racial violence perpetrated by the KKK and other white supremacist groups declined, police brutality remained steady.[6] Police brutality and "police crime" sparked resistance and urban insurrections in the 1960s. The Black Panther Party and other Black nationalist and anti-racist groups were formed to address the police violence and terrorism, and the social, political, and economic control of white supremacists.[7] After the Panthers and other Black activists were illegally and unconstitutionally suppressed by the FBI's Counter Intelligence Program (COINTELPRO), police departments in Chicago and other cities obtained what amounted to free license to terrorize African Americans; and they carried out the torture, forced confessions, and murder of Panther leader Fred Hampton and other militant men and women.[8]

Throughout the 400-year period, Africans and their descendants have fought against this inhumane treatment and put forth demands that these criminal practices be halted, redressed, and repaired. Twice in the second half of the twentieth century, in 1957 and 1997, charges of "genocide" were made to the United Nations Human Rights Commission (in 2014 and 2016 a new generation of activists reissued the charges). In 1969 civil rights leader James Forman presented the "Black Manifesto" to the predominantly white churches and denominations demanding reparations to be used for Black economic development and various institutional programs and projects.[9] Mass-based organizations arose in the 1980s to stimulate a grassroots demand for reparations. The National Coalition of Blacks for Reparations in America (N'COBRA) was formed by organizations and individuals in the National Conference of Black Lawyers (NCBL), the Republic of New Afrika (RNA), and the New Afrikan Peoples Organization (NAPO).[10] In 1989 Congressman John Conyers introduced the legislative measure HR 40, "The Commission to Study Reparations Proposals for African Americans Act," and reintroduced it into each session of Congress.[11] N'COBRA publicized and developed support for the measure throughout the United States and currently has chapters throughout the United States and in the Caribbean and Africa.

In 2001, N'COBRA joined the December 12th Movement (D-12), and the National Black United Front (NBUF) and led a delegation of nearly 400 from the United States to Durban, South Africa to the "World Conference Against Racism, Xenophobia, and Related Intolerance." Over 14,000 participants attended the conference, including governmental delegations from 195 countries. The conclusion of the conference affirmed many fundamental human rights for people of African descent, particularly "the right to be repaired from criminal and injurious acts of one's government." In the "Durban Declaration and Program of Action," the official document released following the conference, the delegates declared that the Trans-Atlantic Slave Trade, slavery, apartheid, and colonialism were *"crimes against humanity."* It emphasized that there was an economic basis for these crimes that is evident today in the former slave-trading nations that are also currently the wealthiest in the world. The declaration noted that "the effects and persistence of these structures and practices have been among the factors contributing to lasting social and economic inequalities"—poverty, underdevelopment, marginalization, social exclusion—"found in many parts of the world today." It declared that there is an obligation on the part of those nations that were enriched by these crimes to engage in redress for the inequities and injuries that resulted.[12]

This historic victory by those in the global reparations movement marked a new phase in the struggle for reparations and agreed that the Trans-Atlantic Slave Trade, slavery, colonialism, and apartheid were not just bad/immoral acts, they were crimes against humanity—"the most egregious crimes a government can commit or allowed to be committed against a civilian population." Globally we became aware that reparations for crimes against humanity have no statute of limitations and this strengthened our resolve and efforts to organize. The Durban Conference confirmed what N'COBRA already knew—that the enormous economic theft and exploitation was still occurring today in the Global South.

The wealth accumulated by families and individuals through slavery, slave trading, colonization, and economic exploitation was passed down from generation to generation. The crimes committed against humanity by their ancestors have continued and remain harmful to this day. There are increasing numbers of public figures and others who are acknowledging their support for African and African American "reparations" and proclaiming the rightness of this cause. In the 2020 presidential contest, Democratic candidates Marianne Williamson, Senators Elizabeth Warren, Corey Booker, Kamala Harris, Julian Castro, and even Speaker of the House of Representatives Nancy Pelosi, who may have blocked the congressional discussion of Congressman John Conyers's reparation bill during the Obama presidency, announced publicly their support for Black reparations.

Where some err, however, is in their attempt to tell people of African descent in the United States the extent and what forms reparations should take. The forms and extent of reparations payments must be determined by African-descended people and their leaders. This has already begun, in part, with N'COBRA's 21ist Century Reparations Manifesto and Five Injury Areas as a place to start. A series of national town hall meetings have already begun to introduce, assess, and debate the Reparations Ten Point Program put forward by the National African American Reparations Commission (NAARC).[13]

We are already in the "Post Durban Era"! In the years following the Durban Conference, Caribbean political leaders through the Caribbean Community (CARICOM) created the "CARICOM Reparations Commission" (CRC) and has initiated the process of bringing a case of "crimes against humanity" before the International Criminal Court against the European nations that participated in the slave trade and slavery in the Caribbean. The charges are Native genocide, enslavement, and colonial oppression of Africans and African descendants in the Caribbean.

The CARICOM initiative sparked formation of NAARC in the United States, spearheaded by the Institute for the Black World 21st Century.[14] That same year, NAARC held an international summit in New York City attracting many of the CRC commissioners and delegates from seventeen nations.

NAARC inspired several of these groups to establish reparations commissions in several nations in Europe.

Black People Against Police Torture (BPAPT) and N'COBRA led the successful reparations campaign for the victims of police torture in Chicago. The "Movement for Black Lives," organized after the numerous "Black Lives Matter" protests in the 2010s, has made reparations a major objective for its programs. It is from all these actions that those who now speak out for reparations have the support and backing to do so. N'COBRA is committed to expanding the base of knowledge about this movement and we look to international law to support our claims for reparations.[15]

Under international norms and law, reparations means "full repair." In *Slavery Reparations Time Is Now: Exposing Lies, Claiming Justice for Global Survival—An International Legal Assessment*, International law professor Nora Wittmann outlined the basis for full repair.

According to Wittmann, the Permanent Court of International Justice laid out the "general and foundational rule" for reparations in the Chorzow Factory Case of 1928. In that ruling, the Court held "that reparation must, as far as possible, wipe out all consequences of the illegal act and re-establish the situation which would, in all probability, have existed if that act had not been committed."[16]

The extent of "all consequences" was fleshed out as *full reparation* in the International Law Commission (2001) *Draft Articles on Responsibility of States for International Wrongful Act*. In Article 31: "[T]he responsible state is under an obligation to make full reparation for the injury caused by the internationally wrongful act."[17] The International Law Commission and other established international guidelines further lay out what is considered full and comprehensive reparation. These include:

1. Cessation: Assurances and Guarantees of Non-Repetition- a state responsible for wrongfully injuring a people "is under an obligation to a) cease the act if it is continuing, b) offer appropriate assurances and guarantees of non-repetition."[18]
2. Restitution and Repatriation: To "re-establish the situation which existed before the wrongful act was committed." To restore the victim to the original situation before gross violations of international law occurred. How includes restoration of freedom, recognition of humanity, identity, culture, repatriation, livelihood, and wealth.[19]
3. Compensation: The injuring State is obligated to compensate for the damage, if damage is not made good by restitution. Compensation is

"any financially assessable damage suffered." Proper compensation is such that is "appropriate and proportional to the gravity of the violation and circumstances."[20]

4. Satisfaction: Is needed "as a means for reparations for moral damage, such as emotional injury, mental suffering, and injury to reputation."[21]

5. Rehabilitation: "This consists of mind, body, emotional, and spirit healing for the lasting effects of the trauma of enslavement and segregation."[22]

The revisions made to HR 40 in 2017 by Congressman John Conyers and NAARC were based on the international structures described by Wittmann. The revised H. R. 40, introduced in the 115th Congress called for a commission to develop programs, policy, and practices consistent with these elements and intended outcomes. Congresswoman Sheila Jackson Lee has introduced it in the 116th Congress. In NCOBRA's Manifesto and NAARC's Ten Point Reparations Platform, these outcomes are fleshed out to demonstrate how N'COBRA's Five Injury Areas and NAARC's Ten Point Reparations Platform conforms to the five outcomes for full repair.

N'COBRA's Manifesto, broken down in these outcome areas, offers more recommendations on the scope of reparations. One particular policy of redress that we must pursue is the release of Black political prisoners. These men and women have been vindicated. They fought against a government that used all manner of illegality, committed crimes against their humanity and that of their people. Like the Japanese who were imprisoned who fought against their people's internment and were released as part of their reparations deal, Black political prisoners must be set free! Now!

This is what reparations means, and what reparatory justice looks like—*full repair.*

Notes

1. Haile Gerima, Negod-Gwad Productions, *Sankofa* (Washington, DC: Mypheduh Films, 1993).

2. Albert Broussard, "First Africans arrive at Jamestown Colony (1619), *The Black-Past* https://www.blackpast.org/african-american-history/first-africans-in-the-james-town-colony-1619/; Brenda E. Stevenson, "They Called Her Angela," *The Journal of African American History* 105, no. 4 (2020): 673.

3. Frederick Douglass, "What to the Slave Is the Fourth of July?," In *The BlackPast*, https://www.blackpast.org/african-american-history/speeches-african-american -history/1852-frederick-douglass-what-slave-fourth-july/.

4. Herbert Shapiro, *White Violence and Black Response: From Reconstruction to Montgomery* (Amherst: University of Massachusetts Press, 1988); Kidada E. Williams, *They Left Great Marks on Me* (New York: New York University Press, 2012).

5. Gillian Brockell, "More than 4,000 People Have Been Lynched in the U.S. Trump Isn't One of Them," *Washington Post*, October 22, 2019, https://www.washingtonpost.com/history/2019/10/22/more-than-people-have-been-lynched-us-trump-isnt-one-them/.

6. Malcolm X Grassroots Movement, *Operation Ghetto Storm*, Malcolm X Grassroots Movement, Updated Edition, November 2014, http://www.operationghettostorm.org/uploads/1/9/1/1/19110795/new_all_14_11_04.pdf.

7. Huey P. Newton, "In Defense of Self-Defense," *The Black Panther* 1, no. 3 (1967): 3–4; Robyn C. Spencer, *The Revolution Has Come* (Durham, NC: Duke University Press, 2016), 48–52; Donna Jean Murch, *Living for the City: Migration, Education, and the Rise of the Black Panther Party in Oakland, California* (Chapel Hill: University of North Carolina Press, 2010), 119–68.

8. Kenneth O'Reilly, *Racial Matters: The FBI's Secret File on Black America, 1960–1972* (New York: Free Press, 1989), 293–324; Huey Percy Newton, *War against the Panthers: A Study of Repression in America*, University of California, Santa Cruz, 1980; Ward Churchill, and Jim Vander Wall, *The COINTELPRO Papers* (Boston: South End, 1990).

9. James Forman, "The Black Manifesto: I Introduction: Total Control as the Only Solution to the Economic Problems of Black People," *The Review of Black Political Economy* 1, no. 1 (1970): 36–44.

10. Adjoa A. Aiyetoro and Adrienne D. Davis, "Historic and Modern Social Movements for Reparations: The National Coalition of Blacks for Reparations in America (N'COBRA) and its Antecedents," *Texas Wesleyan Law Review* 16 (2009): 730–42.

11. John Conyers, "My Reparations Bill," Institute for the Black World 21st Century, https://ibw21.org/commentary/my-reparations-bill-hr-40/.

12. World Conference Against Racism, Racial Discrimination, Xenophobia, and Related Intolerance, "Declaration," World Conference Against Racism, Racial Discrimination, Xenophobia, and Related Intolerance, https://www.un.org/WCAR/durban.pdf.

13. National N'COBRA, Twitter Post, "Five Issue Areas of Systematic Oppression and Systematic Slavery Are," 9:05 AM, December 14, 2020, https://twitter.com/NCOBRA40/status/1338500260059033600. See Adjoa A. Aiyetoro, Hilary Beckles, and the National African American Reparations Commission (chapters in this book).

14. See the Ron Daniels chapter in this book.

15. Movement 4 Black Lives, "Case Study, https://m4bl.org/wp-content/uploads/2020/11/Case-Study-One.pdf; Vickie Casanova Willis, and Standish E. Willis, "Black People Against Police Torture: The Importance of Building a People-Centered Human Rights Movement," *Public Interest Law Reporter* 21, no. 3 (2016): 235; Toussaint Losier, "A Human Right to Reparations: Black People against Police Torture and the Roots of the 2015 Chicago Reparations Ordinance," *Souls* 20, no. 4 (2018): 399–419.

16. *Germany v. Poland (1927) P.C.I.J., Ser. A, No. 9.* http://www.worldcourts.com/pcij/eng/decisions/1928.09.13_chorzow1.htm; Nora Wittmann, "An International Law Deconstruction of the Hegemonic Denial of the Right to Reparations." *Social and Economic Studies* 68, no. 1/2 (2019): 35.

17. International Law Commission. "Draft articles on Responsibility of States for Internationally Wrongful Acts, with commentaries." https://legal.un.org/ilc/texts/instruments/english/commentaries/9_6_2001.pdf, 91.

18. Ibid., 88.

19. Ibid., 96.

20. Ibid., 98.

21. Ibid., 105.

22. Ibid., 105.

8

Pursuing a Reparatory Justice Agenda for Global Africa

SIR HILARY McD. BECKLES

His Excellency Sam Kutesa, distinguished President of this United Nations General Assembly, Excellences of the United Nations, colleagues of the Working Group of Experts on People of African Descent, distinguished members of the General Assembly, colleagues of Civil Society, distinguished Ladies and Gentlemen. What a beautiful moment [on December 14, 2014] we are invited to share by the distinguished President of this assembly this afternoon in this respected Chamber of the United Nations!

What a seminal season it is for women and men of serious disposition to step up and move forward to shape humanity's future in a fashion consistent with its finest values! Critically, we are assembled here, in this world forum, to choose; we are at the crossroads, and we seek the guidance of Legba, African God of the Intersection, to provide the spiritual content of our choice. The importance of this understanding should not be understated in any way.

We are at the dawn of this 21st century, and once again humanity struggles to come to terms with the legacies of the crimes committed against its African family. Aspects of these legacies are as alive today as they were two centuries ago. Everywhere that African enchainment and enslavement became the basis of societies and economies, their descendants today cannot assume the human right to breathe the air of freedom and justice.

Plantation slave drivers and overseers have been replaced by public prosecutors and militarized police, and the human right to life, denied Africans during the 400 years of the barbarity called chattel slavery, continues to be contested. The racism that informs that contestation defines and distorts the primary social relations of humanity. In 1781, the English Law Lord, Judge William

Mansfield, in an effort to purge African enslavement from his homeland, and to confine its vulgarity to the colonies, insisted that his country folks at home should breathe neither the foul air of slavery nor endure the stench of its stain.

Two hundred and thirty-eight years later, millions of African descendants are still breathing the foul air that blows from the stench of slavery. In their quest to inhale the free air of justice and democracy, they are seized by the throat and their breath taken away in a fashion reminiscent of centuries ago. "I can't breathe" has now become the universal ideology of the African diaspora, most vocal in the United States where African descendants are brutally policed in their pursuit of social justice, economic enfranchisement, and existential dignity.

No longer do we have to watch the construction in movies of the destruction of Black life, nor journey to the journals of history to see and read of this deadly mentality, bred in slavery, legally at work, officially sanctioned, and in triumphant celebration. We see it every day in our streets as we go about our daily business. Humanity cries for the victims of these crimes; we cry out for humanity's descent, deeper and deeper into the despair of the dungeon that is the legacy of African enslavement—the greatest crime against it, in and before modernity.

There has been a steadfast refusal by the beneficiaries of these crimes to formally recognize their nature and nurture. It is this refusal of recognition that drives the legacies of these crimes into our social realities and facilitates life-taking policing in our communities. This denial stands undiminished in the face of a mountain of evidence that cries out for ownership, responsibility, and accountability. Denial and silence are now the mother and father of a new generation of hate crimes, squeezing Black life from already impaired lungs. They are today's breath takers, as hate and greed were in earlier times. But the names on the cold, stone-like face of silence and denial must be known and called to account.

Portugal continues to deny its slavery crimes, yet we know that this nation was the largest shipper of enchained African bodies across the Atlantic. To Portugal we say, "Rise to your Responsibility." Great Britain denies, yet we know that it was the greatest profit maximizers and extractor investor in African slavery. To Great Britain we say, "Rise to your Responsibility."

France denies, yet we know that it fought the bloodiest war of all to prevent enslaved Blacks from breathing the air of liberty, equality, fraternity. Haiti emerged the leading global symbol of Black freedom, resilient and respected, but covered in the ash of French retribution. To France we say, "Rise to your Responsibility."

The Dutch deny, yet we know that they were first to develop the trade in enchained African bodies as a modern, global, corporate enterprise. To the Dutch we say, "Rise to your Responsibility." Spain denies, yet we know that the Spanish were the first to conceptualize and practice the idea that African enslavement should follow the genocide they imposed upon the natives of these Americas.

Norway and Denmark, not to be left behind, joined in and prospered, as did the Royals of Russia and the aristocracy of Austria who were as financially enriched as the beyond-the-scenes slave-investing Swiss and Swedes. All of Western Europe combined with their "American" colonies created the cradle of western financial modernization based upon the most lucrative sustainable investment of all times—the enchained, enslaved African body as commercial property.

This silence of the enslaving nations, and their political allies, must be broken and their denials ended. Then, and only then, will African descendants breathe freely the air of life and justice. Mr. President, I wish on behalf of the forward-looking world to express gratitude to this noble and life-empowering institution—the UN General Assembly—for its wisdom in finding a way to declare this decade in recognition of African descendant people. Mr. President, and Assembly members, we thank you.

We thank also all those advocates and champions of this cause, those who constitute the Working Group of Experts on African Descendant Peoples, our diplomats especially, for bringing us to this moment. Ms. Mireille Fanon, Prof. Verene Shepherd, and Ambassador Rhonda King are entitled to our recognition. We thank also our colleagues at UNESCO who have worked without rest to ensure that the Slave Routes Project, and the General History of Africa Projects, stayed alive despite life-threatening budget cuts. These are the two programs that have made an enormous impact and difference. I celebrate the effort of Madam Irina Bokova, UNESCO's leader, and urge that she continues to find creative ways to ensure that they remain UNESCO's flagship projects during the decade.

UNESCO has determined that the ninth volume of the *General History of Africa*, to be published in three monographs, be dedicated to the study of African descendants, and that it should carry the title "Global Africa." Going forward, the African descendant people of Asia, the Middle East, the Pacific, and Latin America especially will have a voice and a venue to express their vision. This decade will provide millions of African descendants, hitherto silenced and buried in denial, with opportunities to rise without shame and guilt to claim their African heritage without fear of reprisals. To offer these hitherto "invisibles" an opportunity of engagement and participation must be a major goal of this decade.

In this regard I wish to invite you to celebrate the government of Brazil for its enlightened policy that African history must be taught at all levels of the educational system—primary to tertiary. This policy should be emulated by all countries that have built their economies and societies upon African labor and intellect.

The transglobal slave trade was more than a criminal movement of enchained African bodies. It was a transfer of African cosmologies and epistemologies to slaving societies that were enriched by African minds and hands. The violent recruitment of enchained bodies also enabled the mobilization of intellectual and cultural resources that gave rise to the "West" as a recipient of Africa's best. In this decade resources must be provided UNESCO, Non-Governmental Organizations (NGOs), universities, and museums to research and discuss these traditions of labor and intellectual exploitation, and to illustrate the true role of the African in the making of modernity.

Finally, there is the imperative of "reparatory justice." Dr. Martin Luther King in his iconic "I Have a Dream" speech, said the following: "We have come to our nation's capital to cash a check. . . . America has given the Negro people a bad check which has come back marked insufficient funds." Mr. President, we have been taught to rehearse and rechant the "dream" part of this powerful message to modernity, and to forget or ignore the reparatory justice plea. Today, I call upon the world to take notice that Dr. King's reparatory justice claim is as alive as the power of his dream.

This twenty-first century will be the century in which the world will be called upon to atone with reparatory justice for the crimes against Africans and their descendants. These legacies continue to cripple and squeeze the air from their lungs! It took all of the sixteenth, seventeenth, and eighteenth centuries to establish and globalize these crimes of enchainment and enslavement.

It took all of the nineteenth century, from Toussaint's Haiti in the 1790s to Lincoln's United States in the 1860s, to Brazil and Cuba in the 1880s, to uproot chattel slavery from the modern world. It then took all of the twentieth century for African descendants to convert their legal freedom into citizenship and institutional leadership—gains continually threatened by force, rooted in slavery's enduring legacies. Now, if it will take all of the twenty-first century to achieve reparatory justice, we shall not retreat but will mobilize this decade and begin again to move speedily along the journey to reparatory justice.

Our finest and treasured values—peace, justice, respect, and reconciliation—require that we attain reparatory justice. It will be the basis, the only sustainable foundation upon which twenty-first-century humanity will rebuild this world with peace and prosperity for all.

The CARICOM nations, ancestral homes to the world's first complete slave-based economies, have established national and regional commissions in order to engage the nations of Europe, the owners and operators of these slave economies, in a diplomatic dialogue designed to rebuild trust and respect within the framework of reparatory justice. CARICOM has endorsed the "Ten Point Action Plan for Reparatory Justice" submitted by its Commission. It calls for reparatory justice around issues such as healthcare, education, cultural development, food security, and critically a formal apology as well as debt cancellation. It is a plan which says that the legacies of slavery, and the enduring elements of colonialism, constitute the greatest single drag upon the development efforts of citizens.

It calls upon the nations of Europe to return to the scene of these crimes and to participate in remedial development work that will enable African descendants to free themselves of the cultural and economic shackles that remained in place after the formalities of emancipation. This is the only path that can lead to an end of the shame and guilt that result from the silence and denial. We urge all countries to establish "National Reparations Commissions." We intend that this decade will see these National Commissions coming together as a Global Commission for Reparatory Justice. A war of terror is being waged against reparations advocates in some places. They continue to experience the terrorism of intimidation. Black nations and civil society advocate alike are threatened when supportive of reparatory justice.

UN agencies are denied funding for supporting projects that are reparatory of these legacies. The double speak of open mouth lip support and budget butchery is the strategy of subversion. The financial power of rich countries, built upon slavery, is used to intimidate and punish Black nations into silence. This strategy, this attitude of anger, is not sustainable in this twenty-first century. Many Black nations cannot breathe as a result, but they must find strength to say "No More"—and to say it in here, in this the United Nations.

In the name of Toussaint Louverture, Nelson Mandela, Harriett Tubman, Malcolm X and Dr. King, and Maya Angelou, let us all say in this decade: "The demand for Reparatory Justice will be taken through every diplomatic door, or taken down the corridors of every court."

We are survivors of the African Holocaust. Into these Americas were dragged in chains some 12 million enslaved ancestors. At the end of the barbarity only 6 million had survived. Survivors have a right to Reparatory Justice. The powerful have no right to deprive them.

Let us all, then, raise our *hands* in opposition to the violence that denies us the right to breathe, and to have justice.

Let us all resolve to make decent this decade as the door to a century that must witness the triumph of our collective and shared conception of humanity at its best.

Let us all resolve furthermore to clean up the mess left by slavery and colonization—and *move* on as one humanity in peace and with *Love*.

Mr. President, be assured of my respect, cooperation, and my gratitude. Your generosity this day is acknowledged, and I thank you for your gracious endurance of my intervention in your General Assembly.

9

What Is Reparations?

**THE NATIONAL COALITION OF BLACKS
FOR REPARATIONS IN AMERICA (N'COBRA)**

Reparations is a process of repairing, healing, and restoring a people injured because of their group identity and in violation of their fundamental human rights by governments, corporations, institutions, and families. Those groups that have been injured have the right to obtain from the government, corporation, institution, or family responsible for the injuries that which they need to repair and heal themselves. In addition to being a demand for justice, it is a principle of international human rights law. As a remedy, it is similar to the remedy for damages in domestic law that holds a person responsible for injuries suffered by another when the infliction of the injury violates domestic law. Examples of groups that have obtained reparations include Jewish victims of the Nazi Holocaust, Japanese Americans interned in concentration camps in the United States during WWII, Alaska Natives for land, labor, and resources taken, victims of the massacre in Rosewood, Florida and their descendants, Native Americans as a remedy for violations of treaty rights, and political dissenters in Argentina and their descendants.

What Forms Should Reparations Take

Reparations can be in as many forms as necessary to justly address the many forms of injury caused by chattel slavery and its continuing vestiges in American society. The material forms of reparations include cash payments, land, economic development, and repatriation resources particularly to those who are descendants of enslaved Africans. Other forms of reparations for Black people of African descent include funds for scholarships and community development; creation of multi-media depictions of the history of Black people of African descent and textbooks for educational institutions that tell the story from the African descendants' perspective; development of historical monuments and museums; the return of artifacts and art to appropriate people or institutions; exoneration of political prisoners; and the elimination of laws and practices that maintain dual systems in the major areas of life including the punishment system, health, education, and the financial/economic system. The forms of reparations received should improve the lives of African descendants in the United States for future generations; foster economic, social, and political parity; and allow for full rights of self-determination.

Who Should Receive Reparations?

Within the broadest definition, all Black people of African descent in the United States should receive reparations in the form of changes in or elimination of laws and practices that allow them to be treated differently and less well than white citizens. For example, ending racial profiling and discrimination in the provision of health care, providing scholarship and community development funds for Black people of African descent, and supporting processes of self-determination will not only benefit descendants of enslaved Africans, but all African descendant peoples in the United States who because of their color are victims of the vestiges of slavery. This is like the Rosewood, Florida, reparations package, where some forms of reparations were provided only to persons who descended from those who were injured, died, and lost their homes, though other forms were made available to people of African descent living in Florida.

Why Are African Descendants Entitled to Reparations?

The Trans-Atlantic Slave "Trade" and chattel slavery more appropriately called the Holocaust of Enslavement or Maafa/Maangamizi* was and is a crime against humanity. Millions of Africans were brutalized, murdered, raped, and tortured. They were torn from their families in Africa, kidnapped, and lost to their community. African peoples in the United States were denied

---

*This is a Swahili term meaning disaster that has been used for several years to describe these conditions and has been used most notably in the writings and presentations of Marimba Ani, PhD, noted African-centered anthropologist and activist.

the right to maintain their language, spiritual practices, and family relations, always under the threat of being torn from newly created families at the whim of the "slave owner." Chattel slavery lasted officially from 1660 to 1865. It was followed by one hundred years of government-led and -supported denial of equal and humane treatment, including Black Codes, convict leasing, sharecropping, peonage, and Jim Crow practices of separate and unequal public accommodations. African descendants continue to be denied rights of self-determination, inheritance, and full participation in the United States government and society. The laws and practices in the United States continue to treat African peoples in a manner similar to slavery—maintaining dual systems in virtually every area of life including health care, education, and wealth, while maintaining the myths of white superiority and African and African descendants' inferiority.

10

America Owes Us for the Ongoing Destruction of Afrikan Life! Reparations Now!

NEW AFRIKAN PEOPLE'S ORGANIZATION AND MALCOLM X GRASSROOTS MOVEMENT

The New Afrikan People's Organization (NAPO) is a revolutionary organization dedicated to independence and socialism for Afrikan descendants in the U.S. empire. NAPO is also committed to Pan-Afrikanism and anti-imperialist solidarity.

The Malcolm X Grassroots Movement is the mass association and political action wing of NAPO. MXGM is committed to self-determination, reparations, human rights for New Afrikan people and opposes sexism and genocidal policies of the U.S. empire.

As Pan-Africanists and anti-imperialists, NAPO and MXGM stand firmly in solidarity with the struggle of Afrikan and indigenous peoples for reparations internationally as well as inside the United States. The following statement outlines our understanding of both the importance of an international struggle for reparations for our people's and other people's centuries long struggle to end colonial domination and slavery.

What Are Reparations?

Reparations are compensation for damages inflicted on groups or individuals. The responsible party attempts to bring peace and justice by compensating the afflicted party. Reparations are an established principle in international law. The international community has held violators of human rights responsible to redress the damages for which it was responsible. For example,

Germany was forced to pay Israel because of its genocidal practices against Jewish people in the 1930s and 1940s, and Iraq was forced to compensate Kuwait after the Gulf War. The United States government agreed to compensate Japanese Americans for internment in concentration camps and seizing their property during the second World Imperialist War (a.k.a. World War II).

Why Should Afrikans in the United States Receive Reparations?

The history of Afrikans in the United States is an indictment against the U.S. government in terms of violations of human rights and genocide. The U.S. government is responsible for compensating Afrikans who are descendants of those Afrikans who were held captive in North America. For twenty-five years (1783 to 1808), the United States allowed Afrikans to be legally brought into its borders. They received import duties on each captive Afrikan brought to its shores during that time. In winning its war of independence from England, the United States decided to maintain a system of slavery with Afrikans as its primary labor force. Despite continued individual and collective resistance by Afrikans, the American system of slavery created physical, psychological, and social damage on the Afrikan population.

After slavery was declared illegal (except for punishment for "crimes"), the Americans institutionalized a system of colonial apartheid called segregation or "Jim Crow" which limited the life chances and the social and economic development of the Afrikan population in North America. From the 1870s until the early 1920s, the American government allowed terrorist violence against Afrikans to go virtually unchecked by its "law enforcement."

While the American government has declared its brand of apartheid illegal, this system is so institutionalized it is maintained in most aspects of social life in the United States, including the economic system, health care, housing, and education. Afrikan people are disproportionately targeted for police harassment and mass incarceration. White supremacy continues to affect the political, economic, and social life of Afrikans in the United States.

Is the Demand for Reparations a New Issue?

After the American Civil War, Afrikans began to demand land as a form of compensation for years of unpaid labor. The slogan "Forty Acres and a Mule" is rooted in this aspiration. Fear of an Afrikan uprising for land existed throughout the southern American states. In Virginia, Tennessee, and Georgia, American troops put down attempts by Afrikans to occupy land.

In the 1890s there were several efforts by Afrikans to achieve reparations. The National Ex-Slave Mutual Relief Bounty and Pension Association, headed by Callie House and Isaiah Dickerson, was a southern-based reparations movement composed of over 10,000 members.[1] Henry McNeal Turner, a bishop in the African Methodist Episcopal (A.M.E.) Church, called for reparations to allow our people to repatriate to Afrika.

Queen Mother Audley Moore represents the most tireless worker for Afrikan reparations in the Afrikan descendant movement in the United States. A former member of Marcus Garvey's Universal Negro Improvement Association and the Communist Party of the United States, Queen Mother began to advocate for reparations in the 1950s. She convinced Elijah Muhammad and Malcolm X to include it in the program of the Nation of Islam. She also convinced other nationalists, including Imari Obadele, founder of the Provisional Government of the Republic of New Afrika, Oseijeman Adefunmi, the founder of Oyotunji Village in South Carolina and leader of the Yoruba and traditional African religious revival movement in the United States, as well as Muhammad Ahmad (Max Stanford) of the Revolutionary Action Movement (RAM), to advocate for reparations. Inspired by Queen Mother Moore, Black Power organizations like the Revolutionary Action Movement, Provisional Government of the Republic of New Afrika, the League of Revolutionary Black Workers, and the Black Panther Party advocated for reparations. Most national Black Power gatherings endorsed the concept of reparations. After the Black Economic Development Conference called for reparations in 1970, James Forman and other activists initiated a direct-action campaign targeting predominately white Christian churches demanding reparations. This led to white denominations providing funds to Afrikan communities.

Since 1987, the National Coalition of Blacks for Reparations in America (N'COBRA) has led the effort to achieve reparations for Afrikan descendants in the United States. N'COBRA is a united front of activists who advocate for reparations. The Lost-Found Nation of Islam, under the leadership of Silas Muhammad, has initiated efforts to gain international support for reparations. From 1989 until his tenure in the U.S. Congress ended in 2017, Representative John Conyers submitted H. R. 40, a bill to study reparations and make recommendations. The Conyers bill has never made it to the floor of Congress. Several city governments, including Evanston and Detroit, have established commissions to support reparations. The 2000 release of the book *The Debt: What America Owes Blacks* by human rights advocate Randall

Robinson re-introduced the demand for reparations for public discourse. Journalist Ta-Nehisi Coates's 2014 *Atlantic* magazine article "The Case for Reparations" invigorated the dialogue in the United States.

Global Developments

At the beginning of the twenty-first century, the movement toward the 2001 World Conference Against Racism (WCAR) in Durban, South Africa increased international momentum of African peoples toward reparations. The struggle resulted in a resolution in which the United Nations declared the Trans-Atlantic Slave Trade "A Crime Against Humanity." This was considered a significant victory for the reparations movement. Unfortunately, two events disrupted the forward motion.

First, three days after the conclusion of the conference, the attacks on September 11, 2001, in New York and Washington, DC, overshadowed the victory at the WCAR for U.S.-based reparations activists. Secondly, the follow up Conference Against Racism in Barbados was divided by a conflict over including people of European origin in the conference. Despite these setbacks, Afro-descendant movements in South America, notably Brazil and Venezuela, have achieved momentum post-Durban.

Additionally, a significant blow to the international reparations movement occurred after the U.S.-sponsored coup in 2004 of the Lavalas government headed by Jean Bertrand Aristide in Haiti. The Aristide government had demanded twenty-one billion dollars in reparations from France, which had coerced Haiti to compensate the French government for its liberation from French colonialism. The demand for restitution remains a popular demand in Haiti despite the kidnapping of President Aristide and his seven-year banishment from Haiti.

The 2013 CARICOM nations' Ten Point Plan for reparations from European colonizers is an important development in re-asserting the demand for economic justice and for respect for the lives and humanity of our ancestors. It also inspired reparations advocates inside the U.S. empire.

What Type of Redress Does NAPO and the MXGM Argue Should Be Sought?

There are various proposals for reparations. The relationship between Afrikans and the United States has been an experience of conflict. The New Afrikan People's Organization (NAPO) and the Malcolm X Grassroots Movement

(MXGM) argue that Afrikan people and the United States will never have peace until reparations have been delivered on certain fundamental levels. The United States is in denial in terms of its crimes against the Afrikan population within its borders. Just as individuals engaged in therapy, America must first recognize its role in the oppression. The United States must acknowledge its violations against Afrikan people. Admitting to its role and apologies are necessary but not sufficient acts of justice. Acknowledgment of its human rights violations is a prerequisite to action to resolve the conflict between the United States and Afrikans.

Most reparation proposals offer financial compensation to Afrikans in America in terms of monetary payments, tax relief, or support for education. While all of these are valid there are other elements of redress with which NAPO/MXGM and other forces in the New Afrikan Independence Movement are concerned. We do not believe compensating individuals thousands of dollars is a meaningful way to heal the damages experienced by Afrikans in America. Given the current balance of power and capitalist economic arrangements, individual stipends would primarily stimulate the American economy, not empower the Afrikan community. We are concerned with reparation proposals that encourage our collective development and enable our people to ensure our future. The first things that our enslaved ancestors lost were their freedom and identity. After the end of chattel slavery, our ancestors were never allowed to choose their national identity or their relationship to the government, which sanctioned their captivity and enslavement. We should be allowed to determine what a free existence is for us, through a plebiscite. A plebiscite is a vote taken by a people to determine their national will. Some of us would prefer to be U.S. citizens. Some would prefer to be repatriated to Africa. Those of us in the New Afrikan Independence Movement desire an Afrikan government in North America on territory that our ancestors were enslaved on and forced to work without compensation. As part of our compensation, the United States needs to honor and respect our right to self-determination, our choices of how we want to be free. The United States should not deny us the right to organize a vote to determine how we wish to be free, nor should the United States attempt to manipulate that vote. After we determine our respective objectives, the United States should be obligated to fulfill our demands of freedom. This is real justice!

Another form of redress is for the United States government to release all political prisoners and allow all Afrikan political exiles to return to North America, if they choose to do so. The war the United States waged on the Afrikan freedom struggle in this country is the reason political prisoners and exiles exist. No real redress can exist while there is captivity or isolation of Afrikan freedom fighters.

How Does NAPO and the MXGM Think Reparations Will Be Achieved?

Frederick Douglass once said, "power concedes nothing without a demand." The United States will not do anything unless it is forced to. We might still be in slavery if our ancestors did not strike for their freedom during the Civil War. Without active struggle, Afrikans would not be able to vote or enjoy other things now considered basic rights in the U.S. empire. Reparations will only be achieved through a massive movement by Afrikans militantly challenging the empire. If we don't seriously fight for it, we will never get reparations or anything else important to our existence.

We must as a people reach a consensus on reparations. As we reach a consensus, we must challenge the imperialist state on reparations. If we are serious about reparations we will not allow business as usual to occur within the empire until we get it. Without reparations, we won't have justice, and without justice for our ancestors, and ourselves, we shouldn't allow the U.S. empire to live in peace. This is the only way we will achieve reparations.

FREE THE LAND! RESIST SETTLER COLONIALISM AND U.S. IMPE-RIALISM!

Note

1. The movement was national and federal government surveillance reported it had about 300,000 dues paying members. Also, Dickerson never headed the organization but rather he helped House until his death in 1909. See Mary Frances Berry, *My Face Is Black Is True: Callie House and the Struggle for Ex-Slave Reparations* (New York: Knopf, 2005), 253–254, n. 2.

11

Reparations Plan

NATIONAL AFRICAN AMERICAN
REPARATIONS COMMISSION

The National African American Reparations Commission's Preliminary 10-Point Reparations Program is a document for review, revision, and adoption as a platform to guide the struggle for Reparations for people of African descent in the United States.

1. A Formal Apology and Establishment of an African Holocaust (Maafa) Institute

A. We demand a formal apology for the role the United States Government played by explicitly and implicitly participating in, encouraging, and sanctioning the European Slave Trade and the institution of Chattel Slavery. The apology should be initiated by the President and ratified by the U.S. Congress by roll-call vote.

B. Furthermore, the apology should be accompanied by the establishment of a permanent MAAFA/African Holocaust Institute, charged with providing public education on the origins of enslavement, the role of private and public institutions in initiating and sustaining it; the systems of legal and de facto segregation enacted post-"emancipation" to the present; the damages/harm inflicted on people individually and collectively; and the wealth and benefits to local, state, and the federal government, private institutions and white society in general derived from these white supremacist institutions and structurally racist policies and practices.

2. The Right of Repatriation and Creation of an African Knowledge Program

A. The descendants of the millions of Africans who were stolen from Africa and transported to the strange lands of the "Americas" against their will to enrich their captors have a right to return to the motherland to an African nation of their choice. Africans in America who choose to exercise the right to return will be provided with sufficient monetary resources to become productive citizens in their new home and shall be aided in their resettlement by a Black-controlled agency funded by the federal government to perform this function.

B. The Repatriation Program will be complemented by an African Knowledge Program similar to the one included in the CARICOM Reparations Commissions' Ten Point Program of Reparatory Justice. This Program will serve to bridge the barriers and heal the wounds between Africans in the United States and Africans on the continent, resulting from centuries of enslavement, cultural alienation, misinformation, and divide and conquer/exploit schemes initiated by European and American slave traders, colonialists and neo-colonialists. Emotional Emancipation Healing Circles, research missions, and cultural/educational exchanges to build "bridges of belonging" will be part of such a Program.

3. The Right to Land for Social and Economic Development

After centuries of free labor that fueled the commercial and industrial revolutions in the United States enriched those at the helm of capital and finance and created opportunities and a "sense of privilege" for Europeans of every socio-economic strata, enslaved Africans were "emancipated" without being granted a material stake in the form of land/resources, e.g., "40 acres and a mule," to start anew in this hostile land. Moreover, formerly enslaved Africans were excluded from government programs like the Homestead Act which greatly benefited poor and working-class whites and corporations. Post-emancipation, land owned by Blacks was often stolen though trickery, fraud, and discriminatory policies and practices. These policies and practices were rampant in the Department of Agriculture, especially as carried out by Agricultural Extension Agencies in the South. They drastically stunted the growth and led to the bankruptcy of untold numbers of Black farmers. Therefore, we demand:

A. Substantial tracts of government/public land in the South and other regions of the country be transferred to the National Reparations Trust Authority with full autonomy in terms equivalent to the sovereignty granted to Native people over reservations awarded to them. These lands are to be utilized for major educational, commercial, industrial, economic/business and health/wellness institutions, and enterprises to benefit people of African descent.

B. Funds to support the restoration and enhancement of agricultural development, including grants and loans to limited resource farmers to enable them to expand and compete in the U.S. and global economy.

4. Funds for Cooperative Enterprises and Socially Responsible Entrepreneurial Development

Despite amazing efforts during the colonial, Revolutionary War, Civil War, and post-emancipation eras to the present, historically the quest to build a viable and sustained Black business/economic infrastructure has been thwarted by Blacks being pushed out of sectors of the economy like carpentry, brick masonry, catering, tailoring, and other crafts and skills where they dominated in favor of whites; the malicious destruction of thriving business districts like "Black Wall Street" in Tulsa and towns like Rosewood by white terrorist attacks; the systematic strangulation of Black towns like Hayti, North Carolina; Urban Renewal ("Negro removal") programs that gutted Black business districts in numerous cities and towns; and discriminatory lending policies that denied Black businesses the capital needed to survive and develop on a competitive basis. Therefore, we demand resources to support major cooperative enterprises and socially responsible entrepreneurial development:

A. Funds to develop an infrastructure of strategic financial, commercial, industrial, agricultural, and technology-oriented business/economic enterprises for the benefit of Black America as a whole. These enterprises will be managed by Boards of Trustees appointed by the National Reparations Trust Authority.

B. Funds for the establishment of a Black Business Development Bank to provide grants and loans to socially responsible for-profit entrepreneurships and economic ventures dedicated to building the Black community, utilizing just labor policies and sustainable environmental practices.

5. Resources for the Health, Wellness, and Healing of Black Families and Communities

The intergenerational psycho-cultural, mental, spiritual, and physical damages of Post Traumatic Slavery Syndrome, the daily toll of racism on individuals, families, and communities and the debilitating effects of chronic health disparities resulting from structural/institutional racism are well documented by leading Black psychiatrists, psychologists, and physicians. Moreover, many public hospitals and medical facilities that traditionally served Black communities have either been forced to close or are ill-equipped to offer a full range of services for lack of adequate funding. Therefore, we demand:

A. Funds for the establishment of a regional system of Black-controlled Health and Wellness Centers, fully equipped with highly qualified personnel and the best twenty-first century facilities to offer culturally appropriate, holistic preventive, mental health and curative treatment services.

B. Funds to strengthen existing hospitals and medical centers serving Black communities, e.g., Harlem Hospital, Howard University Medical Center and the reopening of such institutions that previously served Black communities that closed due to lack of funds.

C. Funds to strengthen institutions like Meharry Medical College and scholarships for students interested in attending these institutions who are committed to providing a period of service to Black communities.

D. Resources to fully operationalize and institutionalize the use of Emancipation Healing Circles as a methodology to address and overcome the damages of Post Traumatic Slavery Syndrome and racism as a disease infecting America's culture and institutions.

The aforementioned health and wellness Programs are to be implemented in consultation with the National Medical Association, National Dental Association, National Association of Black Nurses, Black Psychiatrists of America, Association of Black Psychologists, Inc., All Healers Mental Health Alliance, and similar organizations, institutions, and agencies.

6. Education for Community Development and Empowerment

Africans in America have acquired knowledge, produced great inventors, built institutions, and developed extraordinary leaders despite calculated efforts to deny Black people an education and/or the propagation of misinformation designed to destroy identity, self-esteem, and instill obedience to an oppressive system. During enslavement Africans could be punished or even killed for learning to read. Post-emancipation the vast majority of Black young people have been confined to separate and severely under-resourced schools during legal and de facto segregation. These conditions prevail today in what is sometimes called "poor performing schools." In higher education

African Americans have courageously endeavored to build and maintain a system of Historically Black Colleges and Universities (HBCUs), many of which are struggling to survive. Therefore, we demand:

A. The allocation of funds for the expansion and consolidation of the National Board of Education of African Ancestry as the body to devise standards and accredit African-centered educational programming for predominantly Black public schools throughout the country.

B. The provision of monetary and material incentives by the Federal government to school districts that adopt and implement a "Curriculum of Inclusion" of the history and culture of people of African descent in the United States.

C. Funds to strengthen Historically Black Colleges and Universities as the indispensable backbone of the higher educational infrastructure in Black America.

D. The funding of an endowment to provide free education for students attending HBCUs who are committed to providing service to Black communities.

7. Affordable Housing for Healthy Black Communities and Wealth Generation

Historically people of African descent were denied equitable access to programs within agencies like the Federal Housing Administration (FHA) that white Americans utilized to create prosperous suburbs across the nation and create wealth that could be transferred inter-generationally. Blacks were often victimized by discriminatory covenants that restricted them to certain neighborhoods: "redlining" by banks which refused to make loans to individuals and businesses in targeted neighborhoods and most recently, sub-prime lending schemes which resulted in the loss of billions of dollars in wealth in the form of home equity. The persistence of these discriminatory policies and practices produced an intergenerational deficit in terms of wealth creation that has stunted the social and economic development in Black families and communities.

Therefore, we demand the funding of an African American Housing and Finance Authority to:

A. Finance the planning and construction of holistic and sustainable "villages" with affordable housing and comprehensive cultural-educational, health and wellness, employment, and economic services.

B. Function as a source of grants and loans for persons seeking affordable housing.

8. Strengthening Black America's Information and Communications Infrastructure

From the earliest days of the forced migration of Africans to these hostile shores, communications vehicles like the Black press have been critical to the survival and development of Black communities. Black America's information and communications infrastructure was built and survives despite operating in a hostile environment and the absence of substantial public and private resources, more readily available to white individual and corporate information/communication media. The most recent conglomeration of electronic and print media with the blessing of the federal government has been particularly devastating to the maintenance of Black America's information and communications infrastructure. Therefore, we demand:

A. An annual federal set-aside of advertising dollars to support Black- owned newspapers and magazines and radio and television stations. These funds would be administered by the National Newspaper Publishers Association (NNPA) and National Association of Black Owned Broadcasters (NABOB) under the guidance of the Reparations Trust Authority.

B. Funding for a national nonprofit, noncommercial newspaper, radio, and television network dedicated exclusively to cultural-education, economic/ business and civic engagement programming for the benefit of Black America.

9. Preserving Black Sacred Sites and Monuments

The struggle for freedom, dignity, self-determination, and community/national development is a saga of a people in a strange land resisting, surviving, maintaining families, building institutions, and creating a future in the face of unspeakable oppression, exploitation, terror, and violence. All across this land there are slave quarters, hundreds of sites where Black people were lynched, and locales where Black towns and institutions were destroyed. But there are also Black burial grounds, Black towns (e.g., Nicodemus, Kansas, Mound Bayou, Mississippi), houses of worship, meeting halls, one-room schools, and other significant institutions that speak to the triumphant quest of a determined people to create a new African community in this hostile land.

These Black sacred sites and monuments must be preserved as permanent memorials to continuously inform and inspire future generations of people of African descent about this legacy of trials, tribulations and triumph and to remind America of the white supremacist terror employed to obstruct the path to freedom of African Americans.

Therefore, we demand:

A. The federal government via the National Parks Service erect markers on every site where a Black person was lynched, where a massacre of Black people was committed, and sites where Black towns or neighborhood were destroyed.

B. Funds for the preservation of Black burial grounds and other significant cultural/historical sites.

C. Funds to conduct research to identify previously unknown Black sacred sites and monuments.

10. Repairing the Damages of the "Criminal Injustice System"

Ever since the forced arrival of enslaved Africans in the Americas, policing and penal policies and practices were enacted to discipline, control, and acclimate Black people to systems of exploitation. The "Criminal Injustice System" that evolved was/is a direct extension and protector of the interests of the corporate and political elites in the United States. From runaway slave patrols, vagrancy laws, chain gangs, the convict lease system to relentless police violence, killings, and mass incarceration, racist policies and practices have decimated Black communities and severely constrained civil rights, human rights, and the socio-economic and political aspirations of Black people. The "War on Drugs" with its attendant racially biased policies and practices is the most recent manifestation of this longstanding war on Black people. It has disrupted millions of Black families and severely damaged Black communities across the country. The "criminal injustice system" has been a persistent source of resentment, resistance, and rebellion by Black people. Apologies from elected officials, leaders, and institutions responsible for fostering and benefiting politically from this unjust system are not sufficient. The damages to Black families and communities must be repaired.

Therefore, we demand:

A. Substantial resources to establish a Black-controlled Agency for Returning Citizens:
- To fund Centers in Black communities nationwide to provide culturally appropriate counseling, career development services, and job/employment training for formerly incarcerated persons.
- Provide grants to create entrepreneurial/business opportunities in communities damaged by mass incarceration.

B. Restoration of Voting Rights for all formerly incarcerated persons.

C. The exoneration of the Honorable Marcus Mosiah Garvey as the first victim of a "COINTELPRO" type operation by J. Edgar Hoover's FBI.

D. The release of all Political Prisoners and Prisoners of War unjustly convicted of acts of conscious committed while resisting and defending Black people from an oppressive system.

E. Revising/amending the 13th Amendment to the Constitution, which formally abolished slavery, to delete the clause: "except as a punishment for crime whereof the party shall have been duly convicted, shall exist within the United States, or any place subject to their jurisdiction"—which implies that Black people convicted of crimes can be legally held in bondage.

12

Reparations in Higher Education

A Scholars for Social Justice Platform

ADOM GETACHEW FOR

SCHOLARS FOR SOCIAL JUSTICE

Over the last two decades, Black organizers and activists around the world have moved reparations from the margins to the center of the political agenda. Organizers with the Movement for Black Lives included reparations in their ambitious Vision for Black Lives Platform in 2016 and pushed the Democratic candidates for president that year to embrace this demand.

Their effort emerged in the context of important victories. Within the United States, reparations for the victims of forced sterilization in North Carolina and victims of police torture in Chicago have modeled successful local strategies for redress. Internationally, the successful case of reparations for British torture during the Mau Mau rebellion, which resulted in a £20 million payout, has inspired new efforts to seek reparations for colonial injustice. The Herero and Nama peoples in Namibia are currently seeking redress for German genocide between 1904–1908. At the same time, the Caribbean Community has announced that it will be seeking reparations from Britain, France, and the Netherlands for their participation in native genocide and colonial slavery.

The debate over reparations is now shaping the conversation leading up to the 2020 Democratic primaries and has even seeped into an unlikely forum—David Brooks's opinion pages at the *New York Times*. That reparations is thinkable and sayable within the political mainstream marks an important transformation that promises to open new spaces to reimagine racial and economic injustice. Thanks to the work of generations of activists and organizers, it is an acknowledgment that historic injustice must be a consideration in contemporary debates about inequality.

At the same time, we should all be cautious about the uses to which reparations are put in these contexts. We should ask hard questions of the political leaders who have recently proclaimed their commitment to reparations. If reparations is going to be transformative, it must be more than an empty litmus test. As organizers did in 2016, this will require holding candidates' feet to the fire. It will mean asking why Cory Booker initially opposed reparations as he cozied up to the DeVos foundation and other proponents of school privatization, how Kamala Harris seeks to repair her criminalization of poor Black families as Attorney General of California, and how Julián Castro will repair the unprecedented decline of Black home-ownership during Obama's presidency and his tenure as the Secretary for Housing and Urban Development.

Here at Scholars for Social Justice, we believe that one way of deepening the debate about reparations is to proliferate the sites where claims of repair might be made. While the national debate about reparations is important, we must also consider the multiple actors involved in histories of racial violence and injustice. They include local governments, private corporations, and other institutions. They too ought to be sites of reparative justice and can be places to experiment with different versions and means of redress.

As academics, we have been particularly concerned to highlight the role reparations can play in universities and colleges. While universities are often viewed as ivory towers, far from everyday politics, the university is both deeply embedded in structures of racial hierarchy and inequality and remains a crucial site for reimagining education and society more broadly.

On April 7, 2019, Scholars for Social Justice launched a platform called "Reparations in Higher Education" to begin a national conversation about reparations in the context of universities and colleges. Modeled on the Vision for Black Lives platform, it examines the university's different roles such as employer, neighbor, and investor to trace paths toward racial justice and equality. We take the view that reparations is not just a matter of settling past accounts, but of transforming existing institutional structures that reproduce racial hierarchy and inequality. Students, scholars, and organizers can use the framework we have articulated to develop a campus specific account of how universities perpetuate racial injustice and build reparations campaigns that best address those contexts.

Reparations in Higher Education

I. INTRODUCTION

The Reparations in Higher Education platform seeks to reimagine racial justice and equity in universities and colleges across the country. Over the last few years, the politicization of higher education cannot be escaped. Between 2014 and 2020, student protests highlighted campus racism, questioned universities' commitment to equity and inclusion, and put pressure on higher education's now complex financial entanglements. On almost ninety campuses, students of color led demonstrations the demands of which included renaming buildings, the curricular inclusion of ethnic studies, the expansion of faculty of color, support for first-generation and working-class students, and living wage guarantees for all university employees.[1] This student action coincided institutional efforts at Georgetown University and elsewhere to come to terms with the ways in which universities were embedded in histories of land theft and slavery. These developments called for a renewed conversation about the politics of racial inequality across college campuses.

The election of Donald J. Trump and the subsequent appointment of Betsy DeVos and Jeff Sessions to head the Departments of Education and Justice significantly undermined this opening. The Trump administration rolled back regulations on for-profit colleges, relaxed its commitment to Title IX investigations, and eliminated the Public Service Loan Forgiveness Program. The majority, Republican-appointed Supreme Court ruled that considerations of race in college admissions is unconstitutional and also struck down a very limited student loan cancellation program initiated by the Biden administration.

Rather than take a defensive approach to this moment of backlash and retrenchment, Scholars for Social Justice view our current predicament as an opportunity to boldly reimagine racial justice in higher education through a framework of reparations. We consider the multiple roles of the university; analyze how institutions of higher education have reproduced racial inequality; and outline policies, campaigns, and approaches that repair relations of injustice and point toward a future inclusive and egalitarian university.

HISTORY OF THE PROJECT This SSJ platform emerges from the work of the Reparations in Higher Education (RHE) working group. RHE was organized in 2016 after a year of student protests that demanded racial equality. As in other moments, student protests on campuses were inspired and sustained by the larger political context of organizing and activism the Movement for Black Lives (M4BL) ushered. M4BL that has boldly centered anti-Black state violence and put forward a comprehensive platform for political and economic justice.[2] Inspired by this context and composed of students, academics, and activists, RHE came together with the aim of developing a broadly conceived vision of what reparations and racial justice might mean in the context of higher education.

SSJ took up the project with the aim of developing a reparations in higher education platform in terms similar to the 2016 "Vision for Black Lives" platform of the M4BL, which included reparations as a central pillar. The reparatory framework mobilized in this platform also draws on the long history of Black and colonized people who have mobilized for reparations to redress racial injustice. From Belinda Sutton, who successfully petitioned for the payment of a slave pension in 1783, to the recent victories of reparations for colonial violence against the Mau Mau in Kenya and for police brutality in Chicago, people of African descent have demanded a reparative framework for slavery and colonialism. The RHE platform draws on this history and builds on the work of organizations like the National Coalition of Blacks for Reparations in America (N'COBRA) to outline a reparatory framework for racial justice in the university.

While SSJ is especially indebted to the struggles for reparations within the United States, this project also takes inspiration from the adoption of reparative frameworks in the struggles for Indigenous self-determination and transitional justice within the Global South and especially in the context of Latin America. As with calls for reparations in the United States, these movements imagine reparations to require more than direct monetary compensation for past injustice. Instead, these approaches incorporate material, symbolic, legal, and institutional redress for both individual and collective victims.[3] These projects view redress for past harm as a necessary part of reconstituting societies where racial, religious, and ethnic violence has generated deep-seated divisions.

Drawing on this insight, this Reparations in Higher Education platform unearths the ways that racial inequality lives in the past and present of the academy to point toward alternative futures.

THE SITE OF THE UNIVERSITY   While many calls for reparations single out the state as the primary perpetrator of racial harm and thus also as the primary site for demanding redress, universities have also played a historical and ongoing role in perpetuating racial inequality. First, recent historical studies have shown the centrality of slavery and settler-colonialism to the founding and financing of colleges and universities in the United States.[4]

Second, institutions of higher education actively participated in the perpetuation of ideologies of race that naturalized and justified racial exclusion and domination. Theories of racial inferiority developed and sustained within the academy had consequences beyond the ivory towers, as they fueled popular knowledge and shaped the contours of political debate.[5]

Third, while often viewed as gateways for upward mobility, institutions of higher education reproduce and reinforce hierarchies of race and class. Thus, while many institutions have embraced the language of diversity and inclusion, they function as sites for the entrenchment of political and economic power rather than vehicles for its redistribution. This is particularly the case in the contemporary context of massive public divestment from education, spiraling tuition costs, and high levels of indebtedness for working and middle-class students. The university as a site for the reproduction of power is not limited to this question of who can access a university education. As employers,[6] real estate developers,[7] and managers of large endowments,[8] institutions of higher education are deeply implicated in broader circuits of inequality.

THE UNIVERSITY AS NEIGHBOR In framing a demand for reparations on behalf of Black, Indigenous, and Latinx communities, it is crucial to recognize and identify the various ways universities have displaced, exploited, and criminalized their neighbors. All too often colleges and universities—in urban centers and small towns alike—have expanded their acreage, upgraded facilities, and compromised its workers without being held accountable for the impact these choices make on vulnerable communities. Here we consider the "hidden" costs to Black, brown, and working-class communities when institutions of higher education use local ordinances, benefit from state and federal dollars, and form private sector partnerships to expand their interests. As universities play large roles in the town and cities they inhabit, we must ask, "What are the costs when colleges and universities exercise significant power over a city's financial resources, policing, employment, and real estate?" and consider what accountability, justice equity requires in these contexts.[9]

ANALYSIS The following analysis draws on the real estate and labor practices of Yale and Columbia to highlight three pernicious processes: the displacement of residents and the criminalization of surrounding areas, residents, and neighborhoods as well as the exploitation of labor. In these two cases, the surrounding community is predominately Black and working class, giving these processes a distinctive trajectory. However, these patterns fit into a broader practice of urban universities, which have advanced a neoliberal model of urban development. Colleges and universities tend to argue that gentrification and the presence of resource-heavy institutions improve cities. These processes have become so normalized and accepted, that colleges and universities regularly characterize their practices as necessary for revitalizing cities. Institutions become part of an "inevitability" narrative, in which gentrification and displacement are predetermined phenomena.[10]

1. Displacement of Residents

One impact that college and universities have on neighborhoods is displacement through an array of means—including gentrification that inflates housing prices, supporting the removal of public or low-income housing, or capitalizing on tax-exempt statuses.[11] Specifically, Columbia and Yale have widened their neighbor footprints by aggressively purchasing properties in predominantly poor and working-class Black neighborhoods. Private, resource-heavy universities engage in a form of *hyper-gentrification* not only by directly purchasing property, but they also fail to intervene when their students perpetuate housing inequality. In many of the neighborhoods adjacent to urban universities, and within the walls of the amenity-rich, planned apartment communities in smaller college towns, students can often afford to pay higher rents than locals. Landlords seeking to profit from the steady stream of student renters become motivated to push out locals, who increasingly will not be able to afford rising rents.[12] Rarely do residents have the political or economic capital to confront and resist this type of gentrification, and universities have little incentive to stop it, particularly if the private rental market fulfills their student housing shortfalls.[13] Due to the urgency of university-led displacement, activist groups have initiated campaigns to raise awareness and resist gentrification, but institutions have yet to fully account for their role in this problem.[14] Colleges and universities are invested in expansion in order to elevate institutional capacity or to provide more housing for students. These goals may seem innocuous or laudable on their face, but no strategic campus plan or initiative can coalesce without consideration of the disproportionate impact these ideas have on neighborhoods and neighbors.[15] In making a case for reparations in higher education, we call for an explicit recognition of how institutions, in the past and present, contribute to the sedimentation of racialized poverty.

2. Criminalization of Neighborhoods

With increasing expansion, universities perpetuate and reinforce the criminalization of Black and Latinx communities. Urban universities maintain large police and security forces and lobby for city police forces to increase their presence in surrounding neighborhoods.[16] Communities of color near universities are thus subject to the overlapping jurisdictions of university and city police forces, which reinforces the over-policing and surveillance of communities of color. While claiming to be working in service of protecting university property and affiliates, police on campuses have also directed violence toward Black staff, faculty, and students, with little or no recourse for violating their rights.[17] High-profile incidents at Arizona State, Brown, Harvard, and the University of Chicago have illuminated some of the problems between Black employees and students and the campus police, but these incidents have not inspired widespread evaluation of how police forces intersect with those off and on campuses. Instead, following broader national trends, university forces have begun to engage in militarization efforts, receiving military-grade gear from the federal government, which enhances their capacity to surveil and punish Black and Latinx residents in neighboring communities.[18]

3. Exploitation of Labor

The presence and expansion of universities in working-class communities of color is often argued by using neoliberal logic: The expansion of institutions with resources and capital is good for neighborhoods as they create jobs and attract financial resources—state investment, consumers, and improved retail options—to the neighborhoods and cities where they are located. This logic of "revitalization" is rooted in the idea that university presence creates openings for employment, and that these new jobs can be filled, at least in part, by neighborhood residents and locals.[19] Universities do create employment opportunities, but because of their monopoly on the surrounding labor market, they exploit the labor of neighboring residents, resist the demands of campus-based labor unions, and depress wages.[20] Colleges and universities may attract students, faculty, and administrators from around the world, but often local people fill clerical, maintenance, service, and technical positions. Frequently, the university-based, service economy offers wages that may be incommensurate with the cost of living.[21]

Recommendations:

The issues examined above provide a broad overview of how universities have engaged in unethical and devastating practices, which have stripped community members and workers of economic security and rendered them vulnerable to hyper-policing. Colleges and universities in the United States are each uniquely situated in their geographical, economic, and intellectual contexts. Yet, when we uncover how they have consolidated property, financial resources, and prestige over the course of centuries and decades, the themes of Indigenous and Black displacement, labor exploitation, and criminalization resonate across their histories. Whether the forces of racial capital lead to the purchase of property below market value, the building of a sports stadium, a reduction in wage expenditures, or the installation of closed-circuit security cameras, universities are intimately tied to the injustices of the past and our present-day struggles. Universities clearly owe a debt to the communities, workers, and neighbors they have exploited and marginalized in order to grow and attract resources to campuses. We recommend the following actions in service to or repaying those most damaged by higher education's past and current practices.

- City-enforced payment in lieu of taxes: Most colleges and universities are deemed tax-exempt by the IRS; therefore, they do not contribute to the stream of municipal and state revenues necessary for the education, housing, health care, infrastructure maintenance, and transportation needs of the communities where they are located. Following on the pioneering 2012 agreement reached in Boston which required nonprofit groups with more than $15 million in tax-exempt property to volunteer 25 percent of the property taxes they would owe if not exempt, we call for a city-enforced payment in lieu of taxes.[22] Because these payments are not required, universities often shirk on their commitments, even when they have agreed in principle. To enforce such agreements, cities can include consequences for reneging on these commitments such as denying necessary permits and other municipal resources universities require for their expansion and operation.
- Community Benefits Agreement: Colleges and universities must create community benefits agreements to allow their neighbors access to campus resources. Institutions of higher education must prioritize hiring local people, providing job training for service workers, allow for community access to libraries, support and invest

in affordable housing for its employees, subsidize childcare and support caretakers through sick leave and family care leave policies, and provide leadership and financial support for neighborhood improvements, including public spaces and schools. University partnerships can create community gardens, designated graffiti and art spaces, as well as recreational facilities for youth and elders.

- Community Self-Determination: Universities can support community self-determination by assisting in commercial and housing development subsidies to prevent the removal of their neighbors and contract with local businesses to keep resources in the immediate community. Universities are not only major employers, but they are also major consumers. Universities can implement practices to ensure they are seeking out contractors from local communities for construction projects, legal counsel, as well as financial services.
- Community Oversight Boards: Universities can bridge the divide between campus and community by creating community oversight boards to collaborate on development projects, campus police departments, as well as creating impact surveys to guide campus planning.
- Unionization Rights: In keeping with the recommendations on labor to follow, we support the unionization of all higher education workers to ensure due process, collective bargaining, and the protection of employee rights.
- Redistribution of Athletic Revenues: Considering the racial dynamics of college athletics, we recommend the distribution of athletic revenues to community-based initiatives.

III. THE UNIVERSITY AS EMPLOYER

Labor in the contemporary university must be analyzed with two broad conditions in mind. First, higher education and health care (sometimes collectively referred to as "meds and eds") are often interlinked and are fast-growing industries that have, in the context of deindustrialization and unemployment, been championed as tools of urban redevelopment and economic growth.[23] Second, universities and associated health centers are often among the largest employers in a given labor market, making university-hospital complexes in some regions function as "company towns" with outsized political and economic power. Demands for justice and equity for university-hospital workers thus has ripple effects beyond the Ivory Tower.

ANALYSIS With this broad context in mind, we analyze the prevailing labor conditions for four kinds of university workers: 1) academic workers (2) student workers (3) the hospital sector and (4) the large sector of nonprofessional workers who provide essential services on both sides of the complex.

1. Academic Workers

While historically the academic profession has been marked by relative job stability and financial security, there has been a growing trend of casualization. Almost three quarters of the faculty are currently contingent workers with no access to tenure, a disproportionate number of whom are women and people of color.[24] Women now constitute 51–61 percent of contingent faculty,[25] a stark contrast to their continued underrepresentation among the ranks of tenured and tenure-track faculty.[26] Moreover, underrepresented groups continue to see increased representation in contingent academic jobs with the pay disparity to match.[27] According to the Coalition on the Academic Workforce, part-time Black faculty earn significantly less than other racial and ethnic groups. The growing rates of contingent workers along with the central role graduate students play in the work of teaching demonstrates a move toward cheaper sources of instructional labor and inadequate working conditions in academia.

The racialized and gendered dimensions of casualization means that demands for greater faculty diversity on campuses require a structural analysis of labor conditions, a concomitant call for equity and a demand for good academic jobs with job security. Without stemming and reversing the casualization trends, we risk a form of diversity that sequesters underrepresented groups to the lowest ranks of the academic workforce.

2. Student Workers

As higher education increasingly becomes unaffordable for many Americans, students must work on or off campus to partially cover their expenses. This takes the form of work-study programs through which students meet their "student income contribution," which is often calculated separately from their parents' contribution. On campuses, students take on a number of jobs from the library counter to serving at cafés and dining halls. For universities, relying on student workers is often a source of casualized and relatively cheaper labor. For instance, students working in UCLA Dining Halls make $10.50 while the starting wage for full-time workers is $16.32. Over the last year, student workers at UCLA have demanded equal pay for equal work.[28]

At wealthier schools with large endowments, student workers have argued that the student income contribution reproduces class inequalities among students, as wealthier students do not have to work and can dedicate themselves fully to educational and extracurricular opportunities. In a report titled "Why We Can't Wait: The Cost of the Student Income Contribution on the Yale Undergraduate Community," Students Unite Now argued that student contributions amount to an extra fee each year that Yale expects exclusively from students on financial aid. They have called for the elimination of the student income contribution for all students on financial aid.[29]

In addition to work-study, student athletes share the conditions of other campus workers. From the contracts they sign before attending the recruiting university to the 50–60 hours of training and game time a week and the profits their sportsmanship brings, there is little difference between college and professional athletes who are understood as workers and unionized in the NFL and NBA. The unprecedented 2014 effort to organize a union of football players at Northwestern University made clear that "the players spend more time on football—what the NCAA has said is the ancillary portion of their education—than [most people] spend at their nine-to-five jobs."[30] As with organizing efforts in other contexts of the University, at stake in this fight to recognize student athletes as workers is an effort to ensure that they have adequate protections of their basic rights including bargaining over the terms of their work, the necessary health care coverage for the injuries they suffer on the job and protections against the arbitrary revocation of scholarships.[31]

3. Hospital Workers

As on the academic side, labor in university hospitals is hierarchically structured and locates women of color in marginalized positions where they do much of the daily care work. Outside of the doctors, consider the following numbers for the health-care industry: Registered Nurses, which tend to be the most professionalized care workers are 91% women—79% are white, 11% are Black, 8% are Asian, and 5% Latina. Their average pay is about $71,000/year. Licensed Practical Nurses who don't have the same professional status and are increasingly being phased out are 91% women: 68% white, 25% Black, 8% Latina, 4% Asian and make about $40,000/year. Beneath these in the hierarchy are the lowest-status patient care jobs: nursing assistants, medical assistants, personal care assistants. These are the people who help with personal grooming, toileting, washing, and so on. The category "nursing, psychiatric, and home health aides" is 54% white, 37% Black, 13% Latina, 5%

Asian, and 87% women. These positions tend to pay in the range of $10–12 an hour.[32] The stratified nature of health care has proven a difficult place to organize workers and the absence of broad-based union drives (as is the case on the academic side) tend to diminish the power of organized labor. For instance, at Johns Hopkins, while care workers in the lowest ranks are organized, nurses are not. This allows the hospital to "divide and conquer" by relying on the professionalized nurses to ensure smooth operations in the context of work stoppages.[33] It should be noted that hospitals, despite being nonprofit, generate large profits. For instance, Hopkins Hospital rebuffed demands for a $14 minimum wage in the year after it reported an operating surplus of $145 million. The poverty wages paid to marginalized health workers stand in sharp contrast to rising compensation packages of hospital CEOs. In 2013, the CEO of Hopkins Hospital made $1.3 million.[34]

4. Non-professional Service Sector Work

At the crux of universities' smooth operation is the large sector of what is often classified as "nonprofessional" jobs, which are usually considered front-line or lowest-level duties. In turn, pay is relatively lower in the form of either a low hourly wage or salaries that top out below $50,000 in most cases.[35] Though their labor is central to the university, employees such as custodians, food service workers, administrative assistants, security staff, and other nonprofessional staff are the very workers that are often left out of conversations about worker exploitation on college campuses.

Despite their important and hard work, many struggle to support their families with incomes that are often inadequate to pay for food, housing, and health care. This inadequate pay is most felt during the summer breaks. Contrary to their credentialed, professional counterparts, many nonprofessional employees have to find another job in the summertime when campus operations are significantly scaled back. California has provided a partial solution by extending unemployment insurance (UI) to what they call "classified" employees during the summer. While expanding UI benefits for nonprofessional employees is an important move for equity, those gains are offset by the cost-cutting measures of outsourcing and subcontracting services largely provided by an already vulnerable worker class to private companies. Essential services such as dining, custodial services, and administrative functions are dissipating into the private sector with steep social and economic consequences. A 2014 study showed that the substantial reduction in wages caused by outsourcing and contracting exacerbates both the gender and race pay gaps.[36] These cost-savings (which the same study shows vary widely and often diminish over time anyway) value money over people.

While outsourcing has been used in sectors like food services and maintenance, on the clerical and technical side, universities have introduced a model of "shared services" to cut costs. Shared services create centralized business and IT offices and replaces workers who once were located in departments or centers. The idea is that by reorganizing this labor in centralized structures, the university can reduce clerical and technical staff. The model of shared services has drawn lots of criticism because it does not appear to reduce costs and is often a decision made without consulting university stakeholders such as faculty and staff.[37] Beyond these concerns, it is important to remain attentive to the human consequences of shared services: layoffs of workers who may struggle to find adequate work and more work for the same pay for those who are left to work in the shared services centers.

There is much to learn, though, from some sectors of nonprofessional university staff (such as clerical workers) that have turned to organizing and unionizing since the 1980s through widely publicized work stoppages like those at Yale, Columbia, New York University, Wayne State, and Michigan State.[38] Additionally, in 2001 after nearly two years of bargaining, 18,000 clerical, library, and administrative assistants, police dispatchers, and child care workers at the University of California won a contract that gave the right to arbitration for allegations of discrimination and the promise that UC would not require employee background checks (including credit checks) unless there is a "bona fide business purpose." Just last year, after a historic three-week strike, Harvard Dining Hall workers won a minimum annual salary of $35,000, which includes raises in hourly rate and summer pay. In addition, Harvard backed off efforts to increase employee contributions to the health plan.[39] These are but a few signs of resistance against a whole series of exclusions that impair the lives of the most marginalized university workers.

Recommendations:

The fundamental injustice of corporate greed and worker exploitation calls for robust modes of redress that allows for the most marginalized of university workers—and all workers—to thrive. Thus, we draw on the Campus Bill of Rights[40] from Tennessee's Higher Education Union, United Campus Workers, and labor struggles at other campuses to inform this vision of reparatory justice.

- A right to organize: Campus workers have the right to organize labor unions; to official recognition of their union; and the ability to "meet and confer" with officials at the departmental, institutional, and state levels on all issues of concern. Campus workers have the right to freely conduct meetings on nonworking hours; to petition for redress of grievances; to deduct dues from paychecks; and ultimately to bargain collectively in order to protect and advance our collective.

- Health care and adequate benefits: Campus workers have the right to guaranteed comprehensive health care; to an adequate retirement; to paid vacations and/or sabbaticals; to paid family leave; and to tuition remission or adequate funding for educational opportunities for workers and their families, including partner benefits.
- A living wage: Campus workers have the right to a base salary high enough to provide for their families to live a decent life without reliance on governmental assistance or private charity, and to salaries that are equitable with wages paid at peer institutions and in private employment.
- Ban the box bill/ban credit checks: Campus workers have a right to protection against discrimination based on past criminal and financial record. "Ban the box" prohibits or delays inquiries about criminal record history until later in the decision-making process. Both criminal background checks and credit checks constitute an illegitimate barrier to employment.[41]
- Full-time, annual work: Universities should guarantee twelve months of work and pay for all workers rather than furlough staff during the summer months. While the academic year only lasts 9 months, staff need salaries throughout their year to meet their needs and provide for their families. One model of annual work and pay is suggested in the recent victory of striking Harvard dining hall staff whose recent contract includes additional compensation (above their annual salary) paid in three installments during the summer months.[42]
- Non-discrimination: Campus workers have the right to a workplace free from harassment, exploitation, and discrimination. This includes the right to receive fair and equal treatment, opportunities, pay, and benefits regardless of religion, race, nationality, immigration history, gender, gender identity or expression, sexual orientation, age, disabilities, or political orientation. Campus workers have the right to equal pay for equal work.
- Job protection: Campus workers have the right to jobs protected from the threat of privatization, outsourcing, and subcontracting.

- Due process: Campus workers have the right to a grievance procedure that includes the right to grieve all matters that can impact
safety, evaluations, raises, transfers, layoffs, promotions, and disci-
plinary actions, and they have the right to representation of their
choice at all levels.

III. THE GLOBAL UNIVERSITY

In the context of economic globalization, university and colleges have sought
to capitalize on new economic networks to position themselves as global institutions. Beyond the entanglements of university endowments in the global
economy, the new face of the global university has taken a variety of forms
from the rise of study abroad to the creation of satellite campuses and degree
programs. These programs raise several ethical challenges. For instance, an
investigation into labor practices during the construction of NYU's Abu
Dhabi campus found that almost 10,000 workers were not protected by the
university's labor guidelines that set standards for fair wages, hours, and living conditions.[43] More broadly, as critics have argued the global university
is also the imperial university insofar as research in the social sciences, and
STEM is being mobilized in service of U.S. hegemony and warmaking abroad.

ANALYSIS

1. The University and U.S. Empire

Beginning as early as President Dwight Eisenhower's 1961 coinage of the
term "military-industrial complex," the university's autonomy as a "fountain-
head for free ideas and scientific thinking" has been compromised by the
strategic and ideological aims of the military. This concern is exacerbated
by the rising militarism of the United States since September 11, 2001, and
the announcement of a global war on terror. For instance, while Reserve
Officer Training Corps (ROTC) were expelled by many elite schools during
protests against the Vietnam War, Harvard, Columbia, Yale, and Stanford
have recently welcomed ROTC back to campus.[44] Moreover, there are over 150
military-educational institutions and according to the American Association
of University Professors, hundreds of colleges and universities receive Pentagon funding for research, provide classes to military personnel, and create
special programs designed to lead to employment in defense industries and
support military operations.[45] In the context of limited funding resources, the
Pentagon and Department of Defense have stepped up research support and
their relationships to universities now extend to the social sciences and humanities. For example, the Pentagon's controversial "Human Terrain System"

recruited anthropologists and Middle East experts to "decipher" Iraqi and Afghani society at the height of United State's wars in these countries.[46]

At times these relationships with the military-industrial complex are parasitic on universities' rhetoric of diversity, equity, and inclusion. For example, a leaked memorandum of understanding (MOU) between Baruch College-CUNY and the Central Intelligence Agency reveals that the CIA has sought recruitment relationships with colleges and universities that have a diverse student body. According to the MOU, CIA recruitment would focus on "campus chapters of diversity professional organizations such as, but not limited to, Society of Hispanic Professional Engineers, American Indian Science and Engineering Society and/or the Association of Latino Professionals for America." The memorandum also binds Baruch College to assessments of the CIA's "Return on Investment."[47]

2. Endowments

Since the calls for divestment from apartheid South Africa in the late 1970s and 1980s, student activists have highlighted the deep interconnections between university endowments and system of injustice and exploitation at home and abroad. Most prominently, campaigns to divest from private prisons and fossil fuels demonstrate the ways that university investments reproduce logics of inequality and help to bolster an unsustainable economy. These divestment campaigns often face an uphill battle as the structure of investments are often mediated through complex financial arrangements and lack transparency.

3. Expansion

As the University physically expands across the world, the creation of new campuses and degree-granting programs has created opportunities for intellectual engagement and interaction but has also raised a number of ethical questions. For instance, faculty and students criticized Yale's creation of a liberal arts program in collaboration with National University of Singapore both because of concerns about freedom of speech at the campus and because the decision to create a campus, the costs involved, the nature of the partnership were not subject to faculty oversight, review, or approval. Far from growing out of the intellectual mission of the university, these expansions abroad appear to be dictated by Boards of Trustees.

4. Marginalization of Africa and the African diaspora

Given the connections between militarism and higher education discussed above, the "global turn" in universities and colleges has largely followed U.S.

strategic interests with universities prioritizing the Middle East and China as sites for intellectual exchange and collaboration. In keeping with the marginalization of the African and African Diasporic world in the Americas in U.S. foreign policy, these areas have seen comparatively little engagement from U.S. universities. The global university thus remains only partially global, and the consequences of this partiality can be seen in curriculum, faculty hires, and the distribution of resources.

Recommendations:

While critical of features in higher education's global turn, we are committed to universities and colleges engaging ethically and equitably with the rest of the world. We recommend the following as avenues for creating more just global networks.

- Divest/Invest model: University and colleges should divest form their relationships with the U.S. military-industrial complex. This should include banning ROTC programs and other military recruitment as well as rejecting DOD funding for research. The university's global engagements and investments should have the university's core education mission in mind, and as result, should be subject to faculty oversight and governance.
- Investment transparency and setting ethical standards: Unlike the fight for divestment in South Africa where the university's direct investment in companies made the lines of investment clear, most university endowments are now organized through pooled funds that make it more difficult to trace investments. We recommend that universities are more transparent with their investment practices and that they set guidelines for responsible and ethical investments. Such standards should be set by a committee that represents the various stakeholders of the university, including students, faculty, and staff.
- Community Benefits agreements: As with their immediate neighbors, universities and colleges should extend community benefits agreements to their global neighbors. Global expansion should be carried out with the same ethical standards that we advocate in the local setting.
- Engagement with the Black world: Universities and colleges should work to incorporate a more expansive global vision by paying greater attention to the African and African Diasporic world. Black studies departments and their equivalents should play a key role in these ventures.

IV. THE UNIVERSITY AND MASS INCARCERATION

As is now well known, the rate of incarceration has more than quadrupled in the last four decades. Between 1973 and 2009, the number of people incarcerated in federal and state prisons increased from approximately 200,000 to 1.5 million with another 700,000 held in local jails. This unprecedented level of incarceration is severely racialized: 60 percent of the prison population is Black and Latino. Black women are locked up at three times the rate of white women. Between 1980 and 2000, the rate of Black incarceration in the United States tripled, with most of the convictions involving nonviolent drug offenses.

Universities have played a complex role vis-à-vis this social crisis. On the one hand, university research developed and endorsed the policies that have contributed to mass incarceration, they have themselves been involved in criminalization of surrounding neighborhoods as section one of this report discusses and have benefited from endowments and investments in private prisons. On the other hand, due to the efforts of faculty and students, universities have also hosted and supported the growing critical scholarship on incarceration and have pioneered prison education programs.

Recommendations:

The crisis of mass incarceration reaches far beyond the domain of higher education, but universities can play an important role in rectifying this injustice.

An end to criminalization through an invest/divest model: Universities can model what decriminalization and decarceration looks like in their neighborhoods by divesting from private police forces and security apparatuses and investing in the community. This investment can take the form of providing full-time work at a living wage and providing resources for public education. The tax-exempt status of universities often means that their surrounding communities are losing out on property taxes, which would support public goods including K–12 schools. The recommendation for a city-enforced payment in lieu of taxes discussed above should be combined with and enhanced through this divestment from policing.

- Divestment from Private Prisons: From the 2005 Yale Graduate Employees and Student Organization's report "Endowing Injustice" to the recent successful efforts of undergraduates at Columbia, students have directed attention to the ways that universities financially benefit from investments in private prisons.[48] Universities should divest holdings from all private prisons.

- Increasing access to education: Universities should extend access to higher education to those incarcerated and to the formerly incarcerated. Rather than simply a haphazard course offering, prison education programs must be tailored toward the aims of allowing students to receive degrees. Models of this kind include the Bard and NYU prison education programs. Universities should also offer job placement opportunities for those who leave the prison and have completed their coursework. Moreover, universities can also help reintegrate the formerly incarcerated by ensuring equal access in the admissions process and providing adequate financial support that considers their exclusion from Federal Pell grants.

V. STUDENT DEBT

The struggle for education and access to education has been a hallmark of the struggle for Black freedom and racial equality throughout the history of the United States. The heroic fight for racial equality in education lead to the Supreme Court decision in the case of *Brown v. Board of Education* in 1954. At the same time, the expansion of public higher education in the immediate postwar years democratized access to university and colleges to students of color and working-class communities. However, this moment when inclusion and equality were on the table quickly dissipated as public funding of universities shrank, tuition increased, and debt came to play an outsized role in the financing of higher education. Student debt in the United States now exceeds $1 trillion. Astronomical tuition and ballooning student debt ensure that rather than a right, college education in the United States is an increasingly unaffordable luxury. Moreover, because a college degree is the gateway to stable and decent-paying jobs, the denial of access to college essentially relegates a large sector of the population to low wage work.

ANALYSIS: RACE AND DEBT Given the racialized disparities in inherited wealth, a history of discrimination by lending agencies and higher borrowing, the dependence on debt to finance higher education places distinctive burdens on students of color and particularly Black students. According to Demos, "While less than two-thirds (63%) of white graduates from public schools borrow, four-in-five (81%) of Black graduates do so. Latino graduates borrow at similar rates and slightly lower amounts than white students."[49] The same study finds that Black and Latinx students are dropping out with debt at higher rates than white students.[50] Moreover students of color are more likely to be delinquent on loan repayments. As a study by the economists Marshall Steinbaum and Kavya Vaghul found, zip codes with a high concentration of Black and Latinx residents had far higher delinquency rates. The correlation between delinquency and race was most extreme in middle-class neighborhoods.[51] According to Steinbaum, this pattern can be attributed to "segregation within higher education, which relegates minority students to the worst-performing institutions, discrimination in both credit and labor markets, and the underlying racial wealth gap that means Black and Hispanic students have a much smaller cushion of family wealth to fall back on, both to finance higher education in the first place and also should any difficulty with debt repayment arise."[52]

Recommendations:

- Cancel student debt: We endorse the movement to "Occupy the Student Debt" in its effort to cancel all student debt. Canceling the debt requires the federal government to forgive all the student loans it owns (which constitute 90% of all student debt) and to buy out the private holders of student loans. For the same price as the 2017 Republican tax cuts (which were concentrated among the richest 10%), this policy would free 44 million Americans from their debt burdens and increase their ability to reap the economic benefits of college education. A recent study by Levy Economics Institute of Bard College also finds that canceling the debt would have positive consequences for the economy by increasing the purchasing powers of 44 million people, which in turns spurs the consumption that contributes to economic growth.[53]
- Federally guaranteed and tuition-free public college education: Since Bernie Sanders's presidential campaign in 2016, the campaign for tuition-free public college education has spurred action at the state and local level. A growing number of cities and states already offer tuition-free access to community colleges. We call for the scaling of these efforts to the federal level so that all students have free access to a four-year public college and university.
- Reparations scholarships for Indigenous and African American students: We call for $100 million national scholarship fund to be established for Indigenous and Black students to be paid by colleges and universities that benefitted directly from slave labor and from federal

land grants that were made possible through the expropriation of In-digenous communities. These funds, independently administered by a reputable racial justice nonprofit organization, would be distributed on a sliding scale based on need to Black and Indigenous students pursuing undergraduate degrees at four-year institutions and com-munity colleges. While elite private schools would contribute, all Indigenous and Black students would be eligible to receive an award and could attend an institution of their choice.

VI. CONCLUSION

The above is not meant to be a comprehensive account of the university's multiple roles or a complete list of reparations demands. We recognize that higher education is a heterogeneous field with many different kinds of in-stitutions, which will not always exhibit the features identified above and might have distinctive kinds of problems. While the above might not capture all the specific dynamics of a particular institution, it is meant to provide a framework for the multiple ways in which the university functions as a site of reproducing racial hierarchies and how we might imagine more just and egalitarian institutions of higher education. It is our hope that activists and organizers take this document as a roadmap for the kinds of questions they might ask at their respective institutions.

It should be clear that in focusing on higher education, we do not wish to claim this space as a privileged site in struggles for racial justice. It is one of many sites and, as some of the issues discussed above attest, the university is deeply embedded in broader structures of hierarchy and inequality. We hope that this document makes more visible that embeddedness and opens the university to critical scrutiny in the context of more widespread social movements.

Notes

1. Robin D. G. Kelley "Black Study, Black Struggle," *Boston Review*, March 07, 2016, http://bostonreview.net/forum/robin-d-g-kelley-black-study-black-struggle.

2. Movement 4 Black Lives, https://policy.m4bl.org/platform/.

3. Rueth Rubio-Marin, Caludia Paz y Paz Bailey, and Julie Guillerot, " Indigenous Peoples and Reparations Claims: Tentative Steps in Peru and Guatemala," *International Center for Transitional Justice,* June 2009.

4. See for example, Craig Wilder, *Ebony and Ivy: Race, Slavery and the Troubled History of America's Universities* (New York: Bloomsburg Press, 2013). "Report of the Working Group on Slavery, Memory and Reconciliation," Georgetown University,

http://slavery.georgetown.edu/report/, President's Commission on Slavery and the University, University of Virginia, http://slavery.virginia.edu, "A Case for Reparations at the University of Chicago," http://www.aaihs.org/a-case-for-reparations-at-the-university-of-chicago/, Gauri Viswanathan, "Yale College and the Culture of British Imperialism," *Yale Journal of Criticism* 7 (January 1994): 1–30.

5. Wilder, *Ebony and Ivy*, 228.

6. Andrew Ross, "Universities and the Urban Growth Machine," *Dissent Magazine*, October 4, 2012, https://www.dissentmagazine.org/online_articles/universities-and-the-urban-growth-machine, Accessed September 14, 2016.

7. Davarian Baldwin, "The '800 Pound Gargoyle': The Long History of Higher Education and Urban Development on Chicago's South Side," *American Quarterly* 67 (March 2015): 81–103.

8. Victor Fleischer, "Stop Universities from Hoarding Money," *The New York Times*, August 19, 2015, https://www.nytimes.com/2015/08/19/opinion/stop-universities-from-hoarding-money.html?_r=0.

9. Davarian Baldwin, "When Universities Swallow Cities," *The Chronicle of Higher Education*, July 30, 2017, https://www.chronicle.com/article/when-universities-swallow-cities/.

10. For further readings on universities and Black communities, see M. Krause, M. Nolan, M. Palm, and A. Ross, *The University Against Itself: The NYU Strike and the Future of the Academic Workplace* (Philadelphia: Temple University Press, 2008); M. Bousquet, *How the University Works: Higher Education and the Low-wage Nation* (New York: NYU Press, 2008); and Stephan Bradley, *Harlem vs. Columbia University: Black Student Power in the Late 1960s* (Urbana: University of Illinois Press, 2009).

11. "The Hypocrisy of Revitalization: Universities in Black Communities," *The Atlantic*, December 15, 2014, http://www.theatlantic.com/education/archive/2014/12/no-its-not-gentrification-its-something-else/383645/.

12. "A Columbia Study of Amsterdam Avenue Finds Evidence of Hyper-Gentrification," *The Columbia Spectator*, December 12, 2015, http://columbiaspectator.com/news/2015/12/13/gentrification-project.

13. "Gentrification in New Haven, 2000–2014," *Yale Daily News*, November 20, 2015, http://yaledailynews.com/blog/2015/11/20/gentrification-in-new-haven-2000–2014/.

14. "Understanding Columbia University's Expansion into West Harlem," Columbia Student Coalition Against Gentrification," October 2014, https://coalitionagainst gentrification.files.wordpress.com/2014/10/understanding-columbia-university_s-expansion-into-west-harlem.pdf.

15. "Harlem and the Columbia Expansion," *The Harlem Times*, http://theharlem times.com/online-news/harlem-columbia-expansion.

16. "After Harlem Gang Raid, Anti-Violence Advocates Seek to Defuse Tensions," *Columbia Spectator*, June 11, 2014, http://columbiaspectator.com/news/2014/06/11/after-harlem-gang-raid-anti-violence-advocates-seek-defuse-tensions.

17. "Campus Cops: Authority without Accountability," *American Prospect*, November 2, 2015, http://prospect.org/article/campus-cops-authority-without-accountability and "Being a Better Neighbor in Manhattanville," *Columbia Spectator*, October 23, 2014, http://columbiaspectator.com/opinion/2014/10/23/being-better-neighbor-manhattanville.

18. Million Hoodies Movement for Justice, http://millionhoodies.net/the-danger-of-militarizing-campus-police-forces/.

19. Brian Charles, "For College Towns, Having a World-Famous University is a Mixed Blessing," *Governing*, September 27, 2018, https://www.governing.com/archive/gov-university-college-towns.html; IFTIKHAR: Fire! Fire! Gentrifier! *Yale* News, https://yaledailynews.com/blog/2020/10/07/iftikhar-fire-fire-gentrifier/; Lauren Michelle Jackson, "The Hypocrisy of Revitalization: Universities in Black Communities," *The Atlantic*, December 15, 2014, https://www.theatlantic.com/education/archive/2014/12/no-its-not-gentrification-its-something-else/383645/.

20. "Yale Workers Fight the Power," Solidarity-Us.Org, https://www.solidarity-us.org/node/2418 and "New Haven Rising," *Dissent Magazine*, Winter 2015, https://www.dissentmagazine.org/article/new-haven-rising.

21. "Black Workers and the University," *Inside Higher Ed*, https://www.insidehighered.com/news/2020/10/27/black-workers-universities-often-are-left-out-conversations-about-race-and-higher; Pablo Eisenberg, "Campus Workers' Wages: A Disgrace to Academe," *The Chronicle of Higher Education*, September 10, 2012, https://www.chronicle.com/article/campus-workers-wages-a-disgrace-to-academe/; Danielle Douglas-Gabriel and Alyssa Flowers, "The Lowest-Paid Workers in Higher Education Are Suffering the Highest Job Losses," *Washington Post*, November 17, 2020, https://www.washingtonpost.com/education/2020/11/17/higher-ed-job-loss/.

22. Baldwin, "When Universities Swallow Cities," https://www.chronicle.com/article/when-universities-swallow-cities/.

23. Ross, "Universities and the Urban Growth Machine," https://www.dissentmagazine.org/online_articles/universities-and-the-urban-growth-machine.

24. New Faculty Majority, http://www.newfacultymajority.info/facts-about-adjuncts/.

25. Kay Steiger, "The Pink College Workforce of Academia," https://www.thenation.com/article/academias-pink-collar-workforce/.

26. Martha S. West and John Curtis, "AAUP Faculty Gender Equity Indicators, 2006," https://www.aaup.org/NR/rdonlyres/63396944-44BE-4ABA-9815-5792D93856F1/0/AAUPGenderEquityIndicators2006.pdf.

27. American Federation of Teachers, "Promoting Racial and Ethnic Diversity in the Faculty: What can Higher Education Unions Do," http://www.aft.org/sites/default/files/facultydiversity0310.pdf.

28. Mariah Furtek, "Mind Your Business: UCLA's Business-Like Practices Create Exploitative Environment for Student Workers," *Daily Bruin*, July 12, 2022, https://

dailybruin.com/2019/05/14/mind-your-business-uclas-business-like-practices
-create-exploitative-environment-for-student-workers; Catherine Liberty Feliciano,
"Student demands equal pay for full-time and student," *Daily Bruin*, July 12, 2022,
http://dailybruin.com/2016/08/21/student-demands-equal-pay-for-full-time-and
-student-workers/.

29. Students Unite Now!, "Why We Can't Wait: The Cost of the student Income Contribution on the Yale Undergraduate Community," August 2020, https://sunatyale.org/
wp-content/uploads/2020/07/SUN-Financial-Aid-Report-2019_FINAL-copy.pdf#.

30. Jake Simpson, "Of Course Student Athletes Are University Employees," *The
Atlantic*, April 7, 2014, https://www.theatlantic.com/entertainment/archive/2014/04/
of-course-student-athletes-are-university-employees/360065/.

31. College Athletes Players Association, "Why We're Doing It," http://www.college
athletespa.org/why.

32. National Center for Health Workforce Analysis, "Sex, Race, and Ethnic Diversity of U.S. Health Occupations," (2010–2012), U.S. Department of Health and Human Services, Health Resources and Services Administration, National Center for
Health Workforce Analysis. Sex, Race, and Ethnic Diversity of U.S. Health Occupations (2010–2012), Rockville, Maryland; 2014, https://bhw.hrsa.gov/sites/default/files/
bureau-health-workforce/data-research/diversity-us-healthoccupations-2012.pdf.

33. Shawn Gude and Rachel M. Cohen, "Baltimore since Beth Steel: Hopkins Hospital Worker Fight for 15," *Dissent Magazine*, https://www.dissentmagazine.org/online
_articles/baltimore-since-beth-steel-hopkins-hospital-workers-fight-for-15. The place
of doctors and nurses within the labor structure of the hospital is akin to the status
of tenured and tenure-track faculty on the academic side, who are often also not
organized and sometimes hostile to unionization.

34. Michael Sandler, "CEO Pat Sora at Top Not-For-Profits," *Modern Healthcare*,
http://www.modernhealthcare.com/article/20150808/magazine/308089988.

35. Barbara Bean-Mellinger, "Non-Professional Vs. Professional Jobs," *CHRON*, June
28, 2018, http://work.chron.com/nonprofessional-vs-professional-jobs-20537.html.

36. Daphne T. Greenwood, "The Decision to Contract Out: Understanding the Full
Economic and Social Impacts" (March 2014), https://www.inthepublicinterest.org/
wp-content/uploads/contracts.broaderimpacts.greenwood.march-2014.REVISED
-AND-FINAL-2.pdf.

37. Ry Rivard, "Shared Services Backlash," *Inside Higher ED*, November 21, 2013,
https://www.insidehighered.com/news/2013/11/21/u-michigan-tries-save-money
-staff-costs-meets-faculty-opposition.

38. Richard Hurd, "Non-Faculty Unionization at Institutions of Higher Education," Cornell University Library, https://ecommons.cornell.edu/bitstream/handle/
1813/75892/Hurd55_non_faculty_unionization.pdf?sequence=1&isAllowed=y.

39. Adam Vacarro, "In 583–1 Vote Harvard Dining Room Workers OK Labor
Contract," *Boston Globe*, October 26, 2016, https://www.bostonglobe.com/business/

2016/10/26/striking-harvard-workers-got-everything-they-wanted-says-union/
OtLJHHoWcdXeiHbKi1WPIN/story.html

40. United Campus Workers, "The Campus Workers Bill of Rights," https://www
.ucw-cwa.org/system/files/campus_workers_bill_of_rights.pdf.

41. Amy Traub, "Discredited: How Employment Credit Checks Keep Qualified Workers Out of a Jobs," *Demos.org*, http://www.demos.org/discredited-how-employment
-credit-checks-keep-qualified-workers-out-job.

42. Danielle Douglas-Gabriel, "Harvard Dining Hall Workers End Strike," *Washington Post*, October 26, 2016, https://www.washingtonpost.com/news/grade-point/
wp/2016/10/26/harvard-dining-hall-workers-end-strike/?noredirect=on&utm_term
=.740f0e3e9643.

43. Stephanie Saul, "N.Y.U. Labor Guidelines Fail to Protect 10,000 Workers
in Abu Dhabi, Report Says," *New York Times*, April 16, 2015, https://www.nytimes
.com/2015/04/17/nyregion/nyu-labor-rules-failed-to-protect-10000-workers-in-abu
-dhabi.html?mcubz=0.

44. Michael Melia, "ROTC Programs Return to Ivy League Universities," *NBC
News*, October 23, 2011, https://www.nbcnews.com/id/wbna45006571.

45. Ibid.

46. Newsweek Staff, "A Gun in One Hand, A Pen in the Other," *Newsweek*, June 12,
2008, http://www.newsweek.com/gun-one-hand-pen-other-85485; David H. Price,
Weaponizing Anthropology: Social Science in Service of the Militarized State (Petrolia,
CA: CounterPunch and AK Press, 2011).

47. CUNY Struggle, "Leaked Document Reveals Scope of Cooperation Between
Baruch College and Central Intelligence Agency, Furthering CIA's "Diversity and Inclusion Brand," March 15, 2018, https://cunystruggle.org/2018/03/15/leaked-document
-reveals-scope-of-cooperation-between-baruch-college-and-central-intelligence
-agency-furthering-cias-diversity-and-inclusion-brand/.

48. Graduate Employees & Students Organization at Yale, *Endowing Injustice: YALE
UNIVERSITY'S INVESTMENT IN CORRECTIONS CORPORATION OF AMERICA*,
N.D., https://www.privateprisonnews.org/media/publications/yale_geso_yale_univ
_investment_in_cca_exec_summary_.pdf.

49. Mark Huelsman, *The Debt Divide: The Racial and Class Bias Behind the "New
Normal" of Student Borrowing*, Demos, 2015, http://www.demos.org/sites/default/
files/publications/Mark-Debt%20divide%20Final%20(SF).pdf, 2.

50. Ibid.

51. Josh Logue, "Geography, Race and Student Loan Delinquency," *Inside Higher
Ed*, February 18, 2016, https://www.insidehighered.com/quicktakes/2016/02/18/
geography-race-and-student-loan-delinquency.

52. Marshall Steinbaum, "A Radical Solution to the Student Debt Crisis," *Roosevelt
Institute*, February 6, 2018, https://medium.com/@rooseveltinst/a-radical-solution
-to-the-student-debt-crisis-5a354d19ab28.

53. Eric Levitz, "We Must Cancel Everyone's Student Debt, for the Economy's Sake," *New York Intelligencer*, February 9, 2019, http://nymag.com/daily/intelligencer/2018/02/lets-cancel-everyones-student-debt-for-the-economys-sake.html.

PART II

Reparations

Articles and Essays

13

Industrial Slavery and Dietary Deprivation

Expanding the Case for Black Reparations

JAMES B. STEWART

On August 7, 1865, Jourdon Anderson, who formerly was enslaved in Big Springs, Tennessee, sent a letter from Dayton, Ohio, to his erstwhile owner, Colonel Patrick Henry Anderson in response to Anderson's request that he return to Tennessee. In the letter Jourdon describes his current situation noting:

> I am doing tolerably well here. I get twenty-five dollars a month, with victuals and clothing; have a comfortable home for Mandy,—the folks call her Mrs. Anderson,—and the children—Milly, Jane, and Grundy—go to school and are learning well. The teacher says Grundy has a head for a preacher. They go to Sunday school, and Mandy and me attend church regularly. We are kindly treated.

Jourdon Anderson also wryly lays out conditions which would have to be met for him to consider the prospect of returning to Tennessee:

> Now if you will write and say what wages you will give me, I will be better able to decide whether it would be to my advantage to move back again.
>
> As to my freedom, which you say I can have, there is nothing to be gained on that score, as I got my free papers in 1864 from the Provost-Marshal-General of the Department of Nashville. Mandy says she would be afraid to go back without some proof that you were disposed to treat us justly and kindly; and we have concluded to test your sincerity by asking you to send us our wages for the time we served you. This will make us forget and forgive old scores, and rely on your justice and friendship in the future. I served you faithfully

for thirty-two years, and Mandy twenty years. At twenty-five dollars a month for me, and two dollars a week for Mandy, our earnings would amount to eleven thousand six hundred and eighty dollars. Add to this the interest for the time our wages have been kept back, and deduct what you paid for our clothing, and three doctor's visits to me, and pulling a tooth for Mandy, and the balance will show what we are in justice entitled to.

In the conclusion to his letter, Jourdon Anderson seeks information regarding guarantees of safety and security for his family and educational opportunities for his offspring:

In answering this letter, please state if there would be any safety for my Milly and Jane, who are now grown up, and both good-looking girls. You know how it was with poor Matilda and Catherine. I would rather stay here and starve—and die, if it come to that—than have my girls brought to shame by the violence and wickedness of their young masters. You will also please state if there has been any schools opened for the colored children in your neighborhood. The great desire of my life now is to give my children an education, and have them form virtuous habits.[1]

As is evident in his response, Jourdon Anderson meticulously calculates the value of his family's unpaid labor (presumably agricultural) expropriated by his whilom master. This is a concrete example of how the amount of reparations due to descendants of previously enslaved Black folk is typically computed. Specifically, the critical variables are imputed wages, years of service, and imputed interest rates used to determine present values of years of unpaid wages. Notably, Jourdon reports that he worked in a Nashville, Tennessee, hospital after emancipation and currently is employed in Dayton, Ohio, where he receives a regular salary.[2] In calculating the amount of reparations owed, Jourdon equates the value of forced agricultural labor with his present compensation. He also imputes a much lower value to his wife Mandy's expropriated labor, possibly because she is not currently employed or because existing wage imputation practices set higher wage levels for men than women. It furthermore is noteworthy that Jourdon deducts the costs of clothing and medical treatments from the amount of reparations that he determines is owed to him by Colonel Anderson.

Jourdon's computations suggest at least three areas of inquiry relevant for documenting and quantifying reparations claims. First, is it appropriate to determine the value of his labor services expropriated by Anderson based on his agricultural work history or his current employment? Estimating the value of Jourdon's expropriated labor is admittedly challenging. As an example, it would be useful to have specific information about the particular enterprise where Jourdon worked in Dayton and the compensation he received. Whether reparations claims for agricultural labor exploitation should be treated differently from those associated with industrial labor exploitation is one of the central issues explored in this investigation. Second, how are we to understand Jourdon's assessment of compensation owed to Mandy? As will be demonstrated, enslavers found creative ways to expropriate the labor of both enslaved women and children in industrial enterprises.

Another area of inquiry relates to Jourdon's deduction of the value of clothing and medical services from the amount that he claims is owed by Colonel Anderson. Maintenance costs is the term used by economists to characterize these expenditures, which also include food and shelter. Although the concern here is whether food provided to enslaved men, women, and especially children was insufficient to meet basic nutritional needs and, over time, catalyzed adverse health conditions. If this is the case, the medical costs incurred after emancipation to ameliorate conditions emanating from the harsh experience of enslavement should offset any maintenance costs paid by enslavers. To illustrate, in *The Half Has Never Been Told* (2014), Edward Baptist includes formerly enslaved George Strickland's recollections of Sundays on an Alabama plantation: White folk "would give us biscuits for breakfasts, which was so rare that we'd try to beat others out of theirs."[3] Elaborating, Baptist observes: "Children fought for the taste of white flour, to the laughter of enslavers, and some enslaved people old enough to know better acted much the same."[4] In Jourdon's case, if the medical treatments he received resulted from dietary deprivation, why should he reimburse Col. Anderson for the costs of treating an illness caused by the Colonel's actions?

The second section of this chapter examines the nature and the scope of exploitation experienced by bondpersons in industrial enterprises. Rudimentary calculations of the present value of the unpaid labor appropriated from enslaved African Americans who worked in industrial enterprises are also presented. In some cases, southern industrialists were able to exploit enslaved labor and utilize bondpersons as collateral to finance industrial projects. Edward Baptist describes in detail how "the faith bonds of the 1830s generated revenue for investors from enslavers' repayment of mortgages on enslaved people."[5] Robert S. Starobin describes how owners of the Nesbitt Manufacturing Company in South Carolina allowed investors to purchase stock by transferring ownership of enslaved African Americans rather than making direct cash disbursements.[6] Consequently, reparations claims associated with expropriated industrial labor should include both the value of expropriated labor as well as profits derived from slave-financed investments. It is not well known that women and children were significantly represented in several industrial sectors. Starobin reports, for example, that "Slave women and children comprised large proportions of the workforces in most slave-employing textile, hemp, and tobacco factories."[7] which mandates that attention be directed to possible gender and age labor segmentation as well as possible gender and age differences in productivity.

The third section explores the issue of nutritional options available to bondpersons. There is ongoing widespread disagreement regarding the adequacy of the dietary consumption of bondpersons with respect to energy requirements and overall nutritional sufficiency. However, it is widely accepted that women, infants, and children were the principal casualties of malnutrition, resulting in high rates of both morbidity and mortality.[8] Various explanations for this pattern have been proposed. Richard Steckel suggests that the high ratio of mortality among newborn and infant enslaved Blacks was caused primarily by stressors generated by excessive work imposed on pregnant women by overworking of women during pregnancy and after childbirth.[9] In contrast, Philip Coelho and Robert McGuire maintain that the most plausible explanation of the elevated infant mortality rate was the prevalence of debilitating diseases that had disproportionately adverse effects on the health of enslaved pregnant women and their fetuses.[10] To the extent that any of the associated diseases have hereditary dimensions, legitimate reparations claims can be advanced for victims' descendants.

The final section explores the implications of this study for the development of plans to allocate proceeds from successful reparations claims. I argue that the inquiry provides strong support for funding biomedical research to combat hereditary diseases and programs that are designed to improve health outcomes for women, reduce infant and child morbidity and mortality, and foster wholesome adolescent development.

Reparations for Industrial Slavery

Ronald Lewis maintains "the distinctive qualities of business and industry in the Old South have been obscured by the pervasive shadow of the plantation."[11] Of course, the most distinctive feature of southern industry was its extensive reliance on enslaved laborers.[12] Among other endeavors, enslaved workers were exploited to produce textiles and woolens, tobacco, hemp, bricks, rice, sugar, lumber, turpentine, as well as other products. Bondpersons were also deployed in shipyards, and railroad construction.[13] But "few nonagricultural occupations in the Old South . . . made use of slaves so universally, and over such an extended period of time," Lewis declares, "as the production of iron and the mining of coal."[14] Indeed, between 1800 and 1860 approximately 7,000 enslaved workers were employed daily in ironworks in Virginia and in Maryland alone. During peak production years of the 1830s, the number of enslaved persons working in coal mining enterprises in eastern Virginia ranged from 1,600 to 1,900.[15]

By the 1850s, between 160,000 and 260,000 bondpersons worked in industrial occupations, with four-fifths owned directly by investors with operations in various sectors including textile mills, iron manufacturing, tobacco factories, hemp manufacturing, sugar refining, and rice milling.[16] Robert S. Starobin noted that these workers comprised 5 percent of the total enslaved population.[17] He adds: They "lived in rural, small-town or plantation settings, where most southern industry was located, not in large cities," where "about 20 percent of urban slaves were industrially employed."[18] In addition, enslaved labor was used extensively by state and local governments, as well as the federal government for public works projects. As Starobin observed, "The wide use of industrial slaves by state and federal agencies suggests not only the centrality of industrial slavery to the southern economy, but also the extent of southern control of the national political structure."[19]

By the 1850s, the South accounted for approximately 20 percent of all invested industrial capital in the United States with the non-agricultural sector accounting for 40 percent of per capita income growth between 1840 and 1860.[20] The region boasted about one-third of the country's railroad mileage in 1860, and this rail network was financed primarily from southern, as opposed to northern, investment capital.[21]

Southern industry was tied intricately to plantation agriculture. In the case of textile mills, mobilizing enslaved African Americans not only generated profits directly from product sales, but it also increased productivity of the slavery regime. This labor redeployment occurred in part because of the differences between the physical requirements of agricultural and industrial work. As one commentator visiting a southern cotton mill observed, "Slaves not sufficiently strong to work in the cotton fields can attend to the looms and spindles in the cotton mills."[22]

For the most part, reparations for industrial labor exploitation and agricultural labor exploitation should be treated separately for the purposes of quantifying reparations claims. By the early 1800s, "manufacturing, crop processing, and transportation enterprises tended to separate from agriculture and to assume independent existences."[23] At the same time, some planters were involved simultaneously in agricultural and industrial ventures, so they shifted workers between the two sectors to maximize profits. In the early 1800s, for example, Missouri farmers used bondpersons in mining ventures after harvest to supplement the farmers' incomes.[24] By the 1840s, industries where such oscillating deployment of enslaved persons was prevalent included gold mining as well as turpentine extraction and distillation.[25]

If there were significant productivity differences between enslaved males and females as well as children employed in industrial production, it would be necessary to reflect these differences to develop accurate reparations claims. However, it does not appear that such differences actually existed. Starobin found, for example, "In certain light industries, such as manufacturing, slave women and children could be as productive as prime males, and sometimes they could perform certain industrial tasks even more efficiently."[26] Elaborating, he indicated that the absence of productivity differentials between males and females "was especially true in tobacco, hemp, and cotton manufacturing, where efficiency depended more upon sprightliness and nimbleness than upon strength and endurance." Starobin also observed that "enslaved women and children, sometimes worked at 'heavy' industries such as sugar refining and rice milling, and industries such as transportation and lumbering used slave women and children to a considerable extent."[27] Iron works and mines also employed enslaved women and children "to lug trams and to push lumps of ore into crushers and furnaces."[28] The upshot of these observations is that there is little evidence that there were sufficient differences in age-based or gender productivity to warrant special adjustments in reparations calculations.

Reparations claims focusing on wage appropriation are relevant for both rented and industry-owned bondpeople. However, industry-owned enslaved workers were, in effect, unwilling co-investors in many enterprises because their value was used as collateral to obtain financing for the industrial ventures. As a consequence, reparations claims on behalf of these workers should include a prorated portion of the profits made by the enterprises.

Focusing first on the issue of wage expropriation, the annual compensation paid to free white workers can be used as an imperfect proxy for the annual value of appropriated wages. This figure is imperfect because the use of enslaved workers reduced the wages that free laborers could command. The annual wages paid to free white laborers averaged $300 from 1800 to 1861.[29] The cost of hiring bondpersons increased fairly steadily during this period, but it maxed out at approximately $150. This difference highlights the profitability of exploiting hired enslaved labor.

Table 13.1 presents some rudimentary calculations intended to demonstrate the importance of including industrial wage appropriation as part of reparations claims. The total nominal value of wages appropriated from hired and industry-owned enslaved workers exceeds $1 billion. William Darity and Dania Frank's 2005 review of various efforts to quantify losses incurred by African Americans as a result of enslavement found that the present value estimates ranged from $5 trillion to $10 trillion.[30] In 2019 dollars, the range of estimates would be $6.5 trillion to $13 trillion, with buying power approximating $3 trillion. This rudimentary calculation is intended to reinforce the importance of scrutinizing exploitation associated with industrial slavery separately from that associated with plantation agriculture.

There are two major caveats that should be acknowledged in assessing the significance of the preceding computations. First, these calculations do not follow Jourdon Anderson's procedure of deducting the value of maintenance costs incurred by owners/employers.[31] If this adjustment is made, the nominal value of expropriated labor would be reduced by $380 million and the present buying power by about $1 trillion (the rationale for not making this adjustment is discussed in the next section). The second limitation is not accounting for the circumstances of enslaved industrial workers in urban areas.[32] As indicated previously, of the approximately 70,000 urban-based enslaved African Americans in 1860, roughly 20 percent were employed in industrial enterprises. Richard Wade has described how urban location led to public control replacing private supervision by owners because many enslaved African Americans were allowed to "hire their own time" and to "live out" (find their own residence).[33] Hiring out and living out reduced the costs to owners of maintaining involvement in negotiating contractual arrangements for the employment of bondpersons and providing for their subsistence. These arrangements also allowed bondpersons to capture some of the returns from their human capital.[34] The assumptions used to develop the estimates in Table 13.1 are provided in the Appendix at the end of the chapter.

I noted previously that bondpersons owned by industrial enterprises basically were involuntary co-owners of such ventures. This status conferred eligibility for a share of the profits generated from commercial operations that oftentimes were very profitable. Starobin concluded that textile mills employing enslaved labor generated net profits ranging from 10 to 65 percent, with an average of 16 percent.[35] Louisiana sugar mills earned greater than 7

Table 13.1. Preliminary Estimates of Industrial Slavery Wage Appropriation

Year	United States (U.S.) Industry Employment	Estimated Enslaved Industrial Employment	Estimated Enslaved Hirees	Estimated Industry Owned Workers	Total Annual Expropriated Wages ($000)	Appropriated Wages by Decade ($000)
1810	25,000	5,000	1,000	4,000	1,550	15,550
1820	28,000	10,000	2,000	8,000	3,100	31,000
1830	88,000	16,000	3,200	12,800	4,960	49,600
1840	418,000	77,000	15,400	61,600	23,870	238,700
1850	629,000	115,000	23,000	92,000	35,650	356,500
1860	869,000	160,000	32,000	128,000	49,600	496,000

Sources and assumptions provided in the Appendix.

percent in 1830 and about 11 percent in 1845.[36] In many cases, enslavers on plantations also used bondsmen as collateral to facilitate investments. Edward Baptist describes in detail how Louisiana-based enslaver J.B. Moussier spearheaded the establishment of new banking operations in Louisiana, Mississippi, Tennessee, Arkansas, and Florida that facilitated expansion of the plantation economy by securitizing slave mortgages that reduced the risks faced by individual planters.[37] To the extent that there are identifiable surviving or derivative businesses and financial institutions that participated in relevant transactions, they are potential targets for reparations claims from descendants of enslaved persons who were designated as collateral for loans issued by banks.

Many industrial bondpersons did not simply acquiesce to their oppression. Various scholars have described various forms of protest employed by the disaffected. Schemes included negligence, slowdown, feigned sickness, outright refusal to work, and pilferage. Most scholars agree, however, that "these actions did not always represent conscious resistance, but they did reflect underlying discontent with industrial work routines and the restrictions of bondage."[38]

Reparations for Nutritional Deprivation

Although the issue of reparations for nutritional deprivation may seem removed from the preceding discussion of industrial slavery, there is a direct connection. According to Starobin, the "evidence suggests that most industrial bondsmen—rural and urban—had approximately the same standard of living as did the mass of agricultural bondsmen."[39] However, he also suggested that industrial bondsmen were at greater risk of experiencing malnutrition even though "the self-interest of slaveowners often protected bondsmen from inadequate provisioning of food by slave-renters." However, Starobin asserted, "many industrial bondmen, hired or directly owned, suffered from notoriously poor care."[40] Industrial work generally entailed greater energy requirements than agricultural labor. As Starobin declared, "For laborers—slave and free—engaged in southern industries, working conditions were usually worse than for those laborers engaged in southern farming, since industrial development often demanded longer and harder working days than did plantation agriculture."[41]

While the relative nutritional deprivation of industrial versus agricultural slaves is an important topic, the broader issue is that to the extent that such nutritional deprivation occurred, did it propagate inheritable diseases or conditions that are implicated in contemporary racial morbidity and mortality differences. If so, the contemporary health status deficits experienced by descendants constitute legitimate bases for reparations claims.

To put the issue of nutritional deprivation in context, during the early nineteenth century, malnutrition in the United States was a persistant problem. Robert Fogel insists the country, "which was awash in calories, compared to Europe, suffered from serious chronic malnutrition, partly because the high rate of exposure to infectious diseases prevented many of the calories that were ingested from being metabolized and partly because of the large share of dietary energy expended in . . . work."[42] Controversy regarding the quality and the quantity of nutrition available to bondpersons commenced with Fogel and Stanley Engerman's controversial book, *Time on the Cross*. As Ramiro Guzmán notes, their monograph "challenged most of the former [scholarship] about slavery, in [particular] the widespread belief on the 'malnutrition of captives.'"[43] Fogel and Engerman argued that food consumption of enslaved African Americans exceeded that of free whites and further that the diets of bondpersons "exceeded modern recommended daily levels of chief nutrients."[44]

Numerous scholars roundly criticized Fogel and Engerman's statistical methods. According to their critics, Fogel and Engerman drew conclusions based on a very small sample size and made unwarranted extrapolations from indirect evidence. At the same time, it is important to recognize that eighteenth century nutritional options were heavily influenced by migration patterns and the prices of foodstuffs. Extensive rural-urban migration during the first half of the nineteenth century induced by early industrialization created urban food shortages, which generated significant price increases that challenged the resources of many urban dwellers. Many households were forced to reduce consumption of foodstuffs rich in calcium and in protein, thus hampering the physical development of children. This arrested development contributed to the subsequent decline in the average height of adults. However, in rural areas increasing agricultural prices induced planters to offer a greater food allowance to bondpersons to increase productivity and thereby expand production. These forces resulted in some bondpersons experiencing better nutrition than some whites. Nevertheless, this anomaly does not mean nutritional deprivation was not a serious problem among bondpersons. To illustrate, Eugene Genovese proffered, "the diet to which the slaves were subjected must be judged immensely damaging, despite assurances from contemporaries and later historians that the slave was well fed."[45]

Nutritional deprivation had the most deleterious effects on women and on children.[46] Health issues deriving from nutritional deprivation were especially pronounced for enslaved pregnant women who, along with women generally, often experienced complications including "convulsions, retention of placenta, ectopic pregnancy, breech presentation, premature labor, and uterine rigidity."[47] These conditions were exacerbated by nutritional deprivation contributing to high infant mortality rates. Richard Steckel found that the infant-mortality rate among the enslaved populations of 11 large plantations (not accounting for stillbirths) in Alabama, Georgia, Louisiana, and South Carolina was 350 children per thousand at the first year of life.[48] He speculates the high ratio of infant mortality resulted, in part, from overworking of pregnant enslaved women, which increased the risk of infant mortality deriving from what is now characterized as "Sudden Infant Death Syndrome," a term first introduced in 1969 to describe infant deaths that occurred unexpectedly during the postnatal period.[49] Notably, African American infants continue to be disproportionately plagued by such deaths. For the years 2013–2016, the SIDS death rate per thousand for African American children was 74.4 compared to 39 for white children. The rate of infant deaths from all causes for Black children was 171.1 per thousand for Black children versus 85.0 for white children. Pregnancy was also often a death sentence for enslaved women. In the contemporary era, Black women continue to experience disproportionate deaths during pregnancy. From 2011 to 2015, for example, the overall pregnancy-related death rate was 17.2 per 100,000 live births. The rate for Black women was 42.8 compared to 13.0 for white women.[50]

Even if an enslaved woman gave birth to a healthy child, the chances of this baby to survive during the first years of life were low due to deficient feeding.[51] Robert Fogel, similar to Richard Heckel, insists that "excess death rates of children under 5 accounted for nearly all the difference between the overall death rates of U.S. slaves and U.S. whites during the late antebellum era."[52] Fogel contends further that available evidence indicates that surviving infants were disproportionately undersized and that small babies failed "to exhibit much catch up growth between birth and age 3 suggest chronic undernourishment during these ages."[53]

Consistent with Steckel's conclusions, Fogel concludes that infants' postnatal problems originated with the malnourishment of pregnant women who were subjected to "the intense routine of the gang system down to the eve of childbirth" and denied nutritional supplementation, resulting in the failure to achieve sufficient weight gains "that would [normally] yield average birth weights and forestall infant death rates."[54] The deleterious effects of nutritional deprivation were magnified by the prevalence of sickle-cell disease among enslaved African Americans, which significantly increased mortality risks throughout adolescence. Todd Savitt relates that nearly half of enslaved children in the antebellum South died before reaching the age of twenty.[55]

The forces that catalyzed the serious medical issues that disproportionately victimized women and children were not ameliorated by the onset of the Civil War. Jim Downs declares because "many slaveholders cared very little about the health and well-being of their labor force . . . many enslaved people entered the war already sick and suffering."[56] The misery imposed by the conflict wore heavily on women and children who, as Downs recounts, "were left vulnerable to sickness and disease, manipulative slaveholders, and even apathetic Union officers during the Civil War."[57] The combined effects of slavery and the war on the well-being of Black women and children was so mutually reinforcing that "it is virtually impossible to determine if ex-slaves suffering and sickness were the direct result of the war or the result of slavery."[58]

For the purposes of developing reparations claims, the critical question is the extent to which the nutritional deprivation created longer-term medical problems for survivors. Vinicious Martins, among other scholars, has documented that undernutrition "has long-lasting physiologic effects, including an increased susceptibility to fat accumulation mostly in the central region of the body, lower fat oxidation, lower resting and postprandial energy expenditure, insulin resistance in adulthood, hypertension, dyslipidaemia and a reduced capacity for manual work, among other impairments."[59] Nevin Scrimshaw and Robert Suskind explain further: "Malnutrition can interfere with any body mechanism that acts as a barrier to the multiplication or progress of infectious agents" and any resulting infectious diseases can adversely influence "the nutritional state in several indirect ways."[60] In addition to the greater likelihood of manifesting hypertension and/or dyslipidaemia, pregnant enslaved women also were at greater risk of contracting diseases such as anorexia, anemia, malaria, and hookworm. Significantly, these diseases created potential health problems for the fetus in addition to the problems encountered by the expectant mother.[61] Robert Waterland and Cutberto Garza, among others, have documented that childhood malnutrition has lifelong consequences through its effects on the body's metabolism that create increased morbidity and mortality risk associated with obesity, cardiovascular disease, high blood pressure, and diabetes.[62]

Hypertension is another medical condition transmittable from one generation to another that is important to recognize in the context of refining reparations claims. As Merlon Butler has noted, "the heritable component of blood pressure has been documented in familial and twin studies suggesting that 30%-50% of the variance of blood pressure readings are attributable to genetic heritability and about 50% to environmental factors."[63] One implication of this finding is that the contemporary disproportionate hypertension experienced by African Americans is at least partially traceable to hereditary transmission coupled with constant exposure to adverse environmental conditions fueled by systemic discrimination. In the case of industrial bondpersons, workers in extraction industries were exposed to high levels of environmental contaminants now known to cause emphysema (chronic shortness of breath) and pneumoconiosis (black lung disease).[64] In 2015–2016, the prevalence of hypertension among adult non-Hispanic African Americans was 40.3 percent compared to 27.8 percent for non-Hispanic whites, 25 percent for Asians, and 27.8 percent for Hispanics.[65]

Type 2 diabetes also has hereditary characteristics that makes its disproportionate prevalence among African Americans another legitimate subject for reparations consideration. In 2004, Paul McCarron and his research associates published the first scholarly study finding "intergenerational associations between type 2 diabetes in one generation and birth weight in the subsequent two generations." McCarron and his colleagues asserted that their conclusions provided some support for the role of developmental intrauterine effects and genetically determined insulin resistance in impaired insulin mediated growth in the fetus. That hereditary susceptibility to certain diseases can be transmitted to future descendants beyond the victim's immediate offspring is a significant implication of this research.[66] Diabetes prevalence among African Americans is greater than for any other ethnic group except for American Indians/Alaska Natives.[67] National Center for Chronic Disease Prevention and Health Promotion data for 2013 to 2015 indicate the prevalence of diabetes among American Indians/Alaska Natives was 15.1 percent and 12.7 percent for African Americans. Rates for non-Hispanic whites, Hispanics, and Asians were 7.4 percent, 12.1 percent, and 8 percent, respectively.[68]

In addition to inducing the direct transmission of specific diseases across generations, slavery-related nutritional deprivation can also weaken the immune system of subsequent generations. A research team headed by Etienne Patin found that dysfunctional changes in cells associated with innate immunity can be hereditarily transmitted to descendants, thereby reducing the ability of the descendants' immune systems to combat infectious diseases.[69] Health care costs resulting from historical nutritional deprivation that induced compromised in succeeding generations constitutes another basis for reparations claims.

There is disagreement regarding the extent of nutritional deprivation experience by enslaved Blacks. In fact, Ramiro Guzmán goes so far as to totally discount the prevalence of nutritional deprivation, insisting bondpersons "were not passive food recipients, since they actively sought to supplement their diet with opportunistic strategies such as cultivate garden plots, hunt little animals or steal food, which eventually helped them to overcome any food shortage."[70] However, the previous discussions firmly refute Guzmán's claim. And it is certainly true that many bondpersons' attempted to devise strategies to mitigate the nutritional deprivation imposed by enslavers.

Unfortunately, many nutritional adaptions that evolved into contemporary cultural dietary practices have the potential to worsen health status. As an example, fried fare and meat with high fat content are staples of "soul food." Such items are contributory factors with respect to obesity and cardiovascular disease. Strong attachments to southern cooking that incorporates high levels of sugar, sodium, and fat have been difficult to alter, in part, because these dietary practices have important cultural significance that is reflected in traditions passed on from one generation to another. The attractiveness of this nutritional fare persists despite identifiable adverse health consequences.[71] Widespread adherence to potentially harmful dietary practices is itself a legacy of enslavement and does not invalidate reparations claims focusing on adverse health conditions originating during enslavement.

Conclusion

The attention focused on the issue of reparations has increased markedly, even pervading the halls of Congress.[72] Hopefully, these discussions will eventually culminate in actual compensation for myriad forms of exploitation exacted on African Americans in the United States during the era of enslavement. This study has foregrounded industrial slavery and advocated for separate treatment in developing reparations claims. The significant deployment of women and children as industrial slaves was highlighted with particular emphasis on victimization associated with nutritional deprivation. This form of victimization was shared by many enslaved workers who toiled in the fields.

Nutritional deprivation experienced during slavery was shown to be implicated in creating several serious diseases and conditions leading to higher mortality rates, especially among women and children. I argued that historical nutritional deprivation experienced during enslavement, disruptions caused by the Civil War, and subsequent ill-conceived public policies are implicated as contributing causes of the disproportionately high contemporary rates of hypertension and diabetes among African Americans. This line of argument provides a forceful response to arguments by reparations opponents who deny that current generations of African Americans can identify contemporary disadvantages deriving from enslavement imposed on ancestors.

Addressing the persisting legacy of health inequities deriving from racial slavery and post bellum public policies should be accorded high priority in the allocation of any reparations claims proceeds. A significant portion of reparations payments should be committed to supporting biomedical research intended to discover treatments if not cures for diseases known to have hereditary transmission mechanisms. Such an initiative can build on the precedent established in 2005 when the U.S. Food and Drug Administration approved a heart-failure medication specifically for African Americans. This federal act represented the first time the central government sanctioned a drug created for a single ethnic or racial group, though there are other race-specific drugs under development. In clinical trials cosponsored by the Association of Black Cardiologists and Nitromed, there were 43 percent fewer deaths than among those who did not receive the drug.[73] The case for targeted medications is straightforward because ethnic and racial minorities are subject to greater risks if they are prescribed a so-called equivalent medicine when substantial evidence indicates that, in some cases, dosage adjustment may be necessary or that the drug has toxic side effects because they cannot tolerate the standard dosage levels.[74] Although different groups are susceptible to different diseases and respond differently to some drugs and treatments, women and minorities have not been included in health research studies in adequate numbers.[75] Chelsea Weidman Burke maintains that larger enrollments of minority participants in clinical trials could lead to improved access to new therapies, and better understanding of disease biology and differences in medication efficacy across different populations.[76] At the same time, it is critically important that future biomedical and nutritional research be designed and controlled by African American specialists because of the long and the sordid history of abuse by the medical establishment illustrated, for example, by the Tuskegee syphilis experiment of 1932–1972 or by the gene exploitation of Henrietta Lacks.[77]

The allocation of reparations payments should prioritize improvements to women's health, reductions in infant mortality, and systematic intervention designed to foster wholesome child and youth development. Geoffrey Warner emphasizes the need to "reconceptualize infant health as integrated with women's health."[78] He argues, "Infant health should comprise all aspects of women's reproductive health starting from childhood and have the goal of ensuring Black women are healthy enough to bear two or three normal weight full-term children and healthy enough to live long enough with sufficient daily activity to parent the children to adulthood."[79]

The stultifying oppression historically and currently experienced by Black youth has cumulative adverse effects on community life as each cohort progresses through their life cycles, and many of the negative consequences of their restricted life chances are transmitted to subsequent generations. The school-to-prison pipeline is reflective of this pernicious pattern. Recognition of this reality is implicit in the proposal advanced by V. P. Franklin for a "Reparations Superfund."[80] According to him, the superfund could "support positive and successful interventions to prevent African American youths from turning to murderous violence against other African American youths and those in the line of fire."[81]

Franklin envisions the superfund being used to underwrite "projects in public schools to promote the arts and music and in private institutions offering supplemental education in the form of music and arts programs."[82] In addition to this possibility, the superfund "would be used to target and support alternatives to the current emphasis on 'high stakes testing' and test preparation that contributes mightily to the high dropout rates."[83] Consistent with the emphasis advocated by Warner, the superfund would "help to support maternal and early childhood health care program and interventions that target young children and place them in a 'health-care network' administered by health care professionals who have experience implementing these programs successfully in African American communities or neighborhoods."[84]

Besides offering guidance for the allocation of reparations payments, this analysis demonstrates that synthesizing information from diverse disciplines is a useful strategy for refining reparations claims. The present investigation required scrutiny of research in several disciplines including economic history, slavery studies, cliometrics, nutritional science, biomedical research, and stratification economics. The investigation likewise demonstrates current limitations associated with the quantification of some types of reparations claims. These difficulties were most apparent in the discussion of the long-term consequences of nutritional deprivation. Without multigenerational family medical histories, it will continue to be difficult to document the transmission of medical problems across generations and aggregate the associated medical costs incurred to treat ailments. In the case of infant mortality, the critical question is how does one value the loss of a victim of infant mortality? Forensic economists have developed several models used to estimate earnings losses in wrongful death lawsuits. In the state of New York, for example, for a child decedent, the elements of damages are limited to the likely financial contributions the decedent would have provided to his parents and the market value for the replacement of services that the decedent would have likely performed for his or her parents. Hence, the child is seen solely as an economic asset.[85]

Contrast the preceding perspective with Jourdon Anderson's discussion of his children, Milly, Janes, and Grundy, in the 1865 letter he sent to Colonel Anderson. Jourdon describes how all three youth "go to school and are learning well," with Grundy's teacher saying he "has a head for a preacher." Near the end of the letter, Jourdon declares: "The great desire of my life now is to give my children an education, and have them form virtuous habits."[86] It is obvious that Jourdon, his wife, Amanda "Mandy" Anderson, and their northern community view Milly, Jane, and Grundy not as economic assets but as loved members of a neighborhood with the potential to enhance the quality of their social networks as they mature into adulthood. It does not seem possible to put a monetary value on the denial of the opportunity of deceased infants to participate in the type of nurturing experiences described by Jourdon and to contribute to the well-being of their community.

Jourdon and Amanda Anderson eventually had a total of eleven children. Even though the couple escaped the horrors of slavery, all its consequences could not be escaped, including the loss of virginity of his daughters owing to rape. Two daughters, Matilda and Catherine, were not with their parents when the move to Dayton occurred. Curt Dalton speculates that this separation may have resulted from fatal abuse suffered or because they had been sold and could not be contacted by their parents.

The collective life of the Andersons, not unlike those of many of their contemporaries, was directly impacted by the slavery-related health inequities examined in this investigation. The Andersons never received reparations from Colonel Patrick H. Anderson; hence, one is left to ponder whether reparations payments would have enabled their daughters to survive. The deaths of their children were undoubtedly a deeply traumatic experience for the Andersons and is an exemplar of Joy DeGruy's characterization of the enslavement and post-enslavement experience as "one of continual violent attacks on body, mind and spirit."[87] Such violence, DeGruy insists, engendered intense trauma that, in turn, induced both constructive and destructive attitudinal and behavioral adaptations, which she characterizes as the Post Traumatic Slavery Syndrome (PTSS). Identifiable and measurable costs associated with PTSS may well constitute another basis for expanding reparations claims.[88] In this regard, the lyrics of Gil Scott-Heron's classic piece, "Who'll Pay Reparations on My Soul?," seem apropos:[89]

> Many suggestions
> And documents written.
> Many directions
> For the end that was given.
> They gave us
> Pieces of silver and pieces of gold.
> Tell me,
> Who'll pay reparations on my soul?

Appendix

Assumptions Associated with the Calculations of Losses Due to Industrial Slavery

1. Number of Industrial Bondsmen by Decade

The calculation uses the lower bound of Starobin's estimate of the number of industrial bondsmen in 1860 (160,000) as a starting point.

Estimates of the size of the industrial bondperson workforce by decade were developed using the attached table from Stanley Lebergott, Labor Force and Employment, 1800–1960, Dorothy Brady, ed. *Output, Employment, and Productivity in the United States after 1800.* (NBER, 1960). The growth in the number of industrial bondsmen from decade to decade was assumed to be the same as for the overall labor force. The occupations included in the calculations were mining, construction, and manufacturing.

It was assumed that the number of industrial bondsmen was constant for each year within each decade.

2. Imputed Wages for Industrial Bondsmen

The figure of $300 cited in Robert Starobin, The Economics of Industrial Slavery in the Old South, *The Business History Review* 44:2 (Summer, 1970), 140 was used as the value of the unpaid labor provided by industrial bondsmen. Based on Starobin's research, the figure was assumed to be constant for the entire period 1810–1860. The same imputed wage was used to calculate the value of expropriated wages for rented and industry-owned bondpersons.

3. Current Purchasing Power of Expropriated Wages

The CPI Inflation Calculator was used to determine the current purchasing power of appropriated wages for each decade. The end-of-decade year was used to generate the value. The calculator can be accessed at https://data.bls.gov/cgi-bin/cpicalc.pl.

Notes

I am deeply indebted to Dr. Bertis English for his extensive recommendations for improving an earlier draft of this analysis.

1. "To My Old Master: Jourdon Anderson to Patrick Henry Anderson," August 7, 1865, in Shaun Usher, comp., *Letters of Note: An Eclectic Collection of Correspondence Deserving of a Wider Audience* (San Francisco: Chronicle Books, 2014), 57–58.

2. Jourdon Anderson worked in several occupations after relocating to Dayton including servant, hostler, and coachman. See Curt Dalton, "The Life of Jourdon Anderson," *Dayton History Books* Online. URL: http://www.daytonhistorybooks .com/jourdon_anderson.html.

3. Edward E. Baptist, *The Half Has Never Been Told: Slavery and the Making of American Capitalism* (New York: Basic Books, 2014), 165.

4. Ibid., 165.

5. Ibid., 248.

6. Richard Starobin, *Industrial Slavery in the Old South* (New York: Oxford University Press, 1970), 180.

7. Ibid., 164.

8. For a review of research exploring this topic see Ramiro Alberto Flores Guzmán, "The Feeding of Slave Population in the United States, the Caribbean, and Brazil: Some Remarks in the State of the Art," *America Latina en la Historia Economica* 20 (May–August 2013), 5–35.

9. Richard Steckel, "A Dreadful Childhood: The Excess Mortality of American Slaves," *Social Science History*, Duke University 10 (4) (Winter 1986). *The Biological Past of the Black*, 427–66.

10. Philip Coelho & Robert Mcguire, "Biology, Diseases, and Economics: An Epidemiological History of Slavery in the American South, *Journal of Bioeconomics* 1(2) (November 1999), 151–90.

11. Ronald L. Lewis, *Coal, Iron, and Slaves: Industrial Slavery in Maryland and Virginia, 1715–1865* (Westport, CT: Greenwood Press, 1979), 3. For an examination of industrial slavery throughout the Appalachian region, see Ronald L. Lewis, "Industrial Slavery: Linking the Periphery and the Core," chap. 2 in Joe Trotter et al., eds., *The African American Urban Experience: Perspectives from the Colonial Period to the Present* (New York: Palgrave McMillan, 2004), 35–57.

12. Ibid.

13. See Lewis, *Coal, Iron, and Slaves*, 4–6; Robert Starobin, "The Economics of Industrial Slavery in the Old South," *Business History Review* 44 (summer 1970): 131–74; and Gloria Vollmers, "Industrial Slavery in the United States: The North Carolina Turpentine Industry 1849–61," *Accounting, Business and Financial History* 13 (2003): 369–92.

14. Lewis, *Coal, Iron, and Slaves*, 6.

15. Lewis, "Industrial Slavery," 39.

16. Starobin, "Economics of Industrial Slavery in the Old South," 131–32.

17. Ibid., 132.

18. Ibid., 132.

19. Ibid., 133.

20. Robert S. Starobin, *Industrial Slavery in the Old South* (New York: Oxford University Press, 1970), 11.

21. Mark M. Smith, *Debating Slavery, Economy and Society in the Antebellum American South* (New York: Cambridge University Press, 1998), 74.

22. Starobin, "Economics of Industrial Slavery in the Old South," 148.

23. Starobin, *Industrial Slavery in the Old South*, 10.

24. Ibid., 157.

25. Ibid., 157.

26. Ibid., 148.

27. Ibid., 147.

28. Ibid., 147.

29. Ibid., 140.

30. William Darity and Dania Frank, "The Economics of Reparations," in Cecilia A. Conrad et al., eds., *African Americans and the U.S. Economy* (Lanham, MD: Rowman and Littlefield, 2005), 337.

31. The extensive and intergenerational effects of nutritional deprivation make it problematic to deduct so-called maintenance costs in computing reparations claims. While it is true that free African Americans would have incurred such costs, they doubtless would have adopted dietary practices that would have reduced the burden of health risks experienced by succeeding generations.

32. Robert Starobin believed maintenance costs remained fairly constant, approximating $100 per year, during this period.

33. Richard C. Wade, *Slavery in the Cities: The South, 1820–1860* (New York: Oxford University Press, 1964).

34. The adjustments that would be required to compute the reparations due for this subset of enslaved industrial workers would use the difference between their net compensation after payments to owners and the wages of white workers as a basis for the calculations. In addition, if self-hirees were responsible for their own maintenance the issue of maintenance adjustments to the base reparations calculations would not be an issue.

35. Starobin, *Industrial Slavery in the Old South*, 148–49.

36. Ibid.

37. Baptist, *Half Has Never Been Told*, 245–49.

38. Starobin, *Industrial Slavery in the Old South*, 77.

39. Ibid., 50.

40. Ibid., 51.

41. Ibid., 36.

42. Robert William Fogel, *The Escape from Hunger and Premature Death, 1700–2100: Europe, America, and the Third World* (New York: Cambridge, 2004), 17.

43. Ramiro Alberto Flores Guzmán, "The Feeding of Slave Population in the United States, the Caribbean, and Brazil: Some Remarks in the State of the Art," *America Latina en la Historia Economica* 20 (May–August 2013): 6.

44. Robert William Fogel and Stanley L. Engerman, *Time on the Cross: The Economics of American Negro Slavery* (Boston: Little, Brown and Company, 1974), 113. See also John Komlos, "Shrinking in a Growing Economy? The Mystery of Physical Stature during the Industrial Revolution," *Journal of Economic History* 58 (September 1998): 779–802; as well as Robert A. Margo and Richard H. Steckel, "The Heights of American Slaves: New Evidence on Slave Nutrition and Health," *Social Science History* 6 (autumn 1982): 516–38.

45. Eugene Genovese, *The Political Economy of Slavery, Studies in the Economy of the Slave Society*. Second Edition. (Middletown, CT: Wesleyan University Press, 1989), 44.

46. See, for example, Robert Fogel, *The Slavery Debates, 1952–1990. A Retrospective* (Baton Rouge: Louisiana State University Press, 2003).

47. Todd L. Savitt, *Medicine and Slavery, The Diseases and Health Care of African Americans in Antebellum Virginia*. (Urbana: University of Illinois Press, 2002), 117.

48. Richard H. Steckel, "A Dreadful Childhood: The Excess Mortality of American Slaves," *Social Science History* 10 (winter 1986): 427–65. Steckel's findings are based on a rigorous statistical analysis of data from detailed records of eleven large plantations located in South Carolina, Georgia, Alabama, and Louisiana.

49. Ibid. See also Jhodie Duncan and Roger Byard, *SIDS Sudden Infant and Early Childhood Death the Past, the Present and the Future* (Adelaide: University of Adelaide Press, 2018).

50. Emily E. Petersen et al., "*Vital Signs*: Pregnancy-Related Deaths, United States, 2011–2015, and Strategies for Prevention, 13 States, 2013–2017," *Morbidity Mortality Weekly Report* 68 (May 10, 2019): 423–29, https://www.cdc.gov/mmwr/volumes/68/wr/mm6818e1.htm (accessed September 22, 2019).

51. Ibid.

52. Fogel, *Without Consent or Contract*, 144.

53. Ibid., 143.

54. Ibid., 145.

55. Todd L. Savitt, *Medicine and Slavery, The Diseases and Health Care of African Americans in Antebellum Virginia* (Urbana, IL: University of Illinois Press), 33.

56. Jim Downs, *Sick From Freedom, African-American Illness and Suffering During the Civil War and Reconstruction* (New York: Oxford University Press, 2012), 26.

57. Ibid., 26.

58. Ibid., 26.

59. Vinicius J. B. Martins et al., "Long-Lasting Effects of Undernutrition," *International Journal of Environmental Research and Public Health* 8 (June 2011): 1817–1846.

60. Nevin Scrimshaw and Robert Suskind, "Interactions of Nutrition and Infection," *Progress in Food and Nutrition Science* 8 (1984): 193–228.

61. Robert A. McGuire and Philip R. P. Coelho, *Parasites, Pathogens, and Progress: Diseases and Economic Development* (Cambridge, MA: MIT Press, 2011).

62. Robert A. Waterland and Cutberto Garza, "Potential Mechanisms of Metabolic Imprinting that Lead to Chronic Disease," *American Journal of Clinical Nutrition* 69 (February 1999): 179–97.

63. Merlon G. Butler, "Genetics of Hypertension. Current Status," *Journal Medicine Libanais* 58 (July–September 2010): 175–78.

64. See Lewis, *Coal, Iron, and Slaves,* op cit.

65. Cheryl D. Fryar et al., "Hypertension Prevalence and Control Among Adults: United States, 2015–2016," *National Center for Health Statistics Data Brief* 289 (October 2017), https://www.cdc.gov/nchs/data/databriefs/db289.pdf (accessed September 22, 2019).

66. Paul McCarron et al., "Type 2 Diabetes in Grandparents and Birth Weight in Offspring and Grandchildren in the ALSPAC Study," *Journal of Epidemiology and Community Health* 58 (June 2004): 517–22.

67. *National Diabetes Statistics Report, 2017: Estimates of Diabetes and Its Burden in the United States* (Washington, DC: National Center for Chronic Disease Prevention and Health Promotion, 2017), https://www.cdc.gov/diabetes/pdfs/data/statistics/national-diabetes-statistics-report.pdf (accessed September 2, 2019).

68. Ibid.

69. Etienne Patin et al., "Natural Variation in the Parameters of Innate Immune Cells is Preferentially Driven by Genetic Factors," *Nature Immunology* 19 (March 2018): 302–14.

70. Guzmán, "The Feeding of Slave Population,"6.

71. See Geneva Edwards, "The Health Cost of Soul Food," *Topics in Advanced Practice Nursing* 3 (2003), https://www.medscape.com/viewarticle/453335_2 (accessed September 22, 2019) and Adrian Miller, *The President's Kitchen Cabinet: The Story of the African Americans Who Have Fed Our First Families from the Washingtons to the Obamas* (Chapel Hill: University of North Carolina Press, 2017).

72. Emily Davies and Felicia Sonmez, "Black Writers, Activists, Scholars Testify before House Panel on the Role of Reparations," *Washington Post*, June 19, 2019, https://beta.washingtonpost.com/politics/house-panel-holds-hearing-on-reparations-for-slavery/2019/06/19/b62d708a-92a8-11e9-aadb-74e6b2b46f6a_story.html (accessed September 23, 2019).

73. See Anne Taylor, "The African American Heart Failure Trial: A Clinical Trial Update," *The American Journal of Cardiology* 96 (7), Supplement 2 (2005), 44–48.

74. See "Gender, Race, and Ethnicity—Experiences with Three Health Care Related Issues," chap 3 in *The Health Care Challenge: Acknowledging Disparity, Confronting*

Discrimination, and Ensuring Equality, vol. 1: The Role of Government and Private Health Care Programs and Initiatives (Washington, DC: United States Commission on Civil Rights, 1998), 73–117. URL: https://archive.org/details/healthcarechalleoounse/page/200.

75. Judith H. La Rosa et al., "Including Women and Minorities in Clinical Research," *Applied Clinical Trials* 4 (May 1995): 31; J. Claude Bennett, "Inclusion of Women in Clinical Trials—Policies for Population Subgroups," *New England Journal of Medicine* 329 (July 1993): 288–92.

76. Chelsea Weidman Burke, "The Importance of Diversity in Clinical Trials (Because Right Now, It's Lacking)," *Biospace.com*. (October 8, 2018). URL: https://www.biospace.com/article/the-importance-of-diversity-in-clinical-trials-because-right-now-it-s-lacking-/.

77. James H. Jones, *Bad Blood: The Tuskegee Syphilis Experiment* (New York: Free Press, 1981); Rebecca Skloot, *The Immortal Life of Henrietta Lacks* (New York: Crown Publishing, 2010).

78. Geoffrey Warner, "Black infant Health: Where to in the 21st Century?," chap. 20 in Thomas D. Boston, ed., *Leading Issues in Black Political Economy* (New Brunswick, NJ: Transaction Publishers, 2002), 331–56, (quotation on 352).

79. Ibid., 352.

80. V. P. Franklin, "Introduction—African Americans and Movements for Reparations: Past, Present, and Future," *Journal of African American History* 97 (winter-spring 2012): 1–12; V. P. Franklin, "Commentary—Reparations Superfund: Needed Now More than Ever," *Journal of African American History* 97 (fall 2012): 371–75.

81. Franklin, "Introduction," 1.

82. Ibid., 1.

83. Ibid., 1.

84. Ibid., 1.

85. Center for Forensic Economic Studies, "Pecuniary Losses Under New York's Wrongful Death Statute 5–4.3," n.d., https://cfes.com/recent-cases/ (accessed September 23, 2019).

86. "To My Old Master: Jourdon Anderson to Patrick Henry Anderson," August 7, 1865, in Shaun Usher, comp., *Letters of Note*, 57.

87. Joy DeGruy, *Post Traumatic Slave Syndrome, America's Legacy of Enduring Injury & Healing* (Stone Mountain, GA: Joy DeGruy Publications, 2017), 9.

88. DeGruy, *Post Traumatic Slave Syndrome*, op. cit.

89. "Who'll Pay Reparations on My Soul?," written and performed by Gil Scott-Heron, track thirteen, side two, on *A New Black Poet—Small Talk at 125th and Lenox*, Flying Dutchman/RCA FD-10143, 33⅓ rpm, released originally in 1970.

14

Taking the United States to Court

Callie House and the 1915 Cotton Tax Reparations Litigation

MARY FRANCES BERRY

The United Nations (UN) "International Decade for People of African Descent," which began in 2015, calls on those "that have not yet expressed remorse or presented apologies to find some way to contribute to the restoration of the dignity of victims" of slavery, slave trading, and colonization. The conference on "Repairing the Past, Imagining the Future: Reparations and Beyond," held at the University of Edinburgh, Scotland, in November 2014, reflects the continuation of efforts in many places throughout the world to determine remedies for evils perpetrated for invidious reasons such as caste, race, religion, nationality, and financial profit.[1] Over the years some have approached the problem of remedies though litigation, others through reconciliation formats, others through study commissions and apologies. Demands for financial remuneration for peoples of African descent have been made and gone unmet to date.

In this essay I will discuss one of the activities of the reparations movement organized by African Americans to gain pensions from the federal government for formerly enslaved African Americans in compensation for their long years of enslavement and impoverishment after abolition and point out its connections to reparations movements in the early 21st century. The story, described in *My Face Is Black Is True: Callie House and the Struggle for Ex-Slave Reparations* (2005), forms the basis for some of my conclusions about how to achieve successful reparations strategies. It also tells us about the legacy we are left with when a people have been exploited and the breach is not remedied in their lifetimes and what a delay in reparation can mean.[2]

Callie House, who was born a slave, worked as a washerwoman at the bottom of America's social and economic ladder, was a widow with five children, and became the leader of the largest grassroots movement among African Americans at the end of the nineteenth and beginning of the twentieth centuries. According to the federal government's surveillance records, at least 300,000 African Americans joined the Ex-Slave Mutual Relief Bounty and Pension Association, organized in 1898. They paid dues and signed petitions, or had others sign for the illiterate, asking the federal government to provide pensions to African American men and women for their unrequited labor and suffering during slavery. Callie House believed strongly in self-help, and she organized local branches for mutual assistance to aid the sick and bury the dead and succor the families left behind with very meager resources. The petitions to the U.S. Congress were collected through these branches.[3]

The legislation for which Callie House and the formerly enslaved people lobbied was introduced repeatedly in the U.S. Congress and considered in the Pension Committee, but never passed. It called for a pension of $15 per month, and a bounty of $500, for each ex-slave seventy years of age and older. Those under seventy would receive $300 as a bounty and $12 per month until they reached the age of seventy, when it would increase to $15. Those under sixty years old would receive a $100 bounty and $8 a month until they reached age sixty. Those less than fifty years of age would receive $4 per month, and then at age fifty, $8 per month. Ex-slaves, and such persons as "may be charged by laws of consanguinity with the maintenance and support of freedmen who are unable by reason of age or disease to maintain themselves," were also eligible. Relatives who cared for freedpeople could, upon providing satisfactory proof to the U.S. Secretary of the Interior, receive the pension. "Ex-slaves," under the terms of the bill included only those freed by Lincoln's 1863 Emancipation Proclamation, by state constitutional amendment, or "by any law, proclamation, decree or device." The plan appeared uncomplicated, requiring only that a claimant had been enslaved. Under the law anyone alive before 1861 was presumed to be a slave in the South unless proof to the contrary was presented.[4] Frederick Douglass, the most important African American leader of the day, supported reparations. He declared, if land had been given as promised during the Civil War, "the [N]egro would not today be on his knees, as he is supplicating the old master class to give him leave to toil." If reparations had been adopted "untold misery might have been prevented."[5]

As Callie House described the cause, the association acted on behalf of "four & half million slave[s] who was [were] turn[ed] loose ignorant bare footed and naked without a dollar in their pockets without a shelter to go under out of the falling rain but was force[d] to look the man in the face for something to eat who once had the power to whip them to death but now have the power to starve them to death." She pointed out, "We, the ex-slave, feel that if the government had a right to free us she had a right to make some provision for us as she did not make it soon after our emancipation she ought to make it now."[6]

It does not matter so much now that the Federal Pension Bureau and Post Office Department harassed the movement and regarded Callie House as a "dangerous radical" who might inspire formerly enslaved people to rebel if they did not get reparations. It does not matter that she was jailed in 1917 for her persistence and the petition effort failed. But even after her jailing and her death from cancer in 1931, many chapters continued to work. As late as 1931 the Atlanta chapter's mutual assistance work was covered in the local press. In addition, some ex-slave pension association agents and members became prominent in Marcus Garvey's Universal Negro Improvement Association which supported reparations.[7]

However elusive seems the possibility of obtaining financial recompense for the descendants of enslaved African American, lawyers may eventually develop a viable litigation claim against the federal government. For that reason, I call to your attention Callie House's pursuit of the cotton tax case, a claim filed by actual former slaves in the early twentieth century. Despite the federal government's ongoing attacks on the movement, House continued to lecture to local chapters and mobilize membership in the national ex-slave mutual relief and pension association. But House could see that the efforts on behalf of the poor rural and urban African Americans could only go so far. The association could have pension legislation introduced, but it did not have the resources to gain its passage. Further, at the Pension Bureau's instigation, the whole reparations idea had been denounced by key members of Congress. In addition, the association's leaders had to worry about fraud charges against local agents brought by state prosecutors, urged on by the U.S. Justice Department. Local chapters maintained their mutual assistance programs, but the communications barriers and attacks on their leaders made effective organizing toward the reparations goal increasingly difficult. The fraud order made fundraising perilous. Through use of expensive commercial delivery services, solicitations at meetings, and occasional mailings to intermediaries, association leaders kept a bare trickle of financial support flowing into the national office. Clearly, the movement needed another strategy. At this juncture, federal officials became disturbed that Callie House "instigated and paid for a reparations lawsuit."[8]

The federal tax payments from the sale of cotton confiscated by federal troops during and after the Civil War had been the subject of reports in many Black newspapers. The reports noted that ex-Confederates who had tracked the funds found that they lay untouched in the U.S. Treasury. When the Civil War began, the cotton had already been picked and stored. Congress enacted the tax first, in 1862, at two and one-half cents per pound on raw cotton, for the ostensible purpose of paying war debts. In 1866, Congress increased the tax to three cents a pound. This time Congress designated no specific purpose for the money. The newspapers also reported that southern Senators unsuccessfully sought legislation to return the funds to the former slaveholders. Callie House wanted this identifiable fund distributed among the aged former slaves. House claimed that the Treasury Department owed African Americans $68,073,388.99 collected in cotton taxes between 1862 and 1868.[9]

This new tactic taken after federal officials had practically destroyed the movement infuriated them; and it provided yet another reason to harass Callie House. They denounced the litigation publicly as part of a continuing money-making scheme to defraud "credulous" ignorant ex-slaves, even though they knew better. House saw the courts as responsible for deciding claims of injustice when legislative lobbying failed. Even though the courts had proved inhospitable to suits seeking protection for African Americans under the Fourteenth Amendment, judicial protection of minority rights was firmly embedded in the U.S. Constitution. And the Constitution was the rock on which all of House's claims of political agency and citizenship rights for African Americans stood. This lawsuit offered another route to establish their claims legally. Besides, even if the effort failed, it might engender more public understanding of the pensions cause. Turning to the judiciary was just another example of using whatever weapons came to hand.[10]

From Callie House's perspective, the national political climate after the election of Woodrow Wilson on the Democratic Party's ticket in 1912 had made bad matters worse. The formerly enslaved African Americans who resided in the poor communities where she lived and worked were without the right to vote, without land, and without means of support beyond meager wages for their labor. But many were disabled and suffered from the feebleness of old age. House understood that some leading African Americans had shifted parties to vote for Wilson, hoping to attract more attention to the need to end the ongoing racial violence and lynching and disenfranchisement of Black southerners. However, the Wilson administration's "New Freedom" agenda did not extend to African Americans. In Washington, DC, where Black employees had worked freely with whites in the federal workforce, the Wilson administration instituted segregation. The downturn in the fortunes of African Americans coincided with the continued harassment of the ex-slave pension movement by federal officials during the Wilson years.[11]

Callie House understood that the people she represented needed inspiration. They must not give up in discouragement. She thought that recording ex-slaves' claims in the petitions continued to be important and the movement effectively served local ends. Members helped one another to survive and the movement also gave formerly enslaved workers and their families a larger vision: namely, that the experience of slavery validly justified compensation for their suffering. The courts offered another venue to argue their case.

The Ex-Slave Pension Association had been in court supporting Isaiah Dickerson's, one of the group's organizers, successful appeals of his Georgia criminal conviction, and this marked its first foray into civil litigation. They knew that in *Plessy v Ferguson* (1896), Homer Plessy had achieved a victory in a civil case in the lower court before ultimately losing at the appellate level.[12] After deciding on a lawsuit, House faced the challenge of identifying a competent lawyer to handle the case. She soon identified Cornelius Jones, an experienced litigator, and one of two African Americans acknowledged as the best-known and most successful Black attorneys in the Mississippi bar. Both he and Wilford Smith had gained bar admission at the same time, and both argued separate cases before the U.S. Supreme Court on December 13, 1895, challenging the exclusion of African Americans from grand juries. Newspaper publisher Calvin Chase's widely read *Washington Bee* reported that this marked the first time that more than one Black lawyer had appeared before the Supreme Court in different cases on the same day. It was a time when, among the small number of African American lawyers, few had argued before the nation's highest court. Chase considered this a major indication of "racial progress."[13]

Cornelius Jones, an active politician as well as a practicing lawyer, had also served one term in the Mississippi legislature in the 1890s. He lost a disputed contest for a Congressional seat in 1896 after claiming unsuccessfully that he had been elected with votes from 40,000 Black voters and 10,000 whites. Hailing Jones as "a superb constitutional lawyer," publisher Edward Cooper's *Colored American* lamented the failure of Congress to act on Jones's 1896 election challenge and noted Jones's role as one of the first African Americans to openly oppose disenfranchisement measures. The paper identified him as "the first and only Negro lawyer appearing in the Supreme Court of the United States, unsupported by a white lawyer" in defense of the rights of African Americans under the Thirteenth, Fourteenth, and Fifteenth Amendments. For House, engaging Jones to seek compensation, she hoped, would not only ensure effective representation, but might encourage the support of leading African Americans who had ignored or denounced the pension movement.[14]

Jones agreed with House that Congressional action afforded the most reasonable approach to gaining reparations, but since that strategy had failed, he would develop the best possible case to bring before the courts. She and Jones decided to aim the court attack at the widely discussed cotton tax. First, Jones wanted to make sure the cotton tax funds still existed. In May 1915, before filing the suit, he wrote to Secretary of the Treasury William G. McAdoo, asking about cotton tax revenue. Assistant Secretary William S. Malburn responded that courts had never decided whether the tax had been constitutional in the first place. Malburn concluded that "though bills for a refund of the cotton tax have been introduced in Congress from time to time, no legislation has been enacted; and the subject is one within the jurisdiction of the Congress."[15]

In July 1915, attorney Jones filed the Ex-Slave Association's class action suit in federal court in the District of Columbia against Secretary of the Treasury William McAdoo, claiming a specific debt owed from the production of cotton crops during slavery. Because this cotton had been identified when it was taxed, it could be traced in the Treasury, and thus the suit avoided the issue of whether Congress would appropriate funds to pay for pensions as compensation for the formerly enslaved workers who produced it. Jones cited by analogy Indian monies held in the Treasury that were payable under specific Indian treaties. Jones wanted this identifiable fund distributed among formerly enslaved African Americans.[16]

Jones avoided specific reference to developments during or immediately after slavery to support the claim for debt repayment to African Americans. In general, Callie House, Frederick Douglass, and other Black spokespersons did not discuss specific policies initiated during the Reconstruction era. They knew that the Freedmen's Bureau, in operation between 1865 and 1872, had never really controlled any significant amounts of land in the South. Besides, President Andrew Johnson's amnesty proclamation of 1865 had forced the restoration to former Confederates' property that the agency did control. Frederick Douglass, in insisting on reparations, emphasized that "the Russian serf was provided with farming tools and three acres of land with which to begin life,—but the Negro has neither spoils, implements, nor lands." House talked routinely about how the enslaved workers had received nothing for their labor.[17]

Cornelius Jones avoided novel arguments and strategically formulated the suit in the formal legal terms common in the period. His strategy reflected the negative racial climate of the times. He and Callie House knew that by the time they brought the lawsuit, African Americans had endured the reversal of positive uses of civil rights legislation passed during the Reconstruction era. By early twentieth century, the courts had routinely affirmed the use of the Fourteenth Amendment to defend corporations, not African Americans.[18] Jones knew that legal rules, such as governmental immunity—the legal principle that the government cannot be sued without its consent—limited his case. That is why he kept insisting that though the government held the tax revenue, the proceeds always belonged to the formerly enslaved workers. Surely, he argued, they had a right to the funds generated by their labor, even though they could not exercise that right as unfree laborers.

In response, the Treasury Department went on a public relations offensive. In a press statement on 15 October 1915, the department insisted the government had a right to keep the tax money and that if former slaves "had any claim, it would be against their masters." The Treasury department expected to win based on governmental immunity since "the usual fate of such suits is to be thrown out of court because of lack of jurisdiction." The statement warned those persons who contributed to a fund to pay for pursuing the case were "throwing their money away."[19]

Despite an earlier letter to Jones from Malburn, the Treasury Department not only slammed the lawsuit but denied the existence of the monies sought by the plaintiffs. Secretary of the Treasury McAdoo wrote to Jones denying the existence of the cotton tax revenue. He also asserted that "the United States Supreme Court decided the tax of 1862–68 was unconstitutional, and that the money collected as a Civil War revenue tax has been treated as part of the general receipts of the government and applied to payment of government debts." McAdoo stated, "There is no fund of $68,000,000 or any other sum in the Treasury of the United States for ex-slaves, or those who worked in the cotton fields of the South."[20] Jones denounced McAdoo's response, insisting that either sometime after writing to him in June, Treasury officials had spent the funds, or the government still had them in the account, and that McAdoo was denying their existence to defeat the lawsuit. The District of Columbia Court of Appeals rejected Jones's claim in the cotton tax case on the grounds of government immunity. The United States could not be sued without its consent. Jones filed an appeal to the U.S. Supreme Court but lost. The justices upheld the lower court's decision.[21]

The freedpeople lost the case because the court would not let them overcome the government's procedural objection to having a trial to determine who owned the funds. Currently, waivers of governmental immunity might allow such a claim to avoid immediate rejection in the courts. However, Jones's plea failed because the courts decided that governmental immunity superseded a determination as to whether African Americans might receive the funds.

Out of regard for Cornelius Jones's prestige, Black newspapers that usually ignored or denounced Callie House and the Ex-Slave Pension Association commented favorably on the suit when it was filed. However, the *Washington Bee*, still deeply committed to denigrating Callie House and the ex-slaves' campaign and knowing of the federal government's enmity toward the pension movement, insisted the case had no connection with the "agitation of freedmen" for pensions. Other African American papers expressed the same view or did not mention the Ex-Slave Association at all in the news coverage about the lawsuit.[22]

Although the case was lost, by representing the freedpeople, Cornelius Jones made himself a target of governmental officials already attacking Callie House and the Ex-Slave Pension Association—the hostile Post Office Department and Pension Bureau officials. Angered by the lawsuit, government officials used a strategy against Jones that they had planned to use against Callie House. Just as they could not harass her for exercising her right as a U.S. citizen to petition the government, they could not persecute Jones for litigating the cotton tax suit at her instigation. Instead, Post Office Department officials decided to prosecute him for violating the postal code for using the mail to defraud. They made this decision while Jones was appealing the cotton tax case to the U.S. Supreme Court. The government charged Jones with fraud for mailing letters seeking support from African Americans who might benefit from the lawsuit. The government officials sought to punish Jones for having the temerity to bring the lawsuit against the federal government, and for his connection to the Ex-Slave Pension Association. Jones was convicted, but instead of accepting the jury verdict, Judge John Ethridge McCall, who presided over the case, ordered a new trial. Judge McCall appeared uneasy about the government prosecution of a lawyer on such a minor charge while the lawyer was suing the government in the underlying matter of the tax case then before the U.S. Supreme Court. Eventually, the prosecution was not pursued; it is likely that the prosecutors and judge backed off because of Jones's political connections and respectable reputation.[23]

The effort to gain pensions had failed again, but the litigation helped to expand the movement. Formerly enslaved African Americans were even more firmly convinced that they should continue to gather petitions seeking pensions and to continue to strengthen the association's local chapters. In addition, the cause gained favorable publicity among African American leaders based on Jones's respectable reputation. Because he was a successful male professional, African Americans applauded his leadership role. With the failure of the litigation, the movement again concentrated on pursuing legislation. But soon the government successfully entrapped Callie House. She lacked Jones's status as a respectable Black male attorney representing a client in a case before the federal courts. Indeed, House was just an African American woman with no money, but the audacity to stand firmly on claims of citizenship rights for herself and other freedpeople. House was eventually arrested by federal officials, tried, and in September 1917 convicted by an all-white and all-male jury of using the mail to defraud and was sentenced to a year in prison.[24]

The twenty-first-century interest in reparations stems from African Americans' continued discontent. Many African Americans see the slow rate of progress toward equal treatment by the criminal justice system, educational systems, and almost every aspect of their lives; as well as successful attacks on remedial measures such as Affirmative Action and contract set-asides, as showing the need for more drastic solutions. The "Reparations Superfund" proposal has gained some traction and Ta-Nehisi Coates's June 2014 article in *The Atlantic* magazine "The Case for Reparations" stimulated great interest, though not much policy response.[25]

The resurgent interest in reparations in the legal and political community was aroused in the 1980s by the Japanese American redress ordered by the U.S. Congress. The federal government made several efforts to address the unjustified internment of Japanese Americans during World War II. In 1983 in *William Hohri et al. v. United States,* nineteen Japanese Americans, former World War II internees or their living representatives, brought a class action suit against the United States seeking damages and a declaratory judgment on twenty-two claims based on constitutional violations, tort, and breach of contract and fiduciary duties. The U.S. District Court dismissed the claims, holding that all but one based on the Fifth Amendment ban against the government taking private property without compensation, were excluded by "sovereign immunity," the rule that the government cannot be sued without its permission. The appellate court then held that even the Fifth Amendment "takings clause" claim could not proceed. It was too old and barred by the statute of limitations. The court also found the government had not waived its immunity to being sued without its consent.[26]

The decision was eventually upheld by the U.S. Supreme Court, but District Court Judge J. Skelly Wright suggested in his lower court ruling that by exhausting their judicial options, the Japanese Americans had made a case for Congressional action. Congress passed the Civil Liberties Act of 1988 providing for a formal apology and benefits, including redress payments of $20,000, to citizens and permanent residents of the United States interned during World War II. It established an office of redress administration in the Civil Rights Division of the Department of Justice to administer it.[27]

We have not been able to get this far with African Americans' reparations claims. In recent years, there have been lawsuits against the federal government, but so far they have been confounded by "sovereign immunity" as in the cotton tax and Japanese internment cases.

Some lawyers have instead targeted insurers or employers of enslaved workers. Attorney Deadria Farmer-Paellmann sued Aetna Insurance Company, Fleet Boston Financial, the CSX Railroad, and Wachovia Bank among other companies, claiming that these companies conspired with slave traders and illegally profited from slavery. The advocates hoped the public relations impact might give momentum to the reparations cause.[28]

Farmer-Paellmann successfully gained apologies from several companies, including Wachovia Bank, which in June 2005 conceded that they had employed hundreds of enslaved workers on railroads and accepted enslaved people as collateral for loans after 1830. They have agreed to funding scholarships as reparation. Beginning with Brown University, some institutions of higher education financed with profits from slavery and slave trading have started to respond. Some experts argue that the government's immunity to lawsuit without its consent that confounded Callie House and Cornelius Jones is no longer a barrier because the federal government agreed to be sued to protect freedpeople when it passed legislation to assist formerly enslaved people during the Reconstruction era (1867–1877). These lawyers cite the Freedmen's Bureau courts and the Civil Rights Act of 1866, which gave African-descended people the same rights as European Americans to sue and be sued, own property, make contracts, and other routine activities. Even today because of ongoing discrimination the statute of limitations has not run out.

Other experts argue that the Administrative Procedure Act of 1946 (APA) may be used to overcome the government's immunity to lawsuits. The APA provides that a person who is wronged by the actions of a government agency may have the government's activities reviewed in the courts. The act clearly states that the court cannot dismiss the action solely on the grounds that the government is being sued. The United States may be named as a defendant and the court can issue a judgment against the United States. The person suing has the opportunity, unlike the formerly enslaved people in the cotton tax case, to prove they have been harmed under a law permitting monetary damages in order to win payment. In such a case today one of the civil rights acts passed during Reconstruction, which include money damages, might be used to make a claim under the APA.[29]

Some advocates have proposed arguing that international law has been violated by the United States government because a universal consensus exists against genocide, enslavement, and systematic racial discrimination. Furthermore, the Nuremberg trials in the late 1940s established that under international law, a state could be held criminally liable for the treatment of its own citizens. At Nuremberg, the four victorious powers of World War II tried German officials for "crimes against humanity." The German leaders' crimes against its own Jewish citizens were found to be retroactive under international law. In 1951, the Civil Rights Congress presented a petition to the United Nations charging "genocide by the federal government" against African Americans, but to no avail. Under international law, arguably to continue legal segregation under the UN charter meant a waiver of sovereign immunity. However, the United States only signed the covenant on civil and political rights, with reservations, in 1992.[30]

The continuity in the reparations cause from Callie House to the twenty-first century offers graphic historical testimony of the indelible memory of the decades of unrequited labor of African Americans. Today those who argue against reparations, or even the notion of studying the idea, argue that the formerly enslaved workers are all dead so why consider a remedy for their descendants. By 1900, only 21 percent of the African American population, or about 1.9 million persons, had been born in slavery. Their numbers, like the Civil War veterans under the lucrative Union Army pension provisions, were slowly diminishing by death. But those formerly enslaved people still alive were not able to gain pensions, even for the small number of obviously deserving individuals. Those who continue to support reparations today point to the intergenerational effects of leaving slavery as a people without compensation, not even the promised "forty acres and a mule."

Callie House wanted African Americans to have economic capital based on their unpaid labor during the era of slavery. Whatever the outcome of the modern case for reparations, there was a time when freedpeople and their descendants believed in that possibility. Those who act in the cause today pay homage to their struggle.

Notes

1. For information on the United Nations "Decade of People of African Descent," see www.un.org/en/events/africandeescentdecade/background.shtml.

2. Mary Frances Berry, *My Face Is Black Is True: Callie House and the Struggle for Ex-Slave Reparations* (New York, 2005).

3. Callie House, "Introduction," *The Constitution and Bylaws of the National Ex-Slave Mutual Relief, Bounty, and Pension Association of the United States of America* (Nashville, TN, 1899).

4. Walter R. Vaughn, *Freemen's Pension Bill: A Plea for the American Freedmen* (Chicago, IL, 1891).

5. Frederick Douglass to Walter R. Vaughn in ibid., 150.

6. Callie House quoted in Berry, *My Face Is Black Is True*, 88–89.

7. Many members of the agents for the pension association were members of the UNIA, see Robert A. Hill, ed., *The Marcus Garvey and Universal Negro Improvement Association Papers*, Vol. 4 and Vol. 5 (Berkeley, CA, 1985 & 1987), Appendices: "List of state ex-slave pension agents filed 13 May 1902."

8. Berry, *My Face Is Black Is True*, 172; *United States v. Augustus Clark* (1916–17).

9. Berry, *My Face Is Black Is True*, 176–78.

10. Mary Frances Berry, "Reparations for Freedmen, 1890–1916: Fraudulent Practices or Justice Deferred," *Journal of Negro History* 57 (July 1972): 219–130; J. Clay Smith, *Emancipation: The Making of the Black Lawyer, 1844–1944* (Philadelphia, PA, 1993).

11. Rayford Logan, *The Betrayal of the Negro: From Rutherford B. Hayes to Woodrow Wilson* (1965; reprt., New York, 1997).

12. See, Thomas J. Davis, *Plessy v. Ferguson* (Santa Barbara, CA, 2012).

13. "Cornelius J. Jones: America Must Redeem Her National Pledge of 'Sacred Honor,'" *Washington Bee*, 23 October 1915.

14. "He Should Be Seated, the Congressional Campaign of Hon. C. J. Jones—A Superb Constitutional Lawyer," *The Colored American*, 16 July 1898.

15. "Cornelius Jones: America Must Redeem Her National Pledge."

16. *Johnson v. McAdoo* (1916); Berry, "Reparations for the Freedmen."

17. Frederick Douglass, quoted in Berry, *My Face Is Black Is True*, 39; Mary Frances Berry, *Black Resistance/White Law: A History of Constitutional Racism in America* (New York, 1971), 69–80.

18. Berry, *Black Resistance/White Law*, 81–96; Alexander Tsesis, *We Shall Overcome: A History of Civil Rights and Law* (New Haven, CT, 2009), 117–31.

19. "No Fund for Ex-Slaves," *New York Evening Post*, 15 October 1915.

20. "The Cotton Tax," *Washington Bee*, 13 November 1915; quoted in Berry, *My Face Is Black Is True*," 180.

21. *Johnson v. McAdoo*, 45 App. D.C. 440 (1916); 244 U. S. 643 (1917).

22. *Washington Bee*, 24 July 1915; "Cotton Tax Suit Has No Merit," *Chicago Defender*, 6 November 1915.

23. U.S. District Court, *United States v. Cornelius Jones* (accounting ledger); Berry, *My Face Is Black Is True*, 183–85.

24. Berry, *My Face is Black Is True*, 200–211.

25. V. P. Franklin, "Introduction to Special Issue-African Americans and Movements for Reparations: From Ex-Slave Pensions to the Reparations Superfund," *Journal of African American History* 97 (Winter-Spring 2012): 1–12; Ta-Nehisi Coates, "The Case for Reparations," *The Atlantic*, June 1914.

26. *William Hohri, et al., Appellants v. United States, 782 F. 2nd 227* (1986).

27. The Civil Liberties Act of 1988 (Pub. L. 100–383, 10 August 1988, 102 Stat. 150).

28. *Farmer-Paellmann v. FleetBoston, Aetna Inc, CSX Railroad* in *Should America Pay? Slavery and the Raging Debate Over Reparations*, ed. Raymond A. Winbush (New York, 2003), 354–66.

29. *The Administrative Procedure Act* (Pub. L. 79–404, 11 June 1946, 60, Stat. 237).

30. Civil Rights Congress, *We Charge Genocide: The Historic Petition to the United Nations for Relief for a Crime of the United States Government against the Negro People* (New York, 1951); see also, Gerald Horne, *Communist Front? The Civil Rights Congress, 1946–1956* (Teaneck, NJ, 1988).

15

This Is What Reparations Could Actually Look Like in America

CHUCK COLLINS AND
DEDRICK ASANTE-MUHAMMAD

The current racial wealth divide is an economic archeological marker, embedded within the multigenerational story of slavery, racial plunder, and discrimination. It is one way the legacy of racism shows up in people's bank accounts and, if they own a home, in home equity. It is where the past is present, where the wound at the center of U.S. history that goes back to the destruction of Indigenous communities, slavery, and Jim Crow is still open and waiting for repair. Notably, the past few decades has "supercharged" historic racial wealth inequalities.

To repair this breach, it's becoming increasingly clear that reparations for Black slavery and its legacy—including Jim Crow—must be part of the equation. Facing what activist Randall Robinson calls "the debt" to people of African descent, those of us who are low on melanin content (aka "white") will have to address the often-uncomfortable history of how lighter skin color conferred, and continues to confer, economic advantage. To do otherwise is to live a destructive lie, perpetuating a perverted myth of deservedness that holds back our entire society and each of us individually.

As Ta-Nehisi Coates wrote in his 2014 *Atlantic* magazine article, reparations are "the price we must pay to see ourselves squarely." "Reparations," he continues, "beckons us to reject the intoxication of hubris and see America as it is—the work of fallible humans. An America that looks away is ignoring not just the sins of the past but the sins of the present and the certain sins of the future." We know from history and science that race is a social construct. And yet it continues to wield outsized societal influence.[1] Imagine that after playing poker for an hour, we discover that we've been playing with a rigged deck—and that for each hand dealt, a couple of us have gotten extra cards, based on something entirely arbitrary such as the color of our eyes or sweaters. Naturally, the beneficiaries of the stacked deck have accumulated big winnings. We all heartily agree to a clean start with a new deck and fair rules. But as the dealer begins shuffling the new deck, one of the players raises an awkward question: "What do we do about that huge pile of chips that a few of you have accumulated?"

This will not be an easy task—practically impossible in today's political climate. Reparations must address the victims of slavery, but they must also provide opportunities for those who were perpetrators or collaborators to offer their own sort of penance. But we also need to continue talking about the possibilities—and planning for a future when reparations might become politically feasible.

To that end, practical and logistical challenges must be worked out now. We argue that the primary source of funds should be a steeply graduated tax on wealth, paid mostly by households in the top 1 percent—those with assets over $5 million. A tax on concentrated wealth and the resulting investments would have a positive impact on the economy for everyone, reducing the distorting impact of concentrated wealth.

The State of the Racial Wealth Divide

While there are substantial *income* disparities by race, wealth in the form of property and other assets reveals more about the multigenerational roots of inequality. Assets provide a buffer against economic downturns, both personal and societal. Wealth also plays an essential role in establishing financial security and opportunity for future generations. According to the Pew Research Center, the median wealth of white households in 2013 was a stunning 13 times greater than the median wealth of Black households—up from eight times greater in 2010. White households, meanwhile, had ten times more wealth than Latino households. The average retirement savings for Black and Latino households is $19,049 and $12,229, respectively, compared to $130,472 for white households.

If average Black wealth grows at the same rate as it has over the last 30 years, 228 years—17 years shorter than the institution of slavery in the United States—will go by before it equals the amount of wealth possessed by white households today, according to a report we co-authored with Prosperity Now, "Ever Growing Gap." This of course presumes white wealth remains static, which it will not. It will grow.

Understanding Affirmative Action for Whites

For whites to understand the racial wealth divide requires some demythologizing of our own narrative of wealth creation. In his book, *Born on Third Base*, co-author Chuck Collins describes how wealth inequality continues to be justified by powerful myths of deservedness. In the case of racial economic divisions, the full horror of dispossession remains difficult to grasp. In 1965, a century after the formal end of slavery, African Americans were still largely excluded from programs that helped build middle-class wealth. In the decades following World War II, our nation made unprecedented public investments to subsidize debt-free college education and low-cost mortgages. But these wealth-building measures benefited millions of mostly white households.

People of color, meanwhile, faced overt discrimination in mortgage lending and separate-and-unequal school systems throughout the United States. Barred from traditional forms of credit, African Americans were pushed into wealth-stripping mortgage scams like "contract for deed mortgages," where a missed payment would lead to eviction and loss of all equity.[2]

So, while many whites were able to board an express train to middle-class wealth between 1945 and 1975, people of color were left standing at the railway station waiting for a train that never showed up. As a result of government subsidies, white homeownership rates steadily rose to as high as 75 percent in 2005, according to the U.S. Census, while Black rates peaked at 46 percent the same year, a 30-point gap that remains today.[3]

White households were able to help their children obtain access to homeownership and stability through what sociologists call the "intergenerational transmission of advantage."[4] Making matters worse, white economic advantage has historically compounded over time while Black disadvantage has compounded or thwarted advancement.

Historical Precedent

While a politically toxic concept today, there is precedent for reparations in the United States—if not on this sort of scale. In 1988, U.S. president Ronald Reagan formally apologized for the U.S. government's internment of Japanese Americans during World War II and, under the provisions of the Civil Liberties Act, paid $20,000 in reparations to over 800,000 victims of internment.[5] Over $1.1 billion was initially allocated and an additional $400,000 was appropriated later to cover claims.[6]

There are also examples of such payout globally. In accordance with a 1952 agreement, Germany has paid over $89 billion in reparations to victims of the Holocaust during World War II. German officials continue to meet with groups of survivors and their advocates to revisit guidelines and ensure that survivors receive the benefits.[7] As recently as 2015, both Greek and Russian parliaments voted to demand that Germany pay them for the damage inflicted by Nazi occupation.[8]

And yet, discussions about reparations in the United States tend to stall before they get started. It's true that questions about the mechanism and source of funds are complicated. Should the focus be on slavery, or should it include the broader manifestations of white supremacy? Who qualifies? Should we allocate direct cash grants or invest in programs that can more broadly work to expand Black wealth? How can reparations lead to a broader understanding and healing between collaborators and perpetrators?

While difficult, however, these questions are not insurmountable.

Who Pays?

Many whites with little in the bank to show for their racial advantage will understandably be frustrated by the concept of reparations. If they never owned slaves—and neither did their ancestors—why should they have to pay? By the same token, many first- or second-generation Americans, whose European ancestors fled their own hardships to come to the United States, feel miles and centuries apart from slavery.

The key point, however, is the unpaid labor of millions—and the compounding legacy of slavery, Jim Crow laws, discrimination in mortgage lending, and a race-based system of mass incarceration—created uncompensated wealth for individuals and white society as a whole. Immigrants with European heritage directly and indirectly benefited from this system of white supremacy. It is true, of course, that many people have not shared in the economic gains equally, thanks to four decades of hyper-inequality. Today, the wealthiest 100 billionaires in the United States have as much wealth as the entire African American population combined. For this reason, we propose two concrete mechanisms to fund a national Reparations Trust Fund. The first is a graduated tax on wealth and inherited wealth. Households with wealth in excess of $5 million would pay a 1% tax, but rates would climb for billionaire households.

Secondly, we propose that the fund be capitalized in part by hefty penalties on wealthy individuals and corporations that attempt to move their funds "offshore" or into complicated trusts to avoid taxation and accountability.

There would also be stiff penalties assessed on wealth managers who aid and abet these wealth escapes by creating trusts and offshore subsidies for the sole purposes of tax dodging. Part of the austerity that many of our communities now face is the result of the estimated 8 percent of the world's wealth that is now hidden offshore. (See Gabriel Zucman's book *Hidden Wealth of Nations: The Scourge of Tax Havens* for more info.)[9] Both a tax on wealth and stiffer penalties on tax dodging would have beneficial impacts on the larger economy for all workers, not just those who faced racial exclusion.

The Road to Reparations

A first step, politically speaking, would be for Congress to create a national commission. The work of such a commission would be to wrestle with the particulars of reparations and repair. Since 1989, Congressman John Conyers repeatedly filed legislation to create this commission—HR40—which was voted out of the House Judiciary Committee, but not taken up in Congress.[10] The number 40 in the bill's name alludes to unfulfilled promises made to formerly enslaved Africans by the Homestead Act of the late 1800s. The act promised formerly enslaved people "40 acres and a mule."

The commission could investigate many different forms of reparations. In his book, *The Debt: What America Owes to Blacks*, the late Randall Robinson talked about a wide range of ways that reparations could be used, including the funding of cultural institutions, community initiatives, direct cash grants, and targeted wealth-building programs.

The commission could also determine eligibility. Economist William Darity argues that eligibility should be tied to those who can demonstrate they have ancestors who suffered from forced migration and slavery, not those who came to the United States voluntarily.[11] For those who do qualify, the money could be paid in a lump sum. But that's not the only form reparations could take shape. Some options include:

> **Direct stakeholder funds.** These could take the form of direct cash grants without conditions to adults. Additional funds could be targeted for matching savings programs, homeownership, business start-ups, and other wealth building opportunities. Funds could be allocated to optional and free financial literacy training programs to enable people to make the most of their "stake." (This is not out of paternalism but rather a recognition that along with unequal wealth comes the unequal knowledge of the workings of capital, saving, and investment—and that these tools can be powerful).

First-time homebuyer programs. The government could offer subsidized home mortgages similar to those that built the white middle class after World War II but targeted to those excluded or preyed upon by predatory lending. Programs should also be available to descendants who were barred from opportunities to get on family wealth creation programs.

Tuition-free higher education. Free tuition and financial support at universities and colleges for first-generation college students could be covered under reparations provisions.

Endowments for historical and cultural institutions. Reparations funds could provide one-time capital endowments to create and sustain museums and historical exhibits that teach the history of slavery and its aftermath, such as the National Museum of African American History and Culture.

National history education programs. Alongside German reparations for Nazi Germany, there has been a national investment in education about the history of the Holocaust. The "Facing History and Ourselves" curriculum is now used in thousands of U.S. high schools. A similar investment should be made to disseminate the history of African Americans to all segments of the society.

Historical monuments and markers. Throughout Germany, there are historical markers informing people about the legacy of the Holocaust. Over 30,000 commemorative bricks have been installed outside homes and apartment buildings where Jews, gays and lesbians, Roma people, and other targets of the Nazi regime lived prior to deportation to death camps. German residents have daily reminders of this history through what are called *Stolperstein*: "stumbling stones." In the U.S., historical markers could mark buildings such as the U.S. Capitol ("Built with Enslaved Labor"), sites of lynchings, and organized pogroms and riots, such as the 1924 attack on the Black business district in Tulsa, Oklahoma. This would be particularly important in terms of broader education and reconciliation of those who were privileged by racially discriminatory policies.

Roots journeys to Africa. Tens of thousands of Jewish young people from the United States go to Israel each year, part of a "making Aliyah" pilgrimage that helps them deepen their religious and cultural identity. These birthright trips are funded by the Israeli government and private agencies in order to promote resettlement in Israel as well as to facilitate deeper ties between that country and U.S. citizens. A similar initiative could enable people with African heritage to visit Africa, learn more about their historical roots, and deepen friendships and understanding with the African continent.

* * *

To ignore the legacy of slavery and discrimination requires a debilitating denial on the part of whites—even those whose ancestors arrived from other lands in more recent times, and especially for those at the top of the wealth pyramid.

Science tells us "There is no such thing as race." Yet for centuries, economic rewards have been allocated based on the level of melanin in our skin. We do not believe that we will ever be able to truly repair and heal from the material and psychological legacy of grouping people by race without an intensive process of introspection and, yes, material reparations.

Notes

1. Megan Gannon, "Race is a Social Construct, Scientists Argue," *Scientific American*, February 5, 2016. https://www.scientificamerican.com/article/race-is-a-social-construct-scientists-argue/.

2. Jeremiah Battle, Jr., Sarah Mancini, Margo Saunders, and Odette Williamson, "Toxic Transactions: How Land Installment Contracts Once Again Threaten Communities of Color," July 2016, National Consumer Law Center, https://www.nclc.org/issues/toxic-transactions-threaten-communities-of-color.html.

3. Homeownership Data: U.S. Census Bureau, "Residential Vacancies and Homeownership in the Fourth Quarter 2016," Tuesday, January 31, 2017, http://www.census.gov/housing/hvs/files/currenthvspress.pdf.

4. See John Ermisch, Markus Jantti, Timothy M. Smeeding, *From Parents to Children: The International Transmission of Advantage* (Russell Sage Foundation, May 2012), https://www.russellsage.org/publications/parents-to-children. Also see the piece I did adapting this research into a narrative article: Chuck Collins, "The New Politics of Inherited Advantage," http://prospect.org/article/wealthy-kids-are-all-right.

5. Densho Encyclopedia, http://encyclopedia.densho.org/Civil%20Liberties%20Act%20of%201988/.

6. Ibid; Irvin Molotsky, "Senate Votes to Compensate Japanese-American Internees," *New York Times*, April 21, 1988, http://www.nytimes.com/1988/04/21/us/senate-votes-to-compensate-japanese-american-internees.html and later appropriation of $400,000.

7. Melissa Eddy, "For 60th Year Germany Honors Duty to Pat Holocaust Victims," *New York Times*, November 17, 2012, http://www.nytimes.com/2012/11/18/world/europe/for-60th-year-germany-honors-duty-to-pay-holocaust-victims.html.

8. Reuters Staff, "Greece puts a figure on World War II reparation Claims from Germany," *Reuters*, April 6, 2015, http://www.reuters.com/article/us-eurozone-greece-germany-reparations-idUSKBN0MX1DO20150406; Russian Reparation claims: Damien Sharkov, "Russian Parliament Set to Request €4 Trillion in WWII Repa-

rations from Germany," *Newsweek*, February 3, 2015, http://www.newsweek.com/russian-parliament-set-request-eu4-trillion-wwii-reparations-germany-304163.

9. Gabriel Zucman, *Hidden Wealth of Nations: The Scourge of Tax Havens* (Chicago: University of Chicago Press, 2015). http://www.npr.org/2016/04/04/473004992/the-hidden-wealth-of-nations-author-explores-world-of-offshore-tax-havens.

10. U.S. House of Representatives, hearing on HR40–Reparations Bill, February 17, 2021.

11. Adam Simpson and Carla Sandier, "A conversation with William Darity," The Next System Project, March 2017. http://thenextsystem.org/for-reparations/.

16

The Socialist Case for Reparations

BRIAN P. JONES

The socialist movement is gaining steam in the United States, as evidenced by the dramatic growth of the Democratic Socialists of America, the popularity of media platforms like *Jacobin,* and *Black Socialists of America,* the positive attitude young people express toward the broad ideas of socialism in polls, and the popularity of self-described socialist politicians such as Alexandria Ocasio-Cortez and Bernie Sanders.[1] While there are many different trends within the socialist movement, there is a general agreement that working, poor, and oppressed people ought to join together to defend their interests and that capitalism as we presently experience it is intolerable.

But where do socialists stand on the issue of reparations? Award-winning author Ta-Nehisi Coates, whose 2014 article in *The Atlantic,* "The Case for Reparations" helped reignite a renewed public discussion on this topic, famously supported Sanders in his 2016 presidential campaign, yet also criticized Sanders for not supporting reparations.[2] That same year socialist scholar Cedric Johnson and I briefly exchanged articles in *Jacobin* debating the point. Johnson accused Coates of operating as part of a Black managerial elite whose calls for reparations are really about carving out their "piece" of the American capitalist pie.[3] I responded by explaining why I think a class analysis should lead socialists to support reparations (this chapter is an updated and expanded version of that argument).[4] Johnson wrote a rebuttal, addressing my criticisms, and concluding that there is no political constituency that is prepared to mobilize behind the demand for reparations.[5] As the reparations issue reemerged in broader public discussion in 2019, *Jacobin* founder Bhaskar Sunkara, perhaps the best-known socialist of color in the United

States at present, published an article in *The Guardian* challenging the call for reparations as impractical, even if morally just.[6]

Although Coates does not identify as a socialist, he offers useful critiques for the socialist movement to address, in my view. On the other hand, I think Sanders, Johnson, and Sunkara raise thoughtful objections to the idea of reparations that its supporters must answer. What follows is my attempt to do so. In my view, Sanders was wrong to dismiss the issue of reparations (a stance he has maintained as of this writing).[7] Sunkara and Johnson, like Sanders, acknowledge the legacy of slavery and the ongoing problem of institutional racism, but they propose a different solution: universal reforms that provide an economic "floor" for poor and working people, and therefore, they argue, disproportionately benefit Black Americans and other people of color. In fact, they propose that such programs might be a more effective remedy for the effects of institutional racism than reparations. I, too, support the effort to promote universal reforms. We urgently need tuition-free postsecondary education and Medicare For All. My argument is, in short: these reforms are falsely counterposed to the demand for reparations. This false counterposition becomes clearer when we step away from the logic of electoral politics and think about these issues from a more grassroots perspective. There will never be a socialist movement in the United States that is large enough to win universal programs until its membership consists of millions of non-Black people who see reparations for Black people as justified and righteous. As socialist authors Khury Peterson-Smith and brian bean recently put it, "The battle against class exploitation must also be a struggle against anti-Black racism and vice versa."[8] Socialists should support reparations for Black people as part of building a movement to redistribute wealth and power to all people who are oppressed and exploited under capitalism.

As contemporary socialists work to build the largest, broadest possible movement against exploitation and oppression, the question of how to address the needs and demands of particular sub-groups deserves our attention. "Is [reparations] really the basis that we can build a majoritarian coalition?" Sunkara asks. He counterposes reparations to what he calls "solidaristic policies" that he and Johnson rightly point out have been championed by African Americans for decades. But how do we achieve solidarity? The old socialist slogan, "An injury to one is an injury to all" is worth reconsideration in this context. Socialism is about seeing our collective fates as linked, if not identical. The slogan is meant to rally socialists to the goal of building solidarity, which is not the same thing as unity. People can have unity when their circumstances are identical, and they have identical interests. But solidarity is something different. Solidarity is about realizing the need to support someone else's fight, even if you are not directly affected, because you realize that your fates are linked, and that an injury to someone else today may eventually become a more direct injury to you tomorrow.

The particular "injury to one" in this case—the historic injury to Black Americans is very clearly linked to the development of the system socialists love to hate: capitalism. A bounty of new scholarship on American history has very clearly established slavery's role in birthing a world of generalized commodity production, in the development of innovative financial instruments, and the plantation's role in establishing systems of labor organization for factories, to name a few of the findings.[9] As Matthew Desmond noted in *The New York Times'* "1619 Project," it was slavery that shaped the ruthless style of American capitalism. "Given the choice between modernity and barbarism, prosperity and poverty, lawfulness and cruelty, democracy and totalitarianism," Desmond wrote, "America chose all of the above."[10] Rather than view American slavery as a "mistake" or an oddity, or an issue restricted geographically or temporally to the U.S. South or the seventeenth, eighteenth, and nineteenth centuries, socialists must learn to view it as central to the growth and development of this nation and its political and economic systems, up to the present. Repairing this injury is deeply connected to the project of challenging capitalism.

The right wing conservatives understand that a lot is at stake here. They rightly do not see the new investigations of slavery as a narrow concern, but as a broad issue that threatens the entire edifice of American exceptionalism. Perhaps the most breathless and hyperbolic reaction to the 1619 Project came from conservative commentator Erick Erickson's Twitter account. "If the land in which the United States was founded has been tainted by racism since the 1600s and everything derived therefrom is therefore tainted," Erickson wrote in a tweet, "then the US is illegitimate, the constitution is illegitimate, and revolution is the answer."[11] Putting aside for a moment the fact that the project's lead article by Nikole Hannah-Jones argued that Black people have worked for 400 years to make American democracy a reality, there is an important grain of truth in Erickson's response.[12] Likewise, President Donald Trump's reaction to the removal of a statue of Confederate leader Robert E. Lee was to note that many other so-called Founding Fathers were slave owners and therefore to ask if their statues should come down, too. The president then raised a rhetorical question that, as I noted at the time, was revealing: "Where does it stop?"[13] Essentially the conservative right fears that pulling too hard on this slavery/racism thread threatens to unravel the United States' ideological clothing as inherently righteous, always well-intentioned, only using its military to spread democracy, never harming innocent people on purpose, and so on.

And, unfortunately, the end of slavery did not equal the end of institutional racism. It is now well-documented that this country's pattern of residential segregation was not the result of random, individual choices in the housing market, but a conscious policy enforced at all levels of government, from the municipal to the federal. As Richard Rothstein has argued in a recent book, *The Color of Law,* since rising property values have been the principal method by which people accumulated wealth in the United States in the twentieth century (and particularly after the Second World War), and since Black people were, by government action (de jure, not de facto, in violation of the 14th Amendment) excluded from full participation in the housing market, the U.S. government is obligated to remedy the results what he calls "government-sponsored segregation."[14] "Real estate investment has been the great wealth-generating machine of my parents' generation," legal scholar Katherine Franke writes, "yet African-Americans have been systematically locked out of this unique opportunity to buy, sit tight, and get rich."[15] She cites an estimate of the total wealth that she and other children of baby boomers will inherit from 2007 to 2061: $59 trillion.[16] But what about all of the fair housing legislation that aimed to turn this around? Keeanga-Yamahtta Taylor looks at the workings of the post-1968 U.S. market and argues that once lenders were forced to end the practice of excluding Black people from homeownership, they (in partnership with banks and the federal government) created new financial instruments— such as the now-infamous mortgage backed securities—to prey on them: a method she calls *predatory inclusion.*[17]

The list of injuries is long. Besides the 250 years of uncompensated labor, we can add exclusion from the opportunity to accumulate trillions of dollars through government-subsidized home ownership, followed by several decades of predatory lending. We should also mention mass incarceration, the disproportionate patterns of policing and sentencing that have torn millions of Black Americans from their homes and communities, deprived them of the ability to make a living, and separated them from the right to vote.[18] To this list we should add forced sterilization, racist child welfare policies, and the historic pattern of throwing up obstacles to providing equitable educational resources to Black students.[19]

We can learn from this that racism is flexible and dynamic. It is not merely a vestigial product of slavery, not some phantom from the past, but something which survives because it can be adapted in new forms to serve new functions. Its original purpose was the justification of enslavement in the land of the "free," but it survived the destruction of slavery because it was adapted to new purposes—plural. We cannot reduce racism's function as a matter of divide and conquer. Racism was a useful weapon in the struggle to restore the South's single-crop commodity agriculture system.[20] Racism was and is useful in justifying imperial violence abroad.[21] Racism has been useful as a means of suppressing radical domestic social movements.[22] Racism remains a useful way to create domestic scapegoats to deflect anger away from elites (yes, dividing and conquering).[23] And racism remains profitable, creating markets in education, housing, and employment for people made vulnerable by its logic.[24]

Since racism is so central to the functioning of capitalism, anti-racism must be central to any movement that hopes to challenge it. The specific legacy of racism in the United States must be addressed if we are to ever have any hope of winning the kinds of progressive legislation that Bernie Sanders is proposing. Indeed, if we had to sum up in a single word the reason we have thus far failed to adopt a national social welfare system on anything approaching the scale of other advanced industrialized countries, the answer would have to be: racism.[25] Rather than counterpose these agendas, we should fuse them: we need to push for the redistribution of wealth on a vast scale and argue that such an effort should aim specifically to repair the legacy of anti-Black racism. Doing one without the other is a recipe for disaster.

But how to repair a historic injury whose participants on both sides are no longer present? Johnson and Sunkara are correct that providing reparations to formerly enslaved people is one thing and providing them to the descendants of formerly enslaved people is another. Sunkara and Johnson conclude that the problem is too difficult or complex to solve. The same legal strategy that successfully won reparations for Holocaust survivors or Japanese internment "in all likelihood" cannot apply here, Johnson argues, because slavery was an intergenerational offense that therefore lacks a legal category of victim. Sunkara, too, wonders what kind of bureaucracy would figure out who was a descendent of an enslaved person, and contemplates the dilemma of asking a poor Latino immigrant to fund, through income tax, reparations payments to those people.

These categorical rejections of the issue are not the way socialists should think about reparations—or any other reforms, for that matter, for three reasons. First, all reforms are narrow, partial, and insufficient, but we don't have to approach them with a narrow perspective. When teachers go on strike and win modest wage increases, we don't chastise them for failing to fight for higher wages for all workers, or for failing to abolish wage labor. The demand for reparation's foremost articulation, at this moment, is the HR 40 legislation that would form a commission to study the effects of U.S. slavery and to propose recommendations for remedies.[26] It would be one thing to speak out against a conservative or problematic formulation of the reparations demand, but for a socialist to vocally oppose even the extremely modest call for studying the issue means that they place all possible proposals for reparations beyond the realm of worthy consideration. That should be an untenable position for a socialist.

There are, we must acknowledge, reparations proposals that are problematic. There exists a group of people who, calling themselves American Descendants of Slaves (#ADOS), support reparations, but on an extremely narrow basis—for themselves only, and not for any other Black Americans. This is essentially a right-wing, anti-immigrant formation and one that socialists should reject and work against. Reparations does not have to take the form of individual cash payments to people who can prove themselves to be American Descendants of Slaves or can prove themselves to be "Black" Americans. Secondly, we don't have to have every detail in place before supporting a general policy, and it's not difficult to imagine reparations proposals that socialists should support. Many advocates of reparations, such as the National Coalition of Blacks for Reparations in America, have argued that they could take the form of collective supports, such as endowments for historically Black colleges and universities, or community development— thereby targeting Black communities collectively but not necessarily Black people individually.[27] Thirdly, there is no reason that reparations must necessarily be an income-tax supported program. There are countless institutions—corporations, banks, universities, and so on—that owe their existence to the profits they extracted from enslaved people: New York Life, AIG, Wells Fargo, Georgetown University, Harvard University, and many, many more.[28]

What about the lack of a political constituency for the reparations demand? Johnson laments the fact that he never hears Black people bringing up this issue in organizing discussions. Yes, reparations may not be the kind of immediate goal that dominates the agenda of weekly union or coalition meetings, but neither is socialism. Socialists shouldn't be afraid of advocating for minority positions and taking up ideas that are, temporarily, not possible or may even be unpopular. But how did this come to be the case? As Ana Lucia Araujo observes in a recent book on the topic, the reparations demand has actually emerged repeatedly in Black American social movements.[29] Beginning in 1897 with the first national organization of formerly enslaved people who demanded reparations in this country in the form of the National Ex-Slave Mutual Relief, Bounty and Pension Association led by Isaiah Dickerson and Callie House, each subsequent attempt to gather mass support for reparations was met with well-documented persecution by the federal government.[30] Even though it could not identify any victims, movement leaders had to repeatedly defend themselves in court. Having built an organization of some 300,000 people, Callie House was arrested for mail fraud in 1916 and convicted by an all-white jury in 1917. Essentially the exact same thing happened to the next wave of leaders to take up the cause in the 1920s, and the pattern continued down to the more recent examples of Black nationalists such as the Black Panther Party and the Republic of New Afrika, which also raised the idea of reparations in the 1960s and 1970s and faced even more brutal repression.[31] If the idea of reparations isn't on everyone's lips, this history is certainly part of the reason.

Furthermore, socialists can and should support all kinds of ideals before we have a mass constituency for them. And when it comes to building that constituency, we have to use our socialist common sense to evaluate what to support and what to reject. Of course, knocking on doors in poor and working-class neighborhoods asking non-Black people to cough up money for reparations is a dead end. But talking to those same people about what J.P. Morgan Chase or Citibank owes to Black people in this country is a different question.[32] That is no different from talking to non-immigrant people about the need to lend material support to the struggle for immigrant rights or talking to men about the need to stand up for equal rights for women. It is about solidarity. What Sunkara calls "solidaristic policies"—programs that promote universal welfare—are not the policies that actually demonstrate solidarity. Solidarity is about recognizing a shared, but not identical, interest. Solidarity is supporting a demand even if you are not the direct beneficiary. If white supremacy is crucial to upholding American capitalism, then socialists should see the task of educating people about what this country owes Black people as an urgent task. Both universal welfare programs and reparations are important, both hold out the prospect of improving people's lives in tangible ways. Sunkara agrees that universal programs alone are insufficient—he supports affirmative action and other remedies specifically aimed at dealing with the legacy of racism. This "both and" approach is how we should view the urgency of fighting for Medicare for All alongside reparations.

It is important to have a socialist movement that is willing to speak and think and act beyond what politicians like Bernie Sanders are willing to support. The kind of redistribution Sanders is talking about falls far short of the genuine democratic control over our own working lives that Karl Marx proposed; it also falls short of what is needed to truly end poverty in this country. But these are not reasons to oppose his proposals. Sanders's proposals are a threat to America's elite because they would shift the balance of power between labor and capital. If there was no such thing as health care bills or college tuition and if every job paid at least fifteen dollars an hour, working class people in general—and Black people, in particular—would be in a much stronger position to speak up, organize, and fight for everything that we are collectively owed. Coates was wrong to argue that Sanders's proposals represent the same kind of "rising tide lifts all boats" concept that Obama followed. Obama was a neoliberal president from the beginning; his policies decisively shifted the balance of power in favor of capital. As I wrote elsewhere, Obama's emphasis on privatizing public education and crippling teachers unions has had a disproportionately negative impact on Black teachers and has been a harbinger of further attacks on one of the last bastions of Black people's wealth—public sector unions.[33]

I assume that reparations left critics—like Sunkara and Johnson—agree with much of what I have written here about the connection between racism and capitalism (Sunkara calls for a "cultural reckoning" with the legacy of slavery[34]). Even if reparations are not winnable in the short term, even if they can't be an immediate priority for organizing, even if majorities haven't yet been won to support them, why speak out against them? Sunkara admits that "the moral case for reparations is undeniable." But millions of people have not yet come around to that point of view, and the socialist movement would be in a better position if it did.

Bernie Sanders is bringing the word "socialism" back into the mainstream and is raising the idea that America needs to redistribute wealth. Those are good things. Unfortunately, he is doing so inside a party that has diametrically opposite goals—the Democratic Party. Whether or not he prevails, I hope a new generation of people rediscover the socialist tradition. We desperately need a large socialist party in this country; the Democrats are never going to be that party, we're going to have to make our own. The reparations discussion is re-emerging now because a new movement of Black people is fighting state-sponsored violence and pushing for a more truthful examination of the country's history. This movement is already rediscovering the brilliant work of Black socialists, such as W. E. B. Du Bois, C.L.R. James, Angela Davis, and many others, holding out the hope that these two trends can be fused, thereby becoming significantly more powerful. These Black socialists teach us that the struggle against racism and the struggle against capitalism cannot be separated from each other and that we will never defeat one without tearing down the other. As Harlem-based socialist Hubert Harrison famously put it one hundred years ago, "the mission of the Socialist Party is to free the working class from exploitation, and since the Negro is the most ruthlessly exploited working class group in America, the duty of the party to champion his cause is as clear as day." This, Harrison continued, "is the crucial test of Socialism's sincerity . . . "[35] Sadly, the socialist movement has not always passed this test, but the trends of the twenty-first century present a new opportunity to do so. If we can do it, many changes and transformations that have long seemed impossible will come within our reach.

Notes

1. Marcy Tracy, "Is 'Bernie or Bust' the Future of the Left?" *The New York Times,* August 6, 2019, https://www.nytimes.com/2019/08/06/us/politics/bernie-sanders -democratic-socialists-america.html; Teddy Ostrow, "Black Socialists of America Is Putting Anti-Capitalism on the Map," *The Nation,* August 28, 2019, https://www .thenation.com/article/black-socialists-of-america-interview-z/; Mohamed Younis, "Four in 10 Americans Embrace Some Form of Socialism," *Gallup,* May 20, 2019, https://news.gallup.com/poll/257639/four-americans-embrace-form-socialism.aspx.

2. Ta-Nehisi Coates, "The Case for Reparations," *The Atlantic,* June 2014; and "Why Precisely is Bernie Sanders Against Reparations?" *The Atlantic,* January 19, 2016. Links: https://www.theatlantic.com/magazine/archive/2014/06/the-case-for -reparations/361631/ and https://www.theatlantic.com/politics/archive/2016/01/bernie -sanders-reparations/424602/.

3. Cedric Johnson, "An Open Letter to Ta-Nehisi Coates and the Liberals Who Love Him," *Jacobin,* February 3, 2016. https://www.jacobinmag.com/2016/02/ta-nehisi -coates-case-for-reparations-bernie-sanders-racism/.

4. Brian Jones, "The Socialist Case for Reparations," *Jacobin,* March 1, 2016. https:// www.jacobinmag.com/2016/03/reparations-ta-nehisi-coates-cedric-johnson-bernie -sanders/.

5. Cedric Johnson, "Reparations Isn't a Political Demand," *Jacobin,* March 7, 2016. https://www.jacobinmag.com/2016/03/cedric-johnson-brian-jones-ta-nehisi-coates -reparations.

6. Bhaskar Sunkara, "To Fight Racism, We Need to Think Beyond Reparations," *The Guardian,* March 28, 2019, https://www.theguardian.com/commentisfree/2019/ mar/28/racism-reparations-democratic-candidates.

7. John Bowden, "Sanders on Reparations: There Are Better Ways Than 'Just Writing a Check,'" *The Hill,* March 1, 2019, https://thehill.com/homenews/campaign/432254 -sanders-on-reparations-there-are-better-ways-than-just-writing-a-check.

8. Khury Peterson-Smith and brian bean, "Socialists and the Case for Reparations," *SocialistWorker.org*, March 3, 2016, https://socialistworker.org/2016/03/03/socialists -and-the-case-for-reparations.

9. Edward Baptiste, *The Half Has Never Been Told: Slavery and the Making of American Capitalism* (New York: Basic Books, 2016); Sven Beckert, *Empire of Cotton: A Global History* (New York: Vintage, 2015).

10. Matthew Desmond, "In order to understand the brutality of American capitalism, you have to start on the plantation," *The New York Times Magazine: 1619 Project*, August 14, 2019. https://www.nytimes.com/interactive/2019/08/14/magazine/slavery -capitalism.html.

11. Erick Erickson Twitter account: @EWErickson, August 18, 2019. https://twitter .com/EWErickson/status/1163210628703707136.

12. Nikole Hannah-Jones, "Our Democracy's Ideals Were False When They Were Written. Black Americans Have Fought to Make Them True," *The New York Times Magazine: 1619 Project*, August 14, 2019, https://www.nytimes.com/interactive/ 2019/08/14/magazine/black-history-american-democracy.html.

13. Brian Jones, "Trump Asked, 'Where Does It Stop?' That's Actually a Good Question," *Verso Blog*, August 18, 2017, https://www.versobooks.com/blogs/3364-trump-asked -where-does-it-stop-that-s-actually-a-good-question.

14. Richard Rothstein, *The Color of Law: A Forgotten History of How Our Government Segregated America* (New York: Liveright Publishing Corporation, 2017).

15. Katherine Franke, *Repair: Redeeming the Promise of Abolition* (Chicago: Haymarket Books, 2019) 137.

16. Ibid., 136.

17. Keeanga-Yamahtta Taylor, *Race for Profit: How Banks and the Real Estate Industry Undermined Black Homeownership* (Chapel Hill: University of North Carolina Press, 2019).

18. Michelle Alexander, *The New Jim Crow: Mass Incarceration in the Age of Colorblindness* (New York: The New Press, 2010).

19. Don Lash, *When the Welfare People Come: Race and Class in the U.S. Child Protection System*. Haymarket Books, 2017; Brian Jones, "The Struggle for Black Education," in *Education and Capitalism: Struggles for Learning and Liberation*, Jeff Bale and Sarah Knopp, eds. (Chicago: Haymarket Books, 2012).

20. Beckert, Empire of Cotton; see also Barbara J. Fields, "The Nineteenth Century American South: History and Theory," *Plantation Society, 2,* No 1 (April, 1983): 7–27.

21. Deepa Kumar, *Islamaphobia and the Politics of Empire* (Chicago: Haymarket Books, 2012).

22. Angela Y. Davis, *Are Prisons Obsolete?* (New York: Seven Stories Press, 2003).

23. Keeanga-Yamahtta Taylor, *From #BlackLives Matter to Black Liberation* (Chicago: Haymarket Books, 2016).

24. See, for example: Noliwe Rooks, *Cutting School: Privatization, Segregation, and the End of Public Education* (New York: The New Press, 2017).

25. Janeen Interlandi, "Why Doesn't the United States Have Universal Health Care? The Answer Has Everything to Do with Race," *The New York Times Magazine: 1619 Project,* August 14, 2019, https://www.nytimes.com/interactive/2019/08/14/magazine/universal-health-care-racism.html.

26. Rep. Sheila Jackson-Lee, H.R. 40, A Commission to Study and Develop Reparation Proposals for African-Americans Act, 116th Congress (2019–2020), January 3, 2019. https://www.congress.gov/bill/116th-congress/house-bill/40/text.

27. National Coalition of Blacks for Reparations in America. http://ncobra.org.

28. Rachel L. Swarns, "Insurance Policies On Slaves: New York Life's Complicated Past," *The New York Times,* December 18, 2016. https://www.nytimes.com/2016/12/18/us/insurance-policies-on-slaves-new-york-lifes-complicated-past.html.

29. Ana Lucia Araujo, *Reparations for Slavery and the Slave Trade: A Transnational and Comparative History* (New York: Bloomsbury Academic, 2017).

30. Ibid., 99–108, 184.

31. Ibid., 143–4.

32. James C. Cobb, "Cleansing American Culture of Ties to Slavery Will Be Harder Thank You Think," *Time,* March 30, 2016. https://time.com/4274901/slavery-traces-history/.

33. Brian Jones, "Keys to the Schoolhouse: Black Teachers, Privatization, and the Future of Teacher Unions," in *What's Race Got To Do With It?: How Current School Reform Policy Maintains Racial and Economic Inequality,* ed., Bree Picower and Edwin Mayorga (New York: Peter Lang, 2014).

34. Sunkara, "To fight racism . . . "

35. Hubert Harrison, *The Negro and the Nation* (New York: Cosmo-Advocate Publishing Co, 1917), 22.

17

Reparations

Democrats, Universalism, and the African American Struggle for Autonomy

SUNDIATA KEITA CHA-JUA

> The way we can best take care of ourselves is to have land, and turn it and till it by our own labor . . . I would prefer to live by ourselves, for there is a prejudice against us in the South that will take years to get over.
>
> —Rev. Garrison Frazier, January 12, 1865

> Both American Indians and African Americans have momentous claims arising from historical wrongs, but their goals sharply diverge . . . Indians seek money claims for past injuries, but most Indian claims are rooted in tribal culture, governance, and land. Indians and tribes are interested in self-determination, the right to live in their traditional homelands and govern that land . . . But while African-Americans eye individual payments, Indian tribes seek control over lands and natural resources taken from them by the United States and state governments. The advantage in the tribal strategy is to make Uncle Sam the bad guy. African-American strategists should take note.
>
> —Matthew Fletcher, *New York Times*, June 9, 2014

I begin this chapter with two epigrams. One from a meeting between twenty delegates from the newly freedpeople in Savannah, Georgia, with U.S. Secretary of War Edwin Stanton and General Tecumseh Sherman on January 12, 1865, and the other by Indigenous scholar Matthew Fletcher. Sherman and Stanton asked the twenty African American delegates twelve questions.

I want to highlight the group's spokesperson the Rev. Garrison Frazier's answers to two questions. In response to a question as to how they could best take care of themselves, Frazier observed, "The way we can best take care of ourselves is to have land and turn it and till it by our own labor." And when asked specifically, "State in what manner you would rather live—whether scattered among the whites or in colonies by yourselves," Frazier declared, "I would prefer to live by ourselves, for there is a prejudice against us in the South that will take years to get over." All but one of the other delegates affirmed Frazier's answer. I believe the delegation spoke for most of the freedpeople across the South. Four days after this discussion, Sherman issued Special Field Order #15.[1]

In June of 2014, Matthew Fletcher, a Chippewa Indian, challenged African Americans to learn from Indigenous peoples' approach to reparations. He commented, "Both American Indians and African Americans have momentous claims arising from historical wrongs, but their goals sharply diverge . . . Indians seek money claims for past injuries, but most Indian claims are rooted in tribal culture, governance, and land. Indians and tribes are interested in self-determination, the right to live in their traditional homelands and govern that land . . . But while African-Americans eye individual payments, Indian tribes seek control over lands and natural resources taken from them by the United States and state governments . . . African-American strategists should take note."[2]

At the heart of Fletcher's criticism lies the tension between the African American and American Indian racial formations, forms of colonialism—internal or domestic and settler colonialism—and social consciousnesses. It is essentially the differences between peoples who have dual sovereignty and a people who experience severely curtailed and degraded inclusion—incorporation into the economy, representation in the polity, and citizenship rights—nonetheless fall completely under the governance of the United States' federal system. Simply put, the various Indian nations exercise semi-sovereignty; they have governments which make binding decisions about a wide range of internal relations and African Americans do not.

Because U.S. law recognizes Indians as both members of distinct nations and as individual citizens of the United States, they have dual citizenship, membership in a tribal nation and citizenship in the United States. Therefore, Indians are accorded limited group-based rights. That is, the federal government interacts with them through "government-to-government relationship[s]," as well as individual U.S. citizens and members of an interest group.[3] As citizens of "domestic dependent nations,"[4] American Indian sovereignty is circumscribed; nonetheless, the U.S. government recognizes them as semi-sovereign corporate entities. Indians' "limited sovereignty" grants them much more autonomy than African Americans exercise. They have the power to regulate their internal affairs; determine their form of government and citizenship requirements; exercise police and judicial powers over members, and in some cases over non-members; administer health-care systems; and manage cultural resources, including schooling.[5] Thus, as Fletcher argues, Indian claims focus on expanding areas of cultural preservation, self-governance, and land.

Following the American Indian model, I argue that as a distinct people, a separate nationality, African Americans' political relationship to the U.S. state should mirror the positives, the more autonomic aspects of the American Indian nations'—dual sovereignty (pending liberation). Black people should be treated as both individual citizens of the United States and as members of an African-American "nation within a nation or more precisely, a nation within an empire," which like American Indian nations should exercise considerable power over our internal social relations. The struggle for reparations is the best pathway toward building dual power and positioning us for a self-determined future.[6]

This chapter has four central goals: (1) to briefly outline the history of the African American reparations movement; (2) to distinguish African American reparations from universalist approaches; (3) to promote reparations as the mechanism for the revitalization and democratization of African American civil society; and (4) to present reparations as *essentially* a *political project* to build collective group power and to advance *autonomic* solutions, for the African American people.

A Brief Historical Sketch of the Reparations Movement and Its Recent Resurgence

The pursuit of reparations is the oldest specific demand by African people in North America. It recurs each generation. The cry for reparations predates the U.S. Constitution. On February 14, 1783, Belinda Sutton petitioned the Commonwealth of Massachusetts claiming that after years of oppression, "she, by the Laws of the Land, is denied the enjoyment of one morsel of that immense wealth, apart whereof hath been accumulated by her own industry, and the whole augmented by her servitude." Sutton clearly understood that her labor had enriched Isaac Royall, her former owner. Moreover, she believed and demanded compensation for the superexploitation of her labor.[7]

Sutton's cry for redress and affirmation of her right to restitution would be rearticulated by Black people throughout the nineteenth century. It would reach its loudest expression in the National Ex-Slave Mutual Relief, Bounty and Pension Association (ESMRBPA), 1896–1918. Since the demise of ESMRBPA, the African American quest for reparations has been primarily pursued by small radical nationalistic organizations such as the Black Panther Party, the Republic of New Africa (RNA), and more recently the National Coalition of Blacks for Reparations in America (N'COBRA) and led largely by nationalist advocates such as Alexander Anderson, Queen Mother Moore, and Muhammad Ahmad (Max Stanford).[8]

In the century since state repression destroyed ESMRBPA, the issue of African American reparations has periodically intruded into mainstream public discourse. The first such incident was when James Forman, the former Executive Director of the Student Non-Violent Coordinating Committee (SNCC), boldly strode into Riverside Baptist Church on May 4, 1969, and delivered *The Black Manifesto*, the National Black Economic Conference (NBEC). Since the heady days of 1960s (1955–1979), the quest for African American reparations has with increasing regularity gushed up from the dark seabed of the *Black counterpublic* into the country's public sphere.[9] Twenty years after Forman issued the *Black Manifesto*, Michigan Congressman John Conyers proposed HR 40. The late 1990s and early 2000s represented another moment in which the quest for reparations coursed into public awareness. Central to the rise of reparations during this moment was the formation of the National Coalition of Blacks for Reparations (N'COBRA) in 1987;[10] the publication of Randall Robinson's *The Debt: What Is Owed Blacks*; Attorney Daedria Farmer-Paellman's groundbreaking suit against capitalist corporations, Aetna, FleetBoston Financial Corporation, and the CSX Corporation; and Mary Frances Berry's *My Face Is Black Is True,* which recovered the life and work of Callie House and the ESMRBPA. And in the second decade of the new millennium, Ta-Nehisi Coates's highly persuasive 2014 *Atlantic* essay "The Case for Reparations" transformed the issue from a joke into a question to be taken seriously.[11]

Reparations for African Americans has recently resurged into mainstream discourse. Most of the top-tier candidates for the Democratic Party's 2020 presidential nomination supported HR 40, a bill to establish a federal commission to study and develop proposals to remedy the legacy of slavery and racial discrimination. Texas Congresswoman Sheila Jackson Lee's revised HR 40 bill proposes Congress create a commission to study, consider an apology, and recommend remedies for enslavement and subsequent racial and economic discrimination.[12] However, despite its current vogue, the issue of redress, restitution, and repair for anti-Black racial oppression/domestic colonialism during and since enslavement remains engulfed in misunderstanding. Many prominent recent converts confuse reparations with universal programs to eliminate poverty, abolish racial discrimination, and create economic opportunity. This confusion characterizes the so-called reparations proposals of most of the former Democratic presidential candidates.

In a discussion with NPR, former Senator, now Vice President Kamala Harris offered African Americans' higher rates of heart disease and high blood pressure as reasons why African Americans should receive reparations. She explained, "It is environmental. It is centuries of slavery, which was a form of violence where women were raped, where children were taken from their parents—violence associated with slavery. And that there was never any real intervention to break up what had been generations of people experiencing the highest forms of trauma." Continuing, she argued, "But it's generational only because the environment has not experienced a significant enough change to reverse the symptoms. You need to put resources and direct resources—extra resources—into those communities that have experienced that trauma."[13] As one solution, Harris proposes the LIFT Act, a plan to provide families who earn $100,000 or less a tax credit. Senator Harris's website describes the LIFT Act as "the largest tax cut for working Americans in a generation" and claims half of Americans would benefit, "including 60% of Black families."[14] This same logic, that a universal program will disproportionately aid African Americans, also frames Senator Elizabeth Warren's American Mobility and Economic Act proposal.

Warren told *Reuters*, "We must confront the dark history of slavery and government-sanctioned discrimination in this country that has had many consequences including undermining the ability of Black families to build wealth in America for generations."[15] She would "confront" the United States history of racial oppression by providing 500 billion dollars through the American Mobility and Economic Act to "build, preserve, and rehab" affordable housing for "low-income families." Warren contends investment in affordable housing development would reduce rental cost by 10 percent, "close the racial wealth gap," and "create 1.5 million new jobs."[16] Harris and Warren promote their universal plans as reparations programs because they expect African American families to disproportionately benefit.

Proposals by other former Democratic presidential contenders such as New Jersey Senator Cory Booker's "Baby Bonds" and South Bend, Indiana, Mayor Peter Buttigeig's "Douglass Plan" are either universal class-based programs or Affirmative Action type plans masquerading as reparations programs. Booker's universal program would grant every child at least $1,000 at birth. And after that, based on family income, with those with lower incomes getting more, as much as $2,000 per year would be deposited in each child's account. Booker and Buttigieg did not publicize their plans as reparations proposals, as such; in fact, both acknowledged *in the fine print* that they were not. However, because politicians, pundits, and the public assume Black people will disproportionately be aided by universalist programs, these types of policy initiatives are confused with reparation proposals.[17]

After more than a century as a meandering tributary barely incorporated into the mainstream of the Black Liberation movement, the struggle for reparations has been transformed into a mighty tidal wave. Today, the issue of reparations is cascading down on the U.S. political landscape. The deluge forced all of the top-tier 2020 Democratic Party presidential candidates to endorse revised HR 40 and S. 1083 bills. And even more significantly, on June 19, 2019, Juneteenth,[18] the House Judiciary Subcommittee on the Constitution, Civil Rights and Civil Liberties held a historic hearing on reparations. Nancy Pelosi, the Speaker of the House of Representatives, and Senate Minority Leader Chuck Schumer both endorsed HR 40 and S. 1083's call for the establishment of a commission to study and recommend remedies for slavery and its legacies of racial oppression.[19]

The contemporary rise of reparations in U.S. politics represents a genuine sea change. It reflects a transformation in consciousness that has gradually swelled since the 1990s. At the end of the twentieth century and during the initial years of the new millennium, the reparations undercurrent burst into the mainstream of the Black counterpublic and gradually emerged as a significant issue on African Americans' political agenda. Since 1991, liberal Black organizations such as the National Association for the Advancement of Colored People (NAACP), the Southern Christian Leadership Conference (SCLC), the National Bar Association, and numerous fraternities, sororities, and professional organizations have endorsed the concept of reparations. *The acceptance and advocacy of reparations by the civil rights mainstream—the liberal and moderate incorporative wings of the Black liberation movement comes with benefits and deficits; it both advances and retards our struggle for redress, restitution, and repair as liberal and moderate civil righters generally substitute universal programs for genuine reparations.*

Universalism v. Race Specific Policies

The notion that African Americans compose a "nation within a nation" sharply contrasts with the United States' foundational premise of universalism. Universalist approaches to abolishing racial inequality reject race-conscious remedies and advocate policies aimed at the entire society, rather than the aggrieved group. Universalism is premised on the alleged equality of all individuals before the law. The idealized U.S. universalist view is false. First, as Harold Cruse forcefully argued in *The Crisis of the Negro Intellectual*, the United States promotes the doctrine of individuality as paramount, but in reality, it is riven by disputes rooted in class and race/ethnicity/nationality as well as gender, generation, and sexuality. It is a class society and has many racial formations. Second, universalism presumes that individuality determines Black peoples' life chances, rather than membership in a racially oppressed group. Yet, the African American sociohistorical experience testifies that the system of racial oppression determines the fate of Black folk more than individual merit. Referencing Dr. Ralph Bunce, the first African American to win the Nobel Peace Prize, Dr. Martin Luther King, Jr., observed, "To the racist, he, like every Negro, lacks individuality. He is a member of a defective group."[20]

Whereas universalist proposals such as Booker's "Baby Bonds," Harris's "Lift Act," Warren's "American Mobility and Economic Act," and Bernie Sanders' "Jobs for All" are mitigated by their attentiveness to class, Andrew Yang's "Freedom Dividend" ignores all social attributes, except age. It "would give $1,000 to every American over the age of 18."[21] While the class-based universalist economic initiatives of Booker, Harris, Warren, and Sanders would be quite helpful and would disproportionately benefit African Americans, none of these policy approaches would be transformative, close the racial wealth gap in a reasonable time, or more importantly, secure Black people's capacity to determine their own fate, because none of them directly address the structure and ideologies of racial oppression. And Yang's proposal would not impact the racial wealth gap or class disparities because it would redistribute the same amount of money to every adult citizen.

In *Why We Can't Wait*, King offered a possible resolution to the universalism versus race conscious solutions to anti-Black racial oppression. In 1964, King advocated for a class-based universalist redistribution of wealth through a "gigantic Bill of Rights for the Disadvantaged." However, because he believed "something special" had been done "*against* the Negro for hundreds of years" he wanted to do "something special *for* him now." Therefore, King advocated, "The payment . . . in the form of a massive program by the government of special, compensatory measures" to the African American people.[22]

While his explicit argument for reparations was significant, especially in 1964, only a year after Queen Mother Audley Moore founded the Committee for Reparations for the Descendants of U.S. Slaves and published *Why*

Reparations? Reparations is the Battle Cry for the Economic and Social Free-dom of More than 25 Million Descendants of American Slaves, King's proposal is flawed. It adheres to the U.S. creed of individualism. Though largely un-specified, his proposition seems to target African Americans as individuals. In that sense it falls short of the community-building policy proscriptions outlined by James Forman in *The Black Manifesto.* Among the ten demands advocated by Forman were a "Southern land bank," "four major publishing and printing industries," "four advanced scientific and futuristic audial-visual network[s]," an organizer training center, $10 million to "assist" the National Welfare Organization, and a $20 million Black Worker Strike and Defense Fund.[23] Furthermore, in contrast to BEDC's program for self-determination, King envisioned reparations as a vehicle to absorb African Americans "into the mainstream of American life."[24]

Unlike universal programs, The Black Manifesto treats African Ameri-cans as both individuals and as a collectivity. It is essential that a reparations policy initiative recognize both aspects of our relationship to the U.S. political economy, polity, civil society, and culture. Since universal programs evade the duality of the African American colonial relationship, we should draw lessons from a framework that acknowledges the historical particularity of racially oppressed peoples, the dual sovereignty model of American Indians.

Learning from Indigenous Nations

One path out of the United States' crippling commitment to an anti-demo-cratic society is to replace its individualist majoritarian state with a conso-ciational polity. The dual sovereignty exercised by American Indians offers a circumscribed version of such a social system. U.S. law, which recognizes American Indians as "domestic dependent nations," is Janus faced in that it simultaneously treats Indigenous people as individual citizens of the U.S. state and as members of separate semi-sovereign nations. In discussing the dual nature of American Indian sovereignty, African American Supreme Court Justice Thurgood Marshall captured its contradictory character when he observed in *SANTA CLARA PUEBLO v. MARTINEZ* (1978), all "aspect[s] of tribal sovereignty . . . [are] subject to the superior and plenary control of Congress," but, because Indians "remain a 'separate people, with the power of regulating their internal and social relations,' they retain a substantial measure of sovereignty."[25] Subordinated by their settler colonial relationships with the United States, American Indian nations exercise a weak form of dual power. Nonetheless, they practice a much higher level of self-determination than do African Americans.

As Fletcher suggests, dual sovereignty pushes indigenous demands for reparations away from individual payments and toward a focus on increasing autonomy, control over cultural practices, and land. I agree with him that African Americans' pursuit of reparations "should take note" of American Indian strategies. To do so would subordinate individual payments to collective endeavors.[26]

The Black Manifesto offers an intriguing starting point. Reacquisition of land taken through racial pogroms, ethnic cleansing, and fraud should be at the top of any African American reparations proposal. BEDC's focus on creating a collectively owned communications infrastructure was also prescient. At the core of any reparations proposal should be policies that accent collective development and political autonomy. The struggle for reparations offers an opportunity to strengthen our institutional infrastructure, and thereby improve the lives of the Black working-class majority by facilitating the creation of an internal governing apparatus.

Conclusion

Many prominent recent converts confuse reparations with universal programs to abolish racial discrimination, eliminate poverty, and create economic opportunity. Attorneys Adjoa A. Aiyetoro and Adrienne D. Davis contend "there can be a tendency to conflate reparations with civil rights, to cast the claims of reparations activists so broadly that it is no longer distinguishable from broader calls for Black equality."[27] The former Democratic presidential candidates and Party leaders who have endorsed remedies for enslavement and its legacies view reparations as *congruent* with the strategic vision of the Civil Rights movement. Nor do any of them envision a role for everyday African Americans in the *construction* and *ratification* of reparation proposals. For the liberal-moderate sector of the Black Liberation movement, reparations are a means to incorporate African Americans into the U.S. capitalist system and state, albeit on a more equitable basis.

The struggle for reparations is both an objective and a process for building autonomy to achieve self-determination. It should serve to revitalize and democratize Black civil society and build a governing apparatus. Reparations requires the Black community to develop a process for making political decisions independent of the U.S. electoral system. It offers a real opportunity to discuss, organize, and initiate policies and programs around fundamental issues of representation, accountability, and political and economic interests. Therefore, it should not be a top-down affair.

What is needed is a democratic process in which the African American people deliberate and develop a reparations proposal. This process requires building mass-based peoples assemblies in each African American community, electing delegates, and holding a convention in which the will of the Black masses is manifested in a reparations proposal. It would necessitate the election of a leadership team who would facilitate the presentation of a proposal to Afro-America for ratification. Only then should it be submitted to Congress.

Afro-America's demand for reparations turns on the need for redress, restitution, and repair for damages inflicted by the U.S. domestic colonial project. I believe reparations must be *transformative*. I view it is a movement to *completely change* African Americans' *social condition* and *political relationship* to the United States. Reparations should *revitalize* and *remake* Black civil society by creating an *autonomous political decision-making apparatus* and cooperative institutions. I contend that reparations should simultaneously be seen as an *objective*, but more importantly, as a *means* for strengthening and democratizing Black civil society. At a minimum, it should generate *dual power*. I believe reparations should *repair* the fundamental wrong—the subjugation of our ancestors, the taking of their autonomy—sovereignty. For me, American Indians dual sovereignty represents a starting point for reimagining African Americans' relationship to the U.S. state. I view the reparations movement as inherently a struggle for self-determination. It is a struggle for autonomy, independent nationhood, emigration, or "a consociational democracy."[28]

Notes

1. "Newspaper Account of a Meeting Between Black Religious Leaders and Military Authorities," Freedman and Southern Society Project, http://www.freedmen.umd.edu/savmtg.htm. Clipping from *New-York Daily Tribune*, [13 Feb. 1865], "Negroes of Savannah," Consolidated Correspondence File, series 225, Central Records, Quartermaster General, Record Group 92, National Archives.

2. Matthew Fletcher, *New York Times*, June 9, 4:09 PM, 2014; https://www.nytimes.com/roomfordebate/ 2014/06/08/are-reparations-due-to-african-americans/american-indians-seek-control-not-just-reparations.

3. Vine De Loria, Jr., and Clifford M. Lytle, *The Nations Within: The Past and Future of American Indian Sovereignty* (Austin: University of Texas Press, 1984), 7; David E.

Wilkins, "African Americans and Aboriginal Peoples: Similarities and Differences in Historical Experiences," *Cornell Law Review* Volume 90 Issue 2 January 2005.

4. *Cherokee Nation v. Georgia*, 30 U.S. 1 (1831), https://supreme.justia.com/cases/federal/us/30/1/; Porter, Robert Odawi. "The Inapplicability of American Law to Indian Nations," *Iowa L. Review* 89 (2004): 1602.

5. Phillip P. Frickey, "Domesticating Federal Indian Law," *Minnesota L. Review* 2092 (1996): 31–32, https://scholarship.law.umn.edu/mlr/2092.

6. V.I. Lenin, "Dual Power," *Lenin Collected Works*, (Moscow: Progress Publishers, *Volume 24*, 1964), 38–41; Delio Vasquez, "Intercommunalism: The Late Theorizations of Huey P. Newton, 'Chief Theoretician' of the Black Panther Party," *Viewpoint Magazine*, 19–22, https://www.viewpointmag.com/2018/06/11/intercommunalism-the-late-theorizations-of-huey-p-newton-chief-theoretician-of-the-black-panther-party/.

7. Going back to the 17th century, enslaved Africans had filed freedom suits before the colonial courts. However, the first freedom petition to a state legislature was submitted by "Felix" on behalf of "many slaves" to the Massachusetts Governor and the legislature. Other petitions followed. Belinda Sutton's petition was filed during the same period. See "Felix's Petition" Africans in America, Part 2: "Revolution," 1750–1805, *PBS*, https://www.pbs.org/ wgbh/ aia/part2/2h22.html; "Four Petitions for Freedom," *History as a Weapon*, https://www.historyisaweapon.com/defcon1/fourpetitionsagainstslavery.html; "The Petition of Belinda Sutton (Previously known as Belinda Royall), Medford Historical Society and Museum, https://www.medfordhistorical.org/medford-history/africa-to-medford/the-mark-of-belinda-sutton/. Also see New England Historical Society, "The Beginning of the End of Slavery in Massachusetts, New England Historical Society, https://www.newenglandhistoricalsociety.com/beginning-end-slavery-massachusetts/.

8. Mary Frances Berry, *My Face Is Black Is True: Callie House and the Struggle for Ex-Slave Reparations* (New York: Knopf, 2005); Lee Harris, "'Reparations' as a Dirty Word: The Norm Against Slavery Reparations," *University of Memphis L. Review* 33 (2005): 446; Aiyetoro and Davis, "Historic and Modern Movements for Reparations," 687–766.

9. Jürgen Habermas considers the public sphere the area of social life characterized by dialogue through either face-to-face conversation in social networks and associations or through the media. Building on Nancy Fraser's feminist critique of Habermas, Michael C. Dawson argues that African Americans were excluded from the U.S. bourgeois public sphere and responded to its hegemonic aspirations by constructing a semi-autonomous "black counterpublic" within African American civil society. See Jürgen Habermas, *The Structural Transformation of the Public Sphere: An Inquiry into a Category of Bourgeois Society*, The MIT Press; Sixth Printing edition (August 28, 1991; 1962); Nancy Fraser, "Rethinking the Public Sphere: A Contribution to the Critique of Actually Existing Democracy," *Social Text*, 25/26 (1990): 56–80; Michael C. Dawson, *Black Visions: The Roots of Contemporary African-American Political Ideologies* (Chicago: University of Chicago Press, 2001), 23–24.

10. In 1987, nationalist organizations such as the Republic of New Afrika and the New Afrikan Peoples Organization joined with the National Conference of Black Lawyers and other groups to form the National Coalition of Blacks for Reparations in America (N'COBRA) in order to jointly build a mass base for African American reparations.

11. James Forman, "The Black Manifesto," in *The Political Thought of James Forman*. (Detroit: Black Star Publishing, 1970), 58–69; James Forman, *The Black Manifesto*, The Archives of the Episcopal Church, 7–11, https://episcopalarchives.org/church-awakens/files/original/c20bd83547dd3cf92e788041d7fddfa2.pdf.

12. New Jersey Senator Cory Booker introduced S. 1083, the U.S. Senate version of HR 40. Representative Sheila Jackson Lee, HR 40: Commission to Study and Develop Reparation Proposals for African-Americans Act, January 3, 2019, Congress 116th Congress (2019–2020), Congress.Gov, https://www.congress.gov/bill/116th-congress/house-bill/40/text; Cory A. Booker, S. 1082: Commission to Study and Develop Reparation Proposals for African-Americans Act, April 9, 2019, Congress 116th Congress (2019–2020), Congress.Gov, https://www.congress.gov/bill/116th-congress/senate-bill/1083/text.

13. Steve Inskeep interview with Kamala Harris, NPR, March 14, 2019, 7:08 AM, https://www.npr.org/2019/03/14/ 703299534/sen-kamala-harris-on-reparations.

14. Kamala Harris, "Fighting for Racial Justice," Kalama HarrisForThePeople, https://kamalaharris.org/issue/fighting-for-racial-justice/; Natasha A. Alford, "Senator Kamala Harris gets backlash over reparations for African Americans, *the Grio*, February 25, 2019, https://thegrio.com/2019/02/25/sen-kamala-harris-gets-backlash-over-question-about-reparations-for-african-americans/.

15. Ginger Gipson, "Senator Elizabeth Warren Backs Reparations for Black Americans," *Reuters*, February 21, 2019, https://www.reuters.com/article/us-usa-election-warren-idUSKCN1QA2WF.

16. Senator Warren persuasively argues that government (federal, state, and local) play a major role in driving up housing costs, in discriminating against African American home buyers, and that rental cost represents a significant aspect of wealth inequality. She believes that a massive affordable housing development program will force down rental costs. Elizabeth Warren, "Safe and Affordable Housing, "WARREN, https://elizabethwarren.com/plans/safe-affordable-housing.

17. Cory Booker, Cory2020, "Baby Bonds," Economic security and opportunity, https://corybooker.com/issues/ economic-security-and-opportunity/; Benjamin Wallace-Wells, "How Cory Booker's 'Baby Bonds' Proposal Could Transform the Reparations Debate," *The New Yorker*, December 6, 2018, https://www.newyorker.com/news/the-political-scene/how-cory-bookers-baby-bond-proposal-could-transform-the-reparations-debate; Nick Corasaniti, "Booker Campaigns on Baby Bonds Programs to Combat Inequality," *New York Times*, April 6, 2019, https://www.nytimes.com/2019/04/06/us/politics/cory-booker-2020-baby-bonds.html.

18. More than two years after President Abraham Lincoln issued the Emancipation Proclamation and six months after the ratification of the Thirteenth Amend-

ment, on June 19th or Juneteenth a quarter of a million African Americans learned of the abolition of slavery. The next year, 1866, freedpeople in Galveston, Texas, sponsored the first Juneteenth commemoration. See Sundiata Keita Cha-Jua, "Juneteenth: Time for Liberation Now," "RealTalk," *New Gazette,* June 18, 2017, https://www.news-gazette.com/opinion/columns/sundiata-cha-jua-real-talk-juneteenth-time-for-liberation-now/article_d6f35ebb-9faa-57f4-a39f-a7dbb6f3ca90.html; James C. Anyike, *African American Holidays: A Historical Research and Resource Guide to Cultural Celebrations* (Chicago: Popular Truths Inc. 1991), 53–60.

19. Beginning in 1989, Michigan Congressman John Conyers introduced HR 40 to the U.S. House of Representatives for 28 straight years until his retirement. In the early days of the 115th Congress (2017–2018), Conyers presented a revised HR 40. The new bill updated HR 40 by acknowledging that the new information uncovered by contemporary legal and historical scholars answers many of the questions posed by the initial HR 40 concerning whether and to what extent African Americans have been injured by the slave trade and slavery. In January 2019, Texas Representative Sheila Jackson Lee reintroduced HR 40. See N'COBRA, "Congressman John Conyers Introduces New HR 40 Reparations Bill," N'COBRA Press Release, January 9, 2017, https://www.ncobraonline.org/ congressman-john-conyers-introduces-new-hr40-reparations-bill/ Sheila Jackson Lee Press Release, "CONGRESSWOMAN SHEILA JACKSON LEE INTRODUCES LEGISLATION FOR A COMMISSION TO CONSIDER REPARATIONS PROPOSALS FOR AFRICANS AMERICANS," January 7, 2019, https://jacksonlee.house.gov/media-center/press-releases/congresswoman-sheila-jackson-lee-introduces-legislation-for-a-commission; NAACP, Action Alert, "NAACP Supports Slavery Reparations Study Legislation, H.R. 40, Now Pending in the 113th Congress, May 28, 2014, https://www.naacp.org/latest/naacp-supports-slavery-reparations-study-legislation-h-r-40-now-pending-in/.

20. Harold Cruse, *The Crisis of the Negro Intellectual* (New York: New York Review Books, 2005; rprt. 1967), 7–9; Martin Luther King, Jr., *Where Do We Go from Here: Chaos or Community?* (Boston: Beacon Press, 1986; rprt. 1968), 126.

21. Lauren Victoria Burke, "Can African Americans Benefit from Presidential Candidate Andrew Yang's Universal Income Proposal," *Black Enterprise* November 20, 2019, https://www.blackenterprise.com/can-african-americans-benefit-from-presidential-candidate-andrew-yangs-universal-income-proposal/.

22. Martin Luther King Jr., *Why We Can't Wait* (New York: Signet Classics, 2000; rprt. 1963), 170.

23. Forman, *The Black Manifesto,* The Archives of the Episcopal Church, 7–9; James Forman, "The Black Manifesto," in *The Political Thought of James Forman,* 58–69; Dye, Keith. "The Black Manifesto for Reparations in Detroit: Challenge and Response, 1969," *Michigan Historical Review* Vol. 35, No. 2 (FALL 2009), 53–83.

24. King, Jr., *Why We Can't Wait,* 165.

25. *United States Supreme Court SANTA CLARA PUEBLO v. MARTINEZ(1978) No. 76–682,* https://caselaw.findlaw.com/us-supreme-court/436/49.html; Judith Resnik,

"Dependent Sovereigns, Indian Tribes, States, and the Federal Courts," *The University of Chicago Law Review* 56 (1989), 671.

26. I favor both individual payments or debt relief and a social transfer of wealth and resources to Afro-America as corporate entity. Matthew Fletcher, *New York Times*, June 9, 4:09 PM, 2014, https://www.nytimes.com/roomfordebate/2014/06/08/are-reparations-due-to-african-americans/american-indians-seek-control-not-just-reparations.

27. Adjoa A. Aiyetoro and Adrienne D. Davis, "Historic and Modern Social Movements for Reparations: The National Coalition of Blacks for Reparations in America (N'COBRA) and Its Antecedents," *Texas Wesleyan Law Review* 16, no. 4 (2010): 763.

28. A consociational state or consociational democracy is constructed on four principles. The most fundamental are power sharing and "segmental autonomy." Power sharing is an arrangement in which the conflicting social groups agree to cooperate through an arrangement in which they apportion decision-making authority among themselves. Segmental autonomy is the other key decision-making feature. This type of political architecture contrasts with a majoritarian system because it provides each fragment with the authority and capacity to make decisions that affect the internal affairs of its constituency. A third central aspect of consocieationalism is the minority veto, which provides numerically smaller or heretofore subordinate groups the means to counter "the tyranny of the majority." In such a political system proportionality is the essential organizing principle for political representation and the distribution of resources. See Arend Lijphart, "Consocation and Federation: Conceptual and Empirical Links," *Canadian Journal of Politics* 12, No. 3 (Sept. 1979): 500–501; Lani Guinier, *The Tyranny of the Majority: Fundamental Fairness in Representative Democracy* (New York: The Free Press, 1994), 1–20.

18

Family Roots of Reparations in the Era of Trump

CHARLES P. HENRY

Rockbridge County, Virginia, gets its name from a natural limestone bridge that crosses Cedar Creek. This Natural Bridge—over 200 feet high and 90 feet long—was a sacred landscape for the Monacan Indians. According to legend, George Washington surveyed the bridge and cut his initials into one of the interior walls. Thomas Jefferson was so enchanted by the site that he purchased the Natural Bridge and 157 surrounding acres from the Crown in 1774.

The Natural Bridge was seen as being at the edge of civilization, and Jefferson considered building a retreat there. It attracted both domestic and foreign visitors including Patrick Henry, Sam Houston, John Marshall, and Daniel Boone. Jefferson did not build there, but he did hire a free Black man as caretaker and to record the names of his guests in a book.[1]

Jefferson's Black caretaker was also named Patrick Henry. It is not known how Henry gained his freedom, but we do know that he left two wills, one freeing his wife Louisa and giving land to his unnamed children. John Henry, another free Black living in Lexington, Virginia, witnessed his will. The 1840 Census lists a William Henry with a young family living next door to Louisa Henry who was most likely his mother. The history of this family, my antecedents, reinforces the validity of the reparations demand for both free Blacks and formerly enslaved Black folk.[2]

Virginia's free Black population was only 4 percent of the state's total Black population; though small it was by far the largest of any state.[3] The number of free Black people was in decline and in the wake of Nat Turner's rebellion in 1831, their situation became even more precarious. It was clear that the ideology of the Revolution as expressed in the Declaration of Independence did not include Black folk. Alexis de Tocqueville wrote prophetically, "[w]hen I contemplate the condition of the South, I can only discover two alternatives which may be adopted by the white inhabitants of those States; viz., either to emancipate the [N]egroes, and to intermingle with them, or, remaining isolated from them, to keep them in a state of slavery as long as possible. All intermediate measures seem to me likely to terminate, and that shortly, in the most horrible of civil wars, and perhaps in the extirpation of one or other of the two races."[4]

In response to the deteriorating conditions, William Henry decided to move his family out of Virginia to New Castle, Pennsylvania. The economy there was booming because of the construction of the Erie Canal beginning in 1828. Henry had taken up barbering, and his family came to know two other families of free Black folk as neighbors—the Normans and the Berrys. Although Pennsylvania's mistreatment of free Black folk was mild compared to Virginia's, any location on or near the Ohio River such as southwestern Pennsylvania was dangerous. Nightriders moved through the region intimidating the local free Black population. The Henry family decided to seek safer ground and followed the Erie Canal to Newark in central Ohio.

Ohio was the frontier, part of the Northwest Territory that excluded slavery as the country expanded westward. Yet while the Northwest Ordinance of 1787 appeared to exclude slavery, there was a loophole that permitted retaining slaves who had that status at the time of its passage. Moreover, states like Ohio, Indiana, and Illinois through their "Black Laws" made it clear that free Black people were not welcome. As Ohio Justice Nathaniel Reed explained, "Black laws" were deliberately exclusionary and encouraged African Americans to leave Ohio by denying them equal rights. "[T]he laws very purpose," he said, was to keep those who remained in the state "miserable and degraded."[5]

When the Henrys moved to Newark, Ohio, along with the Normans and Berrys, there were roughly twenty thousand free Black folks in the state. Prior to the Civil War, William Henry set up a barbershop, bought a home, and sent his children to school. There were no public funds to support schooling for Black children so William, John Norman, and two other free Black folk convinced the local Board of Education to build a schoolhouse on land one of them owned. Funds were raised by the board and the Black community and a frame building constructed, only to be torn down by unknown persons the night after its completion. It was then rebuilt and one of the free Black supporters, Jackson Shackleford, armed himself, and guarded the structure all night. Later, in 1861, a brick schoolhouse was constructed next to the Henry home.[6] Prior to 1829, there were no laws formally barring African Americans from Ohio's schools, but with the establishment of public schools that year such exclusion became formalized.[7]

William Henry and his wife Elizabeth Swaney had three sons—Oren, Charles, and John. In 1864, William sent his two eldest sons off to fight with the United States Colored Troops. On his return from the war, now Sergeant Charles Patrick Henry joined his father's barbershop, but soon Sergeant Henry moved to Coshocton, Ohio, to set up his own barbershop. Oren, who had been wounded in the Battle of Lookout Mountain, also worked as a barber in Newark until his death in 1880. The third Henry son, John, married Elizabeth Norman in 1881 and worked as a barber in Newark until his death by accident in 1898. After Elizabeth's death by consumption in 1900, their four surviving children—Rhea, Hazel, Helen, and Charles—went to live with their Uncle Charles in Coshocton. Only Charles Patrick Henry II survived to adulthood.

A few years after graduating from the eighth grade in Coshocton, young Charles joined Troop C of the United States Tenth Calvary in 1909. The unit was stationed at Fort Ethan Allen in Vermont, and he served with Buffalo soldiers returning from the western frontier and veterans of the Spanish-American War. Leaving the army as a corporal in 1912, he returned to Newark and began a forty-year career as a brickmason. Over those years he became a leader of the masonic lodge and helped fund the building of the African Methodist Episcopal church. In 1940, he married Zanesville, Ohio, native Ruth Holbert and they had two sons. Charles Patrick III (the author) was born in 1947, and Oren John was born in 1953.

As presented here this brief narrative of the Henry family addresses two myths used by opponents of reparations. First, it disrupts the dominant national narrative that white supremacy was a regional problem, an aberration limited to the South. Moreover, Black folk who are not located in the rural South or northern cities could not avoid racial discrimination. No one more elegantly describes the racial environment of Black people growing up in small cities and towns in Ohio in particular and the Midwest in general than the late Toni Morrison, a native of Lorain, Ohio.[8] Second, the Henry family narrative counters the notion that reparations are all about slavery, and slavery is past. This ahistorical view seeks to distance Americans from the consequences of the past and current practices that have always included free Black folk as well as the enslaved. In fact, it attempts to present whites as the true victims of movements for justice.[9] Thus, by space and time, most white Americans avoid any serious consideration of racial reparations.

What constitutes an "American" are not beliefs arrived at inductively and analytically but rather acquired through exposure to narratives of the "American dream." These narratives are competitive and come through mass and social media, formal education, and informal communal and social life. Collective identity narratives associate shared meanings with some, but not other, historical and contemporary actors, whose actions and purposes they interpret and relate to a vision of what unites "us" and creates a group. These narratives do not have to be fact-based, but they must be believable to significant audiences. By naming "our" heroes and "our" enemies and our shared triumphs and tragedies, this collective identity not only represents but also shapes how we act in the present and future.[10]

The dominant American narrative presents Thomas Jefferson and the "white" Patrick Henry as heroic Americans while ignoring the reality that contradicts our stated beliefs. It excludes one fifth of the national population from the collective "we" whether slave or "free." At no time during the antebellum period did our national leaders or the vast majority of white Americans see a future that included Black Americans as equal citizens. Even in the middle of the Civil War, Lincoln was exploring options for the colonization of Black people beyond the United States spatial-political boundaries. And after the war up to our current era, significant populations view the leader of the succession, Robert E. Lee, as a hero, and his cause—the "Lost Cause"—as a noble one. The Confederate monuments controversy is not about remembering the past but rather about claiming white victimhood in the present.

Just as white Southerners seek to distance themselves from slavery through tales of the Lost Cause, Northerners pretend that the absence of legal racial segregation means the absence of racism. Ohio and other northern states no more welcomed "free" Black folk during the Great Migration than they did prior to the Civil War. Historian Thomas Sugrue found that, "[i]n nearly every arena, Blacks and whites lived separate, unequal lives. Public policy and the market confined Blacks to declining neighborhoods; informal Jim Crow excluded them from restaurants, hotels, amusement parks, and swimming pools and relegated them to separate sections of theaters."[11] Northern Black folk typically attended separate and unequal public schools and even today the most segregated schools are in the North, not the South.

The years immediately before and after this author's birth in 1947 marked the beginning of the modern post–World War II era of race relations highlighted by the "rights revolution." Hundreds of thousands of Americans had died to defeat Aryan supremacy, and the colonized peoples watched intently as the United States and the United Nations assumed leading global roles.

Domestically, Black veterans vowed not to return to the racial status quo, while in the academy, race and racism received new attention as central facets of American life. Despite decades of scholarship by W. E. B. Du Bois, Carter G. Woodson, Zora Neale Hurston, and other Black intellectuals, it was Swedish economist Gunnar Myrdal's exhaustive 1944 study *An American Dilemma* that provided a new paradigm for examining "race" in U.S. society.[12]

Myrdal remarked on the pervasive sense of "innocence" among Northern whites. He wrote, "[t]he social paradox in the North is exactly this, that almost everybody is against discrimination in general but, at the same time, almost everybody practices discrimination in his own personal affairs."[13] Nonetheless, Myrdal chose to focus his work on the South arguing that the "American Negro problem" was a "moral dilemma." Change would come about, he believed, when the practices of segregation were confronted by whites' strong belief in the American "creed." Myrdal said all Americans held in common the ideal of the essential dignity of each individual, the fundamental equality of all persons, and certain inalienable rights to freedom, justice, and opportunity. There was nothing Black people could do to advance their cause other than embracing Euro-American culture because ultimately, said Myrdal, "this is a white man's country."[14]

Political scientist Ralph Bunche, Myrdal's chief Black research assistant, was less sanguine about a focus on individual prejudice and the psychology of discrimination. He preferred to emphasize the structural and economic components of racism. Bunche was also concerned about the possible development of American fascism, stating "[i]t must be noted that Americans are a very opportunistic and a very materialistic people. We have no traditional political theory, despite our alleged reverence for our 'traditional institutions.' We have demonstrated, too often, how easily we can push law, constitution and tradition aside when it suits our purpose to do so. No other country in the world boasts such fertile soil for demagogues and crackpots."[15] In short, Bunche's long experience with racists gave him less confidence in White America's willingness to include Black folk in the collective "we" than the Swedish scholar. Current politics seem to prove Bunche right.

Myrdal's perspective of a gradual and inevitable fulfillment of the ideals of the American creed—without any pressure from Black people—is part of the dominant collective narrative of national progress. The Bunche perspective is closer to the Henry family narrative of migration and constant struggle for first-class citizenship. He embraces the concept of reparations as part of a process of repairing the relationship between whites and African Americans. The dominant conservative view rejects reparations as an effort to make current generations pay for the sins of the past. Historian Michel-Rolph Trouillot emphasized that "history means both the facts of the matter and a narrative of those facts, both what happened and what is said to have happened. The first meaning places the emphasis on the socio-historical process, the second on our knowledge of the process or on a story about the process."[16] For Trouillot, the positivist view hides the tropes of power behind a naïve epistemology, while the constructionist perspective denies the autonomy of the socio-historical process.

The symbolic birth of the United States is an excellent example of this process and its relationship to reparations. In the summer of 2019, Senate majority leader Mitch McConnell was asked for a response to the report that two of his great-great-grandfathers were slaveowners. He said in response: "I find myself once again in the same position as President Obama" . . . "We both oppose reparations. We both are descendants of slave-owners."[17] McConnell added that no one currently alive is responsible for slavery. His cynical use of Obama's ancestry contains a couple of important truths. The first is that Obama, like all American presidents, promotes the vision of America that is already a "city on a hill" while at the same time evolving to that "city of a hill." That is, that the Founders, despite their flaws, were enlightened men who set us on a course to make their dream a reality. Second, that Obama's view of racism, like slavery, as a relic of the past supports the ahistoricism of McConnell.

No president has been more successful than Barack Obama in integrating his family narrative into the larger collective identity. In his most significant speeches, such as the 2004 Democratic National Convention keynote that made him a household name, he explained his African name saying, "my story is part of the larger American story, that I owe a debt to all those who came before me, and that in no other country on earth is my story even possible."[18] And while Obama lauds American exceptionalism, his speeches tend to focus on his white grandparents rather than his African ancestors. However, it is not the white slaveholders in his ancestry but rather his grandparents' participation in the "greatest generation" that attracts his interest. For him, their sacrifices and those participants in the civil rights movement serve as emblems of the best American idealism.

In his "More Perfect Union" speech, Obama suggests that the Founders' original intent was evolutionary, and they intended that we adapt their words to our world. From the nation's birth at the Declaration of Independence to his own inauguration, Obama contends, the moral imperative or "creed" embodied in the Declaration's words has driven our constant struggle to become "a more perfect union." In fact, Obama conflates the landing of the Puritans and the Pilgrims with the "scholars and farmers" who founded the nation over 150 years later. This allows him to ignore the religious intolerance of the former while praising the separation of church and state advocated by the latter. Moreover, by emphasizing the religious mythology of the founding, Obama ignores the economic motives of the earliest settlers at Jamestown, as well as those of the Founders and the slavery that followed.[19]

By beginning the American story in 1607 or 1620 rather than 1619, our national mythology embraces the ideal of religious freedom while ignoring the religious intolerance of the Pilgrims and the economic motives of the Jamestown colony. The first settlers at Jamestown were employees and servants of the Virginia Company. Over half were soldiers and their mission was to find gold and other treasures. Later that year, a Dutch Man of War brought into the colony twenty to thirty Africans who were purchased by John Rolfe.[20] And as Ta-Nehisi Coates reminds us in his testimony on HR 40, "[s]ome slaves of 1619 were freed. Some of them intermarried. Still others escaped with the white indentured servants who had suffered as they had. Some even rebelled together allying under Nathaniel Bacon to torch Jamestown in 1676."[21] It was not until the mid-1600s that Virginia law decreed that the status of the child followed the status of the mother, thus burdening future generations with slavery.

By remembering the Gettysburg Address and by extension the Civil War as a rebirth of American democracy, this national mythology distances people from the sins of their slaveholding past. Even the Great Emancipator not only sought to separate himself from his Black compatriots, but also claimed victimhood for the white race. Speaking to a small delegation of Black ministers at the White House to discuss colonization in the summer of 1862, Lincoln noted the broad differences between the races that made it better for both Black folk and white people to be separated. He then proceeded to blame the war on the presence of Black people: "But for your race among us there could not be war, although many men engaged on either side do not care for you one way or another. . . . "[22] Lincoln concluded that slavery had "evil effects on the white race" as well . . . and "it is exceedingly important that we have men at the beginning capable of thinking as white men and not those who have been systematically oppressed."[23] This language is hardly the soaring rhetoric of the Gettysburg Address or of repair and reconciliation.

The final myth supporting the dominant collective identity said to unite us all is related to the Civil Rights Movement. Dr. Martin Luther King Jr.'s birthday commemorations would make it appear that his protests were widely embraced by Black folk and white people alike. Of course, the King celebrated is the King of the 1963 March on Washington and not the more radical anti–Vietnam War and anti-poverty leader. Even then, to promote differing agendas both liberals and conservatives have adopted his "I Have a Dream" speech. Conservatives have taken King's desire for African Americans to be judged by the "content of our character" as justification for purportedly "color-blind" public policy. Although few conservatives supported King's efforts to enact civil and political rights legislation, they now label any race-specific policy as "reverse racism." Thus, those on the right have turned civil rights on its head and argue that whites are the "new victims" and those who were once branded as "racists" are now merely "racial conservatives."[24]

Obama has said, "my commitment to social justice and the sense that serving as an elected official is more than a mere job, but a mission largely informed by Dr. King's life."[25] Like King and Myrdal, Obama believes in the power of words to move Americans toward fulfilling their creed. Yet, as an elected official, he emphasizes the "character" side of Black people's status and not government intervention to address racial disparities. In 2007 during a speech at the commemoration of the 1965 Selma to Montgomery voting rights march, Obama acknowledged the civil rights leaders present as Moses figures who have taken us 90 percent of the way to the Promise Land. He believes his generation, the Joshua generation, has to take us the rest of the way to equal rights, but has lost some of its energy. Obama, echoing John Kennedy, stated, "it's not enough just to ask what the government can do for us—it's important for us to ask what we can do for ourselves." He added that the current generation "has lost a little discipline" and parents need "to turn off the TV and instill a sense of educational achievement." "Cousin Pookie," Obama declared, "needs to get off the couch and vote" and we must instill the values of the Moses generation in our young people.[26]

At a speech at Dr. King's Ebenezer Baptist Church in Atlanta in 2008, Obama repeated the line about turning off the television set and added that our men need to be home with our children. Regarding reforming the criminal justice system, he stated, "we also have to acknowledge the deep-seated violence that still resides in our own communities."[27] He ended the speech with a story about a young white woman who didn't have the money to help her cancer-stricken mother with medical treatment and was working on his campaign because of his commitment to health care. An elderly Black man was inspired to work on the campaign because of her commitment. Thus Obama, at King's church, chastised Black folk for not having energy or discipline and held up a poor white woman as a model of commitment.

These negative views about African American culture are widespread and were not new to Obama. In his book *The Audacity of Hope*, then Senator Obama states, "I think much of what ails the inner city involves a breakdown in culture that will not be cured by money alone and that our values and spiritual life matter at best as much as our GDP."[28] Later in the same work, Obama says two groups require special attention: the inner city Black poor and the undocumented immigrant workers. Only the latter received any special attention from the Obama administration.[29]

Because he talked about racism as largely a relic of the past, as President, Obama was unable to promote programs targeted at correcting the effects of that racism.[30] Government efforts directed toward addressing the problems of the inner city could be shot down by white and Black conservatives as doomed to failure because of "Black pathology." Obama's narrow use of race, in short, served to shift the burden of redressing contemporary racial injustices solely on the shoulders of Black people themselves at precisely the time when they might expect a receptive federal response to their plight. Obama, for example, portrayed President Bush's weak response to Hurricane Katrina more as a class and bureaucratic issue than a racial one. And during his brief time in the Senate, Obama made it clear he did not want to be seen as a leading voice on racial issues.[31] At one point he is quoted as saying, "[n]obody cares if you suffered some discrimination."[32]

Well into his second term Obama did offer a race-specific program aimed at supporting young Black men. In 2014, the White House launched "My Brother's Keeper," an initiative designed to close the opportunity gap facing boys and young men of color. The following year, "My Brother's Alliance" was established as an independent nonprofit company to coordinate the efforts of corporations, charities, and social clubs to sustain the mission of the original initiative. Thus, late in his second term Obama acknowledged an "opportunity gap" for young Black men and chose to address it with a public-private partnership and not a federal program.[33]

Public-private partnerships are a neoliberal approach to social policy that Obama explored as early as law school. At Harvard, he and fellow student Rob Fisher wrote a major paper developing guidelines on how politically progressive movements could use the market mechanism to promote social goals.[34] During this same period, Black neoconservatives Glenn Loury and Robert Woodson were promoting self-help models that were collectivist oriented. Economist Loury was a pioneer in studying social capital while Woodson founded the National Center for Neighborhood Enterprise to provide technical assistance to local businesses in low-income areas. These Black neoconservatives pushed free market and limited government solutions to racial problems with an emphasis on personal responsibility.[35] Their views are closer to those of Obama than they are to Republican Senator Edward Brooke who supported full employment with the government as the "employer of last resort" among other federal programs.[36]

While he promoted My Brother's Keeper as a solution to the opportunity gap for young men of color, Obama ignored the Congressional Black Caucus's push for a Full Employment Caucus in Congress. Neoliberalism taints such policies as full employment alleging it benefits certain racial groups rather than the country as a whole. By ascribing Black pathology as a characteristic of a Black underclass, Black politicians shrink public spaces and public institutions making whites more receptive to privatizing schools, jobs, prisons, welfare, and social services. In short, by focusing on Black pathology, Obama, like Daniel Moynihan's "benign neglect" in the late sixties, reinforces stereotypes of Black welfare recipients held by whites and closes off any discussion of a federal response to their plight. The burden of Black advancement is shifted solely to the shoulders of Blacks themselves.[37]

The recent revival of the reparations movement owes its existence to a rejection of neoliberalism and a backlash to the white nationalism of Trump and the Republican Party. The financial deregulation of the banking industry leading to the subprime mortgage crisis is seen as a major contributor to the wealth gap between Black folk and whites, which quadrupled from 1984 to 2007.[38]Privatization of publicly owned assets and businesses like prisons fueled a for-profit prison-industrial complex. Welfare state retrenchment has redistributed wealth up rather than down. And the racialization of universal programs such as the Affordable Care Act, intentionally labeled "Obamacare," have sharply divided the political parties. In short, Dr. King's claim against "the bounced check of America's promissory note" has come due.

Polling data immediately before and after Obama's election showed Americans to be more optimistic about race relations than they had in recent years. That optimism rapidly receded despite the administration's best efforts to neutralize race as a political issue. Political scientist Michael Tesler declared "the election of President Obama helped usher in a 'most-racial' political era where racially liberal and racially conservative Americans were more divided over a whole host of political positions than they had been in modern times."[39] A Kaiser/CNN poll in 2015 found that respondents believe racial tensions are worse than twenty years before. Sixty-four percent said tensions were increasing in 2015 compared to 47 percent in 1995.[40] Similarly, a 2016

Gallup poll found that for the first time in nearly two decades most African Americans describe Black-White relations as "bad."[41]

This political polarization has pushed many white Democrats leftward. One report contends that white liberals have moved considerably left on questions related to race since 2012. It attributes this shift to a campus- and online-driven cultural awakening that has accelerated in response to Trump. The share of white liberals who say racial prejudice is the main reason African Americans cannot get ahead jumped substantially after 2014. The number of respondents who disagreed with the statement, "Blacks should do like other minorities without special favors," rose from 20 percent in 1994 to 46 percent in 2016. In fact, a 2016 American National Election Survey (ANES) found white liberals warmer toward minorities than their own racial group (80 percent to 70 percent).[42] Gallup reported a 20 percent rise in liberalism among white Democrats (from 34 to 54 percent) with a smaller increase among Hispanic Democrats at 9 percent (from 29 to 38 percent) and among Black Democrats at an 8 percent increase (from 25 percent to 33 percent).[43] A 2017 Pew poll found the share of Americans who say racial discrimination is the main reason Black folk are unable to get ahead was now at its highest level dating back more than two decades.[44]

This shift left among Democrats translates into increased support for reparations for African Americans. A 2019 Gallup poll reported total support for reparations in the form of cash payments from the government for African Americans descended from enslaved workers rose from 14 percent in 2002 to 29 percent. Among Whites support was up from 6 percent to 16 percent and among Black people support rose from 55 percent to 73 percent. In contrast to the last three presidential elections in which Democratic candidates refused to support HR 40, most of the current Democratic candidates in the 2020 election either supported some form of reparations or supported the study of the issue.[45]

The summer of 2019 witnessed the U.S. Congress' first hearing on reparations for African Americans. Every year beginning in 1989 until his retirement from the House of Representatives in 2017, John Conyers of Michigan introduced HR 40, a bill calling for the federal government to study the impact of slavery and make recommendations for reparations to the 35 million American descendants of the enslaved. The bill was modeled after the Civil Liberties Act of 1988, which was successful in granting an apology and reparations to Japanese Americans for their internment during World War II. Despite being the senior Democrat on the House Judiciary Committee,

Conyers was never able to hold hearings on his bill during both Republican and Democratic administrations. In 2017, Representative Sheila Jackson Lee of Texas took over sponsorship of the bill and was successful in holding hearings through the Subcommittee on the Constitution, Civil Rights and Civil Liberties of the House Judiciary Committee. Leading off the testimony was Senator Cory Booker who sponsored the Senate companion bill to HR 40, along with twelve co-sponsors, including Senators Kamala Harris, Amy Klobuchar, Kelli Gillibrand, Bernie Sanders, and Elizabeth Warren. Others testifying in favor of the legislation included Ta-Nehisi Coates, Danny Glover, Julianne Malveaux, Eric Miller, Right Reverend Eugene Taylor Sutton, and Katrina Colston Browne. Opposing the bill were Burgess Owens and Coleman Hughes. Browne highlighted some of the other activities pursuing reparatory justice underway, including the "Coming to the Table" network of descendants of enslaved workers and slavers in dialogue; the Kellogg Foundations' network of local initiatives; the work of the Episcopal Church, Southern Baptist Convention, and National Council of Churches; "Universities Studying Slavery"; the "Middle Passage Ceremonies and Port Makers Project"; the "Slave Dwelling Project"; the "Hope in the Cities/Institutional Change in Richmond, Virginia"; and the "Teaching Hard History initiative of the Teaching Tolerance of the Southern Poverty Law Center."[46]

Rev. Eugene Sutton's comments might have best captured the spirit of the current push for reparations when he declared, "We forgave this country and continue to forgive it, but are not reconciled . . . we need to repair the broken places and wounds."[47] It is striking that a bill to study reparations—meaning to repair that which has been broken—is and has been another racially divisive issue in the country. Of course, if the breach is denied, if we cling to collective myths of what constitutes an American, we will continue to live in denial and hence in conflict.

There is a difference between conservative distrust of governmental abuses of power and distrust of one's fellow citizens. Extreme racial polarization means that citizens no longer think it sensible, or feel secure enough, to place their fates in the hands of democratic strangers. And democracy depends on trustful talk among strangers that, when properly conducted, should overcome any divisions that block it.[48]

When young Rev. Martin Luther King was asked whether the Montgomery Bus Boycott and subsequent Supreme Court decision was a victory for African Americans, he quickly responded that it was a victory for all Americans. "What changed in the late 1960s," states political scientist Michael Dawson, "was that African Americans and others lost for that time the constant political battle to have their claims recognized as intrinsically political, of universal concern to those who want to build democracy, and ones that should be central to, not excluded from, political discourse."[49] President Obama never used his exceptional speaking ability to convince most white Americans that they might see their own stories, their hopes, fears, and values best realized in a nation that uses race-conscious policies for the improvement of the general welfare. Neoliberal policies and color-blind mythologies have done great harm in every area from voting rights to criminal justice.[50]

When distrust among electoral minorities endures and accumulates it can only result in a breach. If the breach is not resolved to the satisfaction of all parties, it can have only three outcomes. The group will leave the polity; the group will resist and rebel; or the group will be repressed by state and private action. All three responses are a part of America's collective identity. Reparations is a struggle to be included in the narrative of the collective "we."

Notes

1. Laura A Macaluso, *Guide to Thomas Jefferson's Virginia* (Washington, DC: Arcadia Publishing, 2018), 115–17.

2. Loretta J. Henry, unpublished Henry Family history.

3. Nell Irvin Painter, *Creating Black Americans: African-American History and Its Meanings, 1619 to the Present* (New York: Oxford University Press, 2006), 73.

4. Alexis de Tocqueville, in Scott Malcomson, *One Drop of Blood: The American Misadventure of Race* (New York: Farrar, Straus and Giroux, 2000), 114–15.

5. Dana Elizabeth Weiner, *Race and Rights: Fighting Slavery and Prejudice in the Old Northwest, 1830–1870* (Dekalb, IL: Northern Illinois University Press, 2013), 35.

6. Felecia Piggott McMillan, "Locating the Neo-black Aesthetic: Playwrights of the North Carolina Black Repertory Company React to the Black Arts Movement," (Chapel Hill: University of North Carolina, 2002), 124.

7. Weiner, Op. Cit., 58. Weiner notes that in 1843 the Ohio Constitution permitted men who officials could identify as "nearer white than mulattoes" to vote. This led White abolitionist editor Benjamin Stanton to mock their discriminatory powers arguing Ohio's election judges would need to invent a "colorometer" to carry out their machinations (p. 34).

8. Craig Fehrman, "How Ohio has Shaped Toni Morrison's Fiction," *Cincinnati Magazine*, October 31, 2017; https://www.cincinnatimagazine.com/artsmindsblog/how-ohio-shaped-toni-morrison-fiction/2017; "Growing up in Northeast Ohio Played a Major Role in the Prolific and Monumental Writing of Toni Morrison," *ABC News 5*, Cleveland, August 6, 2019, https://www.news5cleveland.com/news/local-news/oh-lorain/growing-up-in-northeast-ohio-was-a-big-part-of-the-prolific-and-monumental-writing-of-toni-morrison.

9. Michael I. Norton and Samuel R. Sommers, "Whites See Racism as a Zero-Sum Game That They Are Now Losing," *Perspectives on Psychological Science* 6, no. 3 (2011): 215–18.

10. Clarissa Rile Hayward, *How Americans Make Race: Stories, Institutions, Spaces* (New York: Cambridge University Press, 2013), 14, 21.

11. Thomas J. Sugrue, *Sweet Land of Liberty: The Forgotten Struggle for Civil Rights in the North* (New York: Random House, 2008), xv.

12. Jonathan Scott Holloway and Ben Keppel, eds, *Black Scholars on the Line: Race, Social Science, and American Thought in the Twentieth Century* (South Bend: University of Notre Dame Press, 2007).

13. Gunnar Myrdal quoted in Sugrue, xiv–xv.

14. Gunnar Myrdal quoted in Charles P. Henry, *Ralph Bunche* (New York: New York University Press, 1999), 115–16

15. Ralph Bunche quoted in Henry, *Ralph Bunche*, 115.

16. Michel-Rolph Trouillot, *Silencing the Past: Power and the Production of History* (Boston: Beacon Press, 2015), 3.

17. Marianne Levine, "McConnell: I'm with Obama on Reparations," *Politico,* June 9, 2019, https//www.politico.com/story/2019/07/09/mcconnell-with-obama-on-reparations-1404123.

18. David J. Garrow and Charles Constant, *Rising Star: The Making of Barack Obama* (New York: HarperCollins, 2017), 938.

19. Steven Sarson, *Barack Obama: American Historian* (New York: Bloomsbury Publishing, 2018), 7–8.

20. Ibid., 52.

21. Ta Nehisi Coates, "Testimony," House Judiciary Committee Subcommittee on the Constitution, Civil Rights and Civil Liberties, June 19, 2019, 13.

22. David W. Blight, *Frederick Douglass* (New York: Simon & Schuster, 2018), 371.

23. Ibid., 371.

24. Rogers M. Smith and Desmond King, "America's New Racial Politics: White Protectionism, Racial Reparations, and American Identity," *China International Strategy Review* 2, no. 2 (2020): 169–83.

25. Garrow, op. cit., 690.

26. Barack Obama Selma Voting Rights March Commemoration Address, March 4, 2007, https// www.americanrhetoric.com/speeches/Barack Obama Address.

27. Obama speech at Ebenezer Baptist Church on January 20, 2008. Available online: https// www.americanrhetoric.com/speeches/BararckObama-Ebenezer.

28. Barack Obama, *The Audacity of Hope* (New York: Crown Publishers, 2006), 16.

29. Ibid., 249; Unfortunately, the special attention devoted to Black undocumented immigrants was negative. They were deported at five times their numbers in the total undocumented population. See Todd Shaw C. Shaw et al., eds., *After Obama: African American Politics in a Post Obama Era* (New York: New York University Press, 2021), 321. See also, Ashley Jardina, *White Identity Politics* (Cambridge, UK: Cambridge University Press, 2019) on the centrality of non-white immigration to the Trump campaign for president (pp. 232–33).

30. Randall Kennedy notes an Obama speech that mentions the wealth and income gap but does not mention reparations. See Randall Kennedy, *The Persistence of the Color Line: Racial Politics and the Obama Presidency*. Vintage, 2011, 107–8. Garrow and Constant note Obama thinks there is a good case for reparations but it's not going to happen. *Rising Star*, op. cit., 714, 719.

31. Ibid., 972–74.

32. Ibid., 128; Melanye T. Price, *The Race Whisperer* (New York: New York University Press, 2016), 57; Kennedy, op. cit., 230–32.

33. Barack Obama, "Remarks by the President on 'My Brother's Keeper' Initiative," The White House, February 27, 2014. https://obamawhitehouse.archives.gov/the-press-office/2014/02/27/remarks-president-my-brothers-keeper-initiative; Fredrick C. Harris, "The Challenges of my Brother's Keeper." *Governance Studies at Brookings*. Washington, DC: The Brookings Institution. Retrieved from https://www.brookings.edu/wp-content/uploads/2016/07/my_brothers_keeper.pdf (2015).

34. Garrow and Charles Constant, op. cit., 449–52.

35. Michael L. Ondaatje, *Black Conservative Intellectuals in Modern America* (Philadelphia: University of Pennsylvania Press, 2011), 34, 43, 53, 105.

36. Leah Wright Rigueur, *The Loneliness of the Black Republican: Pragmatic Politics and the Pursuit of Power* (Princeton: Princeton University Press, 2015), 230.

37. See Thomas J. Sugrue, "Not Even Past." In *Not Even Past* (Princeton: Princeton University Press, 2010), 71–79 and Shaw, op. cit., p. 33.

38. Michael Tesler, *Post-Racial or Most-Racial?: Race and Politics in the Obama Era* (Chicago: University of Chicago Press, 2016), 3.

39. Bianca DiJulio, Mira Norton, Symone Jackson, and Molly Brodie, "Kaiser Family Foundation/CNN survey of Americans on Race," Menlo Park, CA: Kaiser Family Foundation, November 2015, 15.

40. Mohamed Younis, "As Redress for Slavery, Americans Oppose Cash Reparations," Gallup, July 29, 2016, https//news.gallup.com/poll/2016/17/22/redress-slavery-americans-oppose-cash-reparations.aspx.

41. Ibid.

42. Eric Kaufman, "Americans Are Divided by Their Views on Race, Not Race Itself," *New York Times*, March 18, 2019, https:www.nytimes.com/2019/03/18/opinion/race-america-trump.html.

43. Thomas B. Edsall, "The Deepening 'Racialization' of American Politics," *New York Times*, February 27, 2019, https:www.nytimes.com/2019/02/27/opinion/trump-obama-race.html.

44. Pew Research Center, October 2017, "Political Typology Reveals Deep Fissures on the Right and Left," 57.

45. By August 2019, the following candidates either favored reparations or a study of the issue: Pete Buttigieg, Julio Castro, John Delany, Tulsi Gabard, John Hickenlooper, Beto O'Rourke, Tim Ryan, Andrew Yang, Cory Booker, Kamala Harris, Amy Klobuchar, Kirsten Gillibrand, Bernie Sanders, and Elizabeth Warren. Joseph Biden

said he favored collecting data on the issue. Maryanne Williams favored the payment of $200 to $500 billion to descendants of slaves over a period of 20 years. See 2020 Candidates Views on the Issues," *Politico,* August 9, 2019.

46. Katrina Colston Browne, Testimony, House Subcommittee, June 19, 2019, 7.

47. Right Reverend Eugene Taylor Sutton, "Testimony," House Subcommittee, June 19, 2019. 1.

48. Danielle S. Allen, *Talking to Strangers: Anxieties of Citizenship since* Brown v. Board of Education, No. 23. Editions Hermann, 2006, xiii–xvi.

49. Michael C. Dawson, "Not in Our Lifetimes," In *Not in Our Lifetimes* (Chicago: University of Chicago Press, 2020), 55.

50. Sundiata Keita Cha-Jua, "The New Nadir: The Contemporary Black Racial Formation," *The Black Scholar* 40, no. 1 (2010): 38–58; Michael C. Dawson and Megan Ming Francis, "Black Politics and the Neoliberal Racial Order," *Public Culture* 28, no. 1 (2016): 23–62; Siddhant Issar, "Listening to Black Lives Matter: Racial Capitalism and the Critique of Neoliberalism," *Contemporary Political Theory* 20, no. 1 (2021): 48–71.

19

Reparatory Justice Campaigns in the Twenty-First Century

V. P. FRANKLIN

One of the most unfortunate economic developments over the last four decades has been the huge increase in income inequality in the United States and other advanced capitalist nations. Larger and larger amounts of the wealth produced in these societies has flowed upward to the top 1 percent of the population. While political progressives in the United States, such as Vermont Senator Bernie Sanders, members of the Democratic Socialist Party, and others, have been advocating socialist approaches to address this inequality, it is increasingly unlikely to occur given the economic power and political influence of conservative capitalists and anti-socialists in both political parties. In the twenty-first century, it is much more likely that social movements for reparations and reparatory justice have a greater likelihood of addressing economic inequalities in U.S. society created by domestic and multinational capitalism in the short term, especially given the political support reparations campaigns have received over the last few years nationally and internationally.

Reparations for Native Americans and U.S. African Americans

It should be noted that "reparatory justice" includes not just African-descended peoples demands for reparations from former colonial powers, governmental agencies, and private institutions and corporations that sanctioned or engaged in slavery, slave trading, convict leasing, redlining, and other forms of economic exploitation and discrimination. In the past, successful reparatory justice campaigns have resulted in the Germans' compensation to Jews in Germany and Israel following the Holocaust and World War II; and to the U.S. federal government's payment of reparations to Japanese Americans who were removed from their homes and placed in internment camps in the western states. When the Japanese military attacked the Aleutian Islands in 1942, the U.S. military ordered the evacuation and internment of the Aleuts in "unheated, crowded barracks and vacant buildings." Historian Haunani-Kay Trask found that given the poor treatment and "inadequate health care . . . 10 percent or more of the Aleuts died in captivity." Under the terms of the Civil Liberties Act of 1988, a formal apology was included and Japanese American internees received $20,000 and Aleut internees received $12,000. More recently, the North Carolina legislature authorized "reparations payments" to victims of "forced sterilization" by state officials seeking to ruin their reproductive capacities. In the case of the Native Hawaiians, following invasion and occupation in 1893, the U.S. government never recognized the indigenous peoples' entitlement to public lands or their right of self-determination; and they are still seeking reparations and recognition as a "native nation" similar to the "American Indian nations."[1]

Some have argued that in terms of "human rights violations," the enslavement of Africans and African Americans in the United States was "somewhat less severe than that suffered by Native Americans." Philosopher J. Angelo Corlett reminds us that "as a general rule African slaves were not the subjects of massive killings or of a genocide, as were Native Americans." Therefore, under the "principle of proportionality," reparations for Native Americans "ought to be greater than reparations paid to African Americans." The recognition of Indigenous peoples' status as "domestic dependent nations" meant that the federal government initially negotiated treaties with the "governing bodies" of Native American ethnic groups and communities. These treaties were soon broken, however, and some funds were distributed to Indian tribes through the Bureau of Indian Affairs (BIA), but with many strings attached. From the standpoint of U.S. politicians and BIA officials, removing Native American children from their families and placing them in boarding schools where they would become "assimilated" was a form of "reparations payment."[2]

With and without formal treaties, the federal government assumed ownership of large swaths of land in the Midwest and Far West claimed by Native Americans. Designated "public lands" by U.S. officials, following the passage of the Homestead Act and Morrill Land Grant College Act in 1862, federal agencies surveyed and sold public lands to white farmers and ranchers resulting in a form of "settler colonialism." Under the Homestead Act, 84 million acres were eventually sold to settlers, and the railroad companies were granted 127 million acres. The taking of Native American land allowed Europeans and

Euro-Americans and their families to stake claims to the land. However, historian Margaret Nash found that over the long term "more land was bought by speculators and large-scale agribusinesses than by individual farmers." And while the establishment of the land-grant colleges was considered "democratizing higher education" by supporting "manual and industrial training," she pointed out that "the sale of public land to support higher education was one side of the more pronounced purpose of settling the West."[3]

An estimated ten million acres of land was sold by the federal government to fund the land grant colleges and each state was allowed thirty thousand acres for each congressional representative. At the same time, the native peoples were removed from their land and placed on small reservations. "The 'harmonious West' was a white-dominated West," Nash concluded, "and the 'common vision' depended on eradicating Native Americans from their homelands." Nash argues that Native Americans have a right to demand reparations from these land grant colleges, given the native peoples' loss of their territories to establish them. There is a need to move beyond "land acknowledgement statements," in which the universities simply note that their "founding came at a dire cost to native nations and peoples" who originally lived on these lands. Ojibwa educator Rachel Mishenene declared, "A land acknowledgement without action is just a statement." What is needed is the funding of scholarships and educational services for Native American students at land grant colleges, the establishment of courses and programs on the cultures of the Indigenous peoples, and economic and educational outreach projects to Native American communities in the area.[4]

In the name of reparatory justice, the internationally recognized "principle" of "morally just acquisitions and transfers" must be applied to the conditions for both Native Americans and African Americans. "For whatever is acquired or transferred by morally just means is itself morally just," J. Angelo Corbett pointed out, "and whatever is acquired or transferred by morally unjust means is itself morally unjust."[5] Reparatory justice requires restitution for the loss of property and lands, but also repair of damage done to people and places in relentless pursuit of financial profit. Beginning in 2012 in the United States, such a reparatory justice campaign was launched against the major pharmaceutical companies for creating and profiting from the devastating opioid epidemic.

Reparations from "Big Pharma"

The attorneys general in forty-eight states sued the pharmaceutical makers who sold highly addictive opioid drugs in large quantities in pursuit of huge financial profits. Purdue Pharma, the maker of the pain medication Oxy-Contin, has been the subject of numerous lawsuits because it downplayed the addictive nature of the drug and lied about its benefits. Privately owned by the Sackler family, prosecutors found that Purdue Pharma's marketing agents encouraged physicians to prescribe the drug in higher and higher doses, leading to a public health crisis. California Attorney General Xavier Becerra declared "Purdue [Pharma] and the Sacklers traded the health and well-being of Californians for profit and created an unprecedented national public health crisis in the process." OxyContin came on the market in 1996 and according to the U.S. Centers for Diseases and Prevention, between 1999 and 2017 nearly 218,000 Americans died from overdoses from prescription opioids.[6]

The broad-based damage created by the opioid crisis in the United States has been documented in numerous newspaper and magazine articles, scholarly articles, and investigative reports.[7] Beth Macy's *Dopesick: Dealers, Doctors, and the Drug Company That Addicted America* documents the impact of opioid addiction on the lives of individuals in three parts of the country: the coal-producing area in Lee County, Virginia; the town of Strasburg in southern Virginia; and Hazelton, West Virginia. Macy quoted Purdue Pharma's point-man, Dr. J. David Haddox, who announced in 1996, "If you take the medicine like it is prescribed, the risk of addiction when taking the opioid is one-half of 1 percent." At that time many health care experts believed that "pain had been grossly undertreated" and Purdue Pharma sought to address this problem with the drug OxyContin. However, the Sacklers' and other pharmaceutical manufacturers' greed led to an opioid epidemic that devastated and destroyed thousands of lives and communities.[8]

The lawsuits filed by private individuals and government officials against "Big Pharma" are manifestations of an ethos of reparatory justice. Not unlike the transatlantic slave traders and the slaveholders in North and South America before 1865, the pharmaceutical companies engaged unscrupulous activities and practices to increase their profits and had deadly consequences and reparatory justice is now being sought.

Reparations from the Petrochemical Companies

Another sector of the economy where powerful multinational corporations seeking huge profits have done great damage to individuals and communities has been the petrochemical industry. For example, the state of Louisiana has the highest proportion of any state of petrochemical companies operating within its borders. Yet given the damage that these oil and gas companies have done to the people and the environment, Louisiana has been dubbed a "Polluters' Paradise."

Extensive investigative reports carried out and published by the *Times Picayune/New Orleans Advocate* revealed that "Louisiana's 100 year romance with the petrochemical companies has come with an undeniably steep human price tag. Tens of thousands of people, living cheek-by-jowl to belching plants along the Mississippi River, are exposed to toxic chemicals at rates that are the highest in the country."[9] The researchers found that "the new chemical plants are being built in the most polluted areas" due to the increased production of "cheap natural gas"; and poor communities in the "chemical corridor" bear "the brunt of Louisiana's toxic pollution, but wealthy ones aren't immune." Moreover, recent Environmental Protection Agency's (EPA) rules for reducing the carcinogenic emissions from the thirteen petrochemical plants operating between Baton Rouge and New Orleans will have no effect because the planned Formosa Chemicals Plant in St. James Parish will soon add to the toxic ethylene oxide already emitted in the area.[10]

Environmental justice advocates have dubbed the chemical corridor "Death Alley" and groups such as the Coalition against Death Alley (CADA) have organized demonstrations, marches, and sit-ins to protest the new plants and demand compensation for those who are being victimized by the pollution. In St. John the Baptist Parish, the Denks/Dupont Plant has been emitting a hundred-times the recommended limit of chloroprene for decades and the low-income Black residents have been suffering the consequences. One study found that those living in St. John's Parish have a risk of having cancer 800 times the national average. Local residents formed social protest organizations, lobbied state officials and industry executives, and organized marches and rallies in an attempt to get limitations placed on plant emissions. In addition, given the huge number of petrochemical plants and workers in St. John Parish, there is even the possibility that should an evacuation be needed, local residents would be crowded out along the highways. Inadequate provisions for emergencies currently exist as plans are being made to construct a new $9.4 billion plastics plant.[11]

Although the environmental activists in CADA and other groups that have organized these protests and called for financial compensation for those living in Death Alley or "Cancer Alley," they have not referred to this grassroots movement as a "reparations campaign," but this is clearly a campaign for reparatory justice. Despite the fact that in a recent settlement Formosa, the Taiwanese Plastics Company, had to pay the state of Texas $50 million because its chemical plant had been polluting the state's waterways, the Louisiana Department of Environmental Quality (DEQ) plans to approve the construction of the plastics plant in St. James Parish, despite receiving over 15,000 letters of complaint from residents and local environmental organizations.[12] From the initial studies published in the 1980s by Robert D. Bullard and others, to the 2019 newspaper series on the "Polluters' Paradise," environmental racism has been exposed and documented and campaigns for reparatory justice have been organized by groups and communities damaged by the petrochemical industry.[13]

Reparations Superfund and Student Loan Debt

The problem of the huge student debt in the United States is not just about young people taking out tens of thousands of dollars in loans to pursue a college degree or professional certification. The federal government created policies that facilitated the financial corruption in the student loan practices particularly at proprietary schools, "technical institutes," and for-profit online "colleges" and "universities" over the last three decades. Many have pointed out that the U.S. Department of Education's policy allowing these online diploma mills to receive up to 90 percent of their annual income from the federally backed student loan funds fueled the student loan debt crisis. The for-profit programs' marketing agents received huge bonuses for signing up young people eligible for federally funded student loans. In addition, these former students have been victimized doubly because the Department of Education in the past refused to forgive the loans, even at schools and programs subsequently closed by federal officials.[14]

The disparities and disadvantages in student loan debt require repair because in many instances the students have been doubly damaged. Not only have they gone into debt, in entering the employment market with these "online degrees" from uncertified programs they have rarely advanced their professional careers. And the disproportionate debt owed by African Americans and other students of color is the result of young people being targeted by educational recruiters hired by these for-profit schools. There was little oversight from educational or government agencies who instituted these practices and billions of dollars in federal funds flowed and continues to flow into the coffers of the owners of the for-profit online schools, while student loan debt cripples the financial future of tens of thousands of young people.[15]

In pursuit of reparatory justice in the twenty-first century, this is an issue on which social activists need to take action. Just as individual philanthropists have agreed to assume the student loan debt of graduating students at More-house College and medical students at New York University, the establish-ment of a national "Reparations Superfund" would accept financial contribu-tions to intervene on a larger scale and provide alternative ways to discharge student loan debt for individuals and specific groups. Over the last few years, several religious and higher educational institutions have acknowledged that much of the wealth accumulated in the eighteenth and nineteenth centuries came from slavery and slave trading. Oftentimes spurred by current student activists, these schools have established "reparations funds" that will make available financial resources for the education of African-descended stu-dents. At Georgetown University the student body voted to contribute to the university's reparations fund through their student fees, while at Virginia Theological Seminary, students unearthed the ties to slavery and slave trad-ing and the trustees agreed to establish a reparations fund aimed at African American students, providing scholarships and other financial resources.[16]

In the twenty-first century, no student of African descent should graduate in debt from colleges and universities whose great wealth and endowments can be traced directly to slavery and slave trading in the eighteenth and nineteenth century. The goal of student activists should be the establish-ment of a "reparations fund" on each campus with the objective of having African-descended students leave debt-free. At the public state universities, reparations funds should be established to address the under-enrollment of students of color compared to their percentage in the state population. In Wisconsin, for example, African Americans are 6 percent of the popula-tion, but in Madison at the flagship university in the 2018–19 school year, there were fewer than 1,000 Black students in a total enrollment of 35,000. The goal of the reparatory justice campaign is to address this racial dispar-ity in enrollment in publicly funded state universities and colleges.[17] Student activists at the University of Wisconsin and other state universities should demand that a nonprofit university foundation be established to serve as the "reparations fund" that would use the financial resources provided by the university, state legislature, and philanthropy to increase the number and percentage of African-descended and other students of color enrolled and to insure that they graduate debt free.

At the same time, the Reparations Superfund would focus on eliminating loan debt by providing scholarship funds for students enrolled at the histori-cally Black colleges, at community colleges and four-year private colleges, and other institutions of higher education where reparations funds have *not* been established. And whereas the reparations funds established at public state universities would seek out financial contributions from that region, the Reparations Superfund would seek donations from national and multinational corporations and from specific industries that have done damage to children and students of color. For example, the corporations that make up the testing industry in the United States should be targeted to provide substantial compensation for the damage that the tests have done to the education and careers of African Americans and other people of color historically and currently.[18]

Reparations from the Testing Industry

It would be difficult to calculate the magnitude of the damage done by the movement for "mental testing" and the proliferation of "intelligence tests" to African-descended men, women, and children, as well as other children of color, in the twentieth century. Whereas the original "Binet-Simon Intelligence Test" was created in the early 1900s to identify "feeble-minded" children in the French public schools, when educators and psychologists translated and introduced them in U.S. public schools, the test results were used to justify racial segregation and discrimination against students and teachers of color. Oftentimes the justification for providing African Americans and other children of color "separate and unequal" public schooling was based on their performance on "intelligence" tests. The argument was made that it would be a waste of (white) taxpayers' money to spend the same amounts on the schooling of Black and white children.[19]

Beginning in the 1930s with the assistance of NAACP attorneys, African American public school teachers who were paid less than comparably trained and experienced white educators in southern school districts filed successful lawsuits to obtain "salary equalization."[20] However, with the introduction of the National Teachers' Examination (NTE) in the early 1940s, legal scholar Scott Baker found that the "new merit system" was based on test results, and 84 percent of the white teachers who took the NTE were placed at the highest salary rank, and 80 percent of the Black teachers were in the lowest rank. In two separate court rulings, in *Turner v. Keefe* (1945) and *Reynolds v. Board of Education of Dade County, FL* (1945), the new merit system was upheld because no evidence was presented to show that the new ratings system was applied in a racially discriminatory fashion. But there has been no evidence that teachers' scores on the NTE could predict performance in the classroom.[21]

The debt owed to students and teachers of color from the testing industry is enormous, especially since the introduction of "high stakes testing" following the implementation of the Bush administration's "No Child Left Behind" program and the funding for "Race to the Top" during the Obama years. The Educational Testing Service, the Pearson Corporation, and other testing companies spent millions lobbying the U.S. Congress to require more and more testing and reaped billions of dollars in profits. And in school systems throughout the country, there has been the widespread substitution of courses and instruction in the arts, music, science, history, and other subjects not included in the high-stakes testing with hours upon hours devoted to "test preparation."[22]

The increasing classroom time spent on "test prep" and the amount of testing taking place has spawned the "Opt-Out" movement in which tens of thousands of middle- and upper-class parents requested that their children not take the "standardized tests" because they do not measure the things they sent their children to school to learn. African American and other children of color have been *the most harmed* by "the testing charade" and they too need to boycott or "Opt out" of the standardized testing until the testing corporations have paid reparations for the damage they have done in the past and currently to African Americans and other children of color.[23] Reparations payments made to individual school districts from the testing corporations should be used to support alternative educational spaces and programs that do not depend on standardized testing to achieve mastery. Indeed, these would be places where the educators are held accountable for their practices and *participate in* the creation of specific forms of evaluation.

The demands for reparations to repair the damage done in the past and currently to African Americans and other people of color by colleges and universities that amassed great wealth from slavery and slave trading should be joined by campaigns mounted by those who have been damaged by the greedy and fraudulent practices of the pharmaceutical industry, the petrochemical companies, the for-profit online schools, and the testing industry. The reparatory justice movement is needed to bring about a redistribution of the wealth in the United States and to repair the damage that corporate capitalists and federal and state governments have done to individuals, groups, and communities in the past and present. In the twenty-first century, reparations movements must address the extreme economic inequality that currently exists in the United States and other developed and developing countries.

Notes

1. Haunani-Kay Trask, "Restitution as a Precondition of Reconciliation: Native Hawaiians and Indigenous Human Rights," in *Who Should Pay? Slavery and the Raging Debate on Reparations*, ed. Raymond A. Winbush (New York: Amistad/ Harper Collins, 2003), quote on 34.

2. David Robert Adams, *Education for Extinction: American Indians and the Boarding School Experience, 1875–1928* (Lawrence: University of Kansas, 1995); Robert A. Trennert, *The Phoenix School: Forced Assimilation in Arizona, 1891–1935* (Norman: University of Oklahoma Press, 1988); Ward Churchill, *Kill the Indian, Save the Man: The Genocidal Impact of American Indian Residential Schools* (San Francisco, CA: City Lights Publishers, 2004).

3. Margaret A. Nash, "Entangled Pasts: Land Grant Colleges and American Indian Dispossession," *History of Educational Quarterly* 59 (November 2019): 440.

4. Margaret A. Nash, "The Dark History of Land Grant Universities," *Washington Post*, November 8, 2019.

5. J. Angelo Corlett, "Reparations for African Americans," in *Redress for Historical Injustices in the United States: On Reparations for Slavery, Jim Crow, and Their Legacies*, ed. Michael T. Martin and Marilyn Yaquinto (Durham, NC: Duke University Press, 2007), quote on 180.

6. Berkeley Lovelace, "Nearly Every U.S. State Is Now Suing OxyContin-Maker Purdue Pharma," *CNBC*, June 4, 2019.

7. Listed in its bibliography are hundreds of sources on the opioid epidemic; see Beth Macy, *Dopesick: Dealers, Doctors, and the Drug Company That Addicted America* (New York: Little Brown, 2018), 313–63.

8. Ibid., quote on 20–21; see also Jonathan M. Metzl, *Dying of Whiteness: How the Politics of Racial Resentment Is Killing America's Heartland* (New York: Basic Books, 2019).

9. Mark Schleifstein, "Louisiana Is Backsliding After Making Environmental Progress," *Times Picayune/New Orleans Advocate*, October 30, 2019.

10. Mark Schleifstein, "New EPA Rules for Reducing Emissions of Ethylene Oxide Won't Apply to Most Louisiana Plants," *Times Picayune/New Orleans Advocate*, November 14, 2019.

11. Gordon Russell, "Corporate Desires or Environmental Protection? In Louisiana, One Takes a Back Seat to the Other," *Times Picayune/New Orleans Advocate*, December 19, 2019.

12. Lylla Younes, "'We're Already Devastated': St. James Parish Residents' Opposition Not Likely to Derail Planned Formosa Plant," *Times Picayune/New Orleans Advocate*, November 14, 2019.

13. Robert D. Bullard, ed., *Unequal Protection: Environmental Racism and Communities of Color* (New York: Random House, 1994); and *The Quest of Environmental Justice: Human Rights and the Politics of Pollution* (New York: Counterpoint Pub-

lishers, 2005); Dorceta Taylor, *Toxic Communities: Environmental Racism, Industrial Pollution, and Residential Mobility* (New York: New York University Press, 2014); Carl A. Zimring, *Clean and White: A History of Environmental Racism in the United States* (New York: New York University Press, 2016).

14. Democrats in Congress pressed the Education Department to discharge the loans of defrauded students; see Erica Bacon, "After Months of Delay, [Betsy] DeVos Touts Limited Student Loan Forgiveness," *Roll Call*, December 12, 2019.

15. Zack Friedman, "Why 100,000 People Never Got Student Loan Forgiveness," *Forbes Magazine*, December 19, 2019.

16. For a summary of the formation of reparations funds at Georgetown and other universities, see Carolyn Thompson, "Reparations Mark New Front for U.S. Colleges Tied to Slavery," *Times Picayune/New Orleans Advocate*, December 15, 2019.

17. Julie Bosman et al., "In a Homecoming Video Meant to Unite Campus, Almost Everyone Was White," *New York Times*, January 1, 2020. While African American students at the University of Wisconsin participated in making the video, they were not included in the final version.

18. V. P. Franklin, "Introduction: African Americans and Movements for Reparations: From the Ex-Slave Pensions to the Reparations Superfund," *Journal of African American History* 97 (Winter-Spring 2012): 1–12.

19. V. P. Franklin, "Black Social Scientists and the Mental Testing Movement, 1920–1940," in *Black Psychology*, 2nd Edition, ed. Reginald Jones (New York: Harper and Row, 1980), 201–15.

20. John A. Kirk, "The NAACP Campaign for Teachers' Salary Equalization: African American Women Educators and the Early Civil Rights Struggle," *Journal of African American History* 94 (Fall 2009): 529–52.

21. Scott Baker, "Testing Equality: The National Teachers' Examination and the NAACP's Legal Campaign to Equalize Teachers' Salaries in the South," *History of Education Quarterly* 35 (Winter 1996): 49–64; Michael Fultz, "The Displacement of Black Educators Post *Brown*: An Overview and Analysis," *History of Education Quarterly* 44 (Winter 2004): 11–45; and V. P. Franklin, "The Tests Are Written for the Dogs: *The Journal of Negro Education*, African American Children, and the Intelligence Testing Movement in Historical Perspective," *The Journal of Negro Education* 76 (Summer 2007): 216–29.

22. Diane Ravitch, *The Death and Life of the Great American School System: How Testing and Choice Are Undermining Education* (New York: Basic Books, 2010); and *Reign of Error: The Hoax of the Privatization Movement and the Danger to America's Public Schools* (New York: Vintage Books, 2013).

23. Daniel Koretz, *The Testing Charade: Pretending to Make Schools Better* (Chicago: University of Chicago Press, 2017).

Acknowledgments

Thanks to the editors and everyone at the University of Illinois Press and my co-editors without whom this project would never have seen the light of day. Also, I owe a special debt to the late Detroit activist Christopher Alston who first told me about the pioneering Callie House, organizer of the post–Civil War reparations struggle.

—Mary Frances Berry

Asante Sana (Thank you very much) to my fellow editors for their contributions to the African American and global struggle of African descendants for reparations and to this important project. Asante to our contributing authors for producing engaging, thought-provoking, and fresh essays on a topic whose time has come. And thanks to the University of Illinois Press, particularly Dawn Durante, for initially recognizing the value of this project and Dominique Moore for seeing it through to fruition.

—Sundiata Keita Cha-Jua

I would like to thank and acknowledge the support and assistance from those in the local, state, national, and global reparations movement in general, and in the production of this volume in particular, including my co-editors Mary Frances Berry and Sundiata Keita Cha-Jua, and Sir Hilary McD. Beckles, Dr. Ron Daniels, Nkechi Taifa, Esq., Kamm Howard, Dr. Joyce E. King, Lionel Baptiste, Esq., Sylvia Cyrus, Bettye Collier-Thomas, Sheila Flemming Hunter, Dr. Cheryl Grills, Robin Rue Simmons, and the other members of the National African American Reparations Commission. A Luta Continua.

—V. P. Franklin

Contributors

Dedrick Asante-Muhammad serves as the Chief of Race, Wealth and Community for the National Community Reinvestment Coalition. Asante-Muhammad has authored numerous studies on the racial wealth gap for organizations such the Institute for Policy Studies and United for a Fair Economy. He has worked for the National Association for the Advancement of Colored People's Economic Department and the National Action Network.

Vice Chancellor of the University of the West Indies, Sir **Hilary McD. Beckles** is a well-respected historian who has chaired the Caribbean Community (CARICOM) Reparations Commissions since its formation in 2013. Beckles is the author of numerous award-winning books in the areas of sports, enslavement, colonialism, and reparations, including his groundbreaking work on reparations, *How Britain Underdeveloped the Caribbean: A Reparation Response to Europe's Legacy of Plunder and Poverty* (University Press of the West Indies, 2021) and *Britain's Black Debt: Reparations for Caribbean Slavery and Native Genocide* (University Press of the West Indies, 2013).

Mary Frances Berry, Ph.D., J.D., is the Geraldine R. Segal Professor of American Social Thought, History, and Africana Studies at the University of Pennsylvania. The recipient of numerous honors for her scholarship and activism, Dr. Berry received the American Historical Society's first Lewis Award for History and Social Justice in 2021, in memory of the late civil rights leader and Georgia Congressman John Lewis. The award recognizes her leadership and engagement at the intersection of historical work, public culture, and social justice. In 2012, she received the Nelson Mandela Award from the South African government for her role in organizing the Free South Africa Movement in the United States. Its advocacy for sanctions against trade with South Africa was instrumental in the passage of legislation that helped end apartheid. She was the chief education official of the United States during the Carter administration and served on the U.S. Commission on Civil Rights during five presidential administrations, first as a member and then as chair. Her books include *Black Resistance/White Law: A History of Constitutional Racism in America* (1971, expanded ed. 1994), *My Face Is Black Is True: Callie House and the Struggle for Ex-Slave Reparations* (2005), and *History Teaches Us to Resist: How Progressive Movements Have Succeeded in Challenging Times* (2018).

Sundiata Keita Cha-Jua teaches in the departments of African American Studies and History at the University of Illinois at Urbana-Champaign. He authored *America's First Black Town, Brooklyn, Illinois, 1830–1915* (2000), co-edited *Race Struggles* (University of Illinois Press, 2009) with Theodore Koditschek and Helen Neville, and has published scores of articles in leading Black/Africana Studies, History, and Left journals. Cha-Jua was President of the National Council for Black Studies, 2010–12, 2012–14; Senior Editor of *The Black Scholar*, 2011–15; and Associate Editor of the *Journal of African American* History, 2015–18. He is currently an organizer for the Malcolm X Grassroots Movement.

Chuck Collins directs the Program on Inequality for the Common Good at the Institute for Policy Studies. He is the author of several books, most recently, *Born on Third Base: A One Percenter Makes the Case for Tackling Inequality, Brining Wealth Home, and Committing to the Common Good.* In 1995, he co-founded United for a Fair Economy.

Ron Daniels is Founder and President of the Institute for the Black World, 21st Century (IBW). He has been a prominent activist in the Black Liberation movement since the 1970s. Daniels was the Executive Director of the National Rainbow Coalition in 1987 and Southern Regional Coordinator and Deputy Campaign Manager for the Jesse Jackson for President Campaign in 1988. From 1993–2005, Dr. Daniels served as first African American Executive Director of the Center for Constitutional Rights (CCR). Following the formation of the Caribbean Reparations Commission in 2014, Daniels convened the National African American Reparations Commission to begin the development of a global reparations program for the 21st century. Dr. Daniels's column *Vantage Point* appears in numerous Black and progressive newspapers and websites. In 2019, he published *Still On this Journey: The Vision and Mission of Dr. Ron Daniels*. Daniels is the Distinguished Lecturer Emeritus, York College, City University of New York.

Allen J. Davis, Ed.D. is a reparationist, racial justice, and democracy activist, and educator. He has been a dean at the Western College of Miami University (OH), Sarah Lawrence College, and Northfield Mount Hermon School, as well as the Executive Director of the United Way of Franklin County (MA), 20/20 Vision, a national peace and environmental organization, and the Greenfield Community College Foundation (MA). Davis serves on the Coordinating Committee of Racial Justice Rising, a grassroots organization in western MA. He organizes educational programs about racism at libraries, community centers, and churches in MA and NH. In 2018, he established the James Baldwin Lecture in conjunction with the History Department at the University of Massachusetts, Amherst, his alma mater. He has also served on many nonprofit boards, including the Greenfield Community College Board of Trustees, the Karuna Center for Peacebuilding, and the Bill of Rights Defense Committee.

V. P. Franklin is the Distinguished Professor Emeritus of History and Education at the University of California, Riverside. Dr. Franklin is the former editor of *The Journal of African American History* (*JAAH*), formerly *The Journal of Negro History*, the leading scholarly publication on African American life and history. During his editorship between 2001 and 2018, five *JAAH* articles received awards for "scholarly excellence in historical research" from national and international organizations. Dr. Franklin is the author or coeditor of eleven books, including *The Education of Black Philadelphia* (1979); *Black Self-Determination: A Cultural History of African American Resistance* (1984, 1992), *Message in the Music: Hip Hop, History, and Pedagogy* (2010), and most recently, *The Young Crusaders: The Untold Story of the Children and Teenagers Who Galvanized the Civil Rights Movement* (2021). He has published over seventy scholarly articles on African American history and education. He has received many awards and honors, and in 2022 the first "V. P. Franklin Legacy Award" will be presented by the Association for the Study of African American Life and History (ASALH) for the best article published in the *JAAH* between 2019 and 2021.

Adom Getachew is the Neubauer Family Assistant Professor of Political Science at the University of Chicago. She is a political theorist whose intellectual interests include the history of political thought, theories of race and empire, and postcolonial political theory. Her work primarily focuses on African and Caribbean intellectual and political histories. She is the author of *World-making After Empire: The Rise and Fall of Self-Determination* (Princeton University Press, 2020). Getachew is a co-chair of Scholars for Social Justice the Reparations Platform.

Actor, director, and human rights activist **Danny Glover** has been at the forefront of humanitarian and social justice campaigns for decades. In 1991, Glover won an Independent Spirit Award for his lead role in *To Sleep with Anger*. He co-founded with Ben Gillery the Robey Theatre in Los Angeles, California. He has been nominated for four Grammy Awards, and two Screen Actor Guild Awards, and he won a Daytime Emmy Award. Glover has received two NAACP Image Awards. He has also won awards for his social justice, humanitarian, and racial justice work, including the NAACP President's Award, the Cuban National Medal of Friendship, and the Academy of Motion Pictures and Arts and Sciences' Jean Hersholt Humanitarian Award.

Charles P. Henry is professor emeritus of African American Studies at UC-Berkeley. He holds a doctorate in political science from the University of Chicago and is the author/editor of nine books including *Long Overdue: The Politics of Racial Reparations*. Henry is also the author of over eighty articles and reviews on Black politics, public policy, and human rights. He is the past president of the National Council for Black Studies and past board chair of Amnesty International USA. President Clinton appointed Henry to a term on the National Humanities Council in 1994, and he was a distinguished Fulbright Chair in Italy in 2003 and France in 2006. He has also taught at Howard and Denison Universities.

Kamm Howard is a Chicago businessman and real estate investor. Kamm is internationally respected for his reparations work. Howard has been a 16-year member of the National Coalition of Blacks for Reparations in America, N'COBRA, the longest running active organization championing the cause of reparations in the United States. In 2017, Howard was elected to lead N'COBRA as its National Male Co-Chair. He was re-elected in 2019, for a second term. He is the author of *Laying the Foundations for Local Reparations: A Guide for Providing National Symmetry for Local Reparations Efforts* (independently published, 2020).

Earl Ofari Hutchinson is a prominent journalist, social commentator, and activist. He hosts *The Hutchinson Report*, a live call-in program on Pacifica

Radio outlet KPFK-FM radio in Los Angeles. Hutchinson is the founder of the Los Angeles Urban Roundtable. The LAUR provides seed grants to grassroots organizations and sponsors community forums. He has authored seventeen books, including the popular *The Myth of Black Capitalism* (970) and is a two-time recipient of the Gustavus Meyers Center Outstanding Book Award for *Blacks and Reds: Race and Class in Conflict, 1919–1990* (1995) and *Betrayed: A History of Presidential Failure to Protect Black Lives* (1996).

Civil rights leader **Jesse Jackson**, founder of People United to Save Humanity (PUSH), has been active in social justice campaigns for over five decades. At the National/International Reparations Summit held in New York City in April 2015, Rev. Jackson delivered the keynote address in which he focused on the exploitation of African Americans under slavery and the failure to protect formerly enslaved workers from exploitation and oppression in the post-emancipation period.

Brian P. Jones is a New York City educator, actor, and activist. He is the inaugural director of the New York Public Library's Center for Educators and Schools and the former Associate Director of Education at the Schomburg Center for Research in Black Culture. A former member of the International Socialist Organization and a candidate for New York Lieutenant Governor in 2014 on the Green Party ticket, Jones has written work appearing in the *New York Times*, *Huffington Post*, *Jacobin*, and *Socialist Worker*.

Sheila Jackson Lee, a Democratic Representative from Texas who was first elected to Congress in 1994, chaired a hearing where she issued her opening statement on the introduction of H.R. 40: the "Commission to study and Develop Reparation Proposals for African Americans Act," on January 7, 2019. Lee makes clear the intent to study slavery's responsibility for the enduring economic inequality experienced by descendants of the formerly enslaved as well as the moral harm done by the institution.

The National African American Reparations Commission (NAARC) was convened and is administered by the Institute of the Black World 21st Century (IBW). NAARC fights for reparatory justice, recompense, and repair of African American communities that were ravaged by the crimes against humanity: the slave trade, enslavement, racial terrorism, and apartheid. In response to the Caribbean Reparations Commission 2014 10-Point Plan for Reparations, NAARC issued its 10-Point Plan for African American reparations in

2015. Organized in 1987, the National Coalition of Blacks for Reparations in America (N'COBRA) is a mass-based coalition composed of both individual members and organizations whose sole mission is to obtain reparations for African Americans. In 2003, N'COBRA incorporated the N'COBRA Legal Defense, Research and Education Fund to educate the public and broaden the support base for Black reparations. N'COBRA played a leading role in the updating of HR 40, an act to "establish a Commission to Study and Develop Reparation Proposals for African Americans."

The New Afrikan Peoples Organization (NAPO) was formed in 1984 by diverse revolutionary nationalists working in different formations in the New Afrikan Independence Movement (NAIM). NAPO seeks to build popular support to pursue the creation of an autonomous Black nation-state more effectively. In 1990, NAPO organized the Malcolm X Grassroots Movement (MXGM) as a mass-based organization whose primary focus was to incorporate the idea of self-determination and the objective of reparations into Black peoples' protracted everyday struggles for basic human rights.

Organized in 2017, **Scholars for Social Justice** (SSJ) is a collective of progressive scholars who are committed to using their knowledge, skills, and resources to defend and fight for justice for all, especially the most marginalized communities. SSJ is especially focused on transforming universities and colleges. It seeks to move universities away from neoliberal policies of austerity that wrap educational objectives and that divert from and diminish marginalized communities' access to educational resources. Therefore, SSJ organizes around elimination of student loan debt, fair treatment of campus workers, downgrading of arts and humanities departments and initiatives, and the diminution of academic freedom for faculty.

James B. Stewart is a Senior Fellow at the New School's Institute on Race, Power, and Political Economy and Director of the Black Economic Research Center for the 21st Century. Both organizations conduct research linked to the Reparations Movement. Stewart, a Professor Emeritus at Penn State University, has published fifteen books, including *Introduction to African American Studies, Transdisciplinary Approaches and Implications*, and over eighty articles in Economics and Africana Studies professional journals. He is a founder of Stratification Economics, a new Economics subfield that integrates insights from multiple disciplines to produce distinctive analyses of inter-group economic inequality.

Index

Alexander, Michelle, 44

American Civil War, 28, 76, 100; and Black migration, 206; democracy, 209; Frederick Douglass on, 97, 158; federal property confiscation and taxation, 160; William Henry, 204; Abraham Lincoln, 206; medical issues, 145; nutritional deprivation, 148; postwar compensation requests, 1–2; postwar forty-acres legislation, 27–28, 93; reparations, 50, 68, 231; veterans, 160

Anderson, Henry Anderson, 19–20, 135–37, 141, 150–51. *See also* Stewart, James B.

Anderson, Jourdan, 19–20, 135–37, 141, 150, 152n2. *See also* Stewart, James B.

Araujo, Ana Lucia, 16, 183

Arbery, Ahmaud, 15

Argentina, 34, 89; and Raúl Alfonsín, 34; Comisión Nacional Sobre la Desaparición de Personas (National Commission on the Disappearance of Persons), 34

Asante-Muhammad, Dedrick, 6, 20, 22, 233; and *Born on Third Base: A One Percenter Makes the Case for Tackling Inequality, Bringing Wealth Home, and Committing to the Common Good* (Collins), 172; Civil Liberties Act of 1988, 172; Ta-Nehisi Coates, 170–71; Chuck Collins, 170–77; John Conyers Jr., 174; "Facing History and Ourselves" curriculum, 175; forty acres, 174; Holocaust, 173, 175; home ownership, 170, 172, 174–75; Homestead Act, 174; House Resolution 40, 174; Jim Crow,

170, 173; mass incarceration, 173; National Museum of African American History and Culture, 175; Nazi occupation (Greece, Russia), 173; Prosperity Now, 171; pro-White affirmative action, 172; reparations trust fund, 173; Randall Robinson, 170; Stolperstein (stumbling stones), 175; tuition, 175; Tulsa, Oklahoma, 175; wealth inequality, 170–75; Gabriel Zucman, 174. *See also* Collins, Chuck

Beckles, Hilary McD., 17–18, 21, 231, 233; and African Holocaust, 88; Maya Angelou, 87; *Britain's Black Debt: Reparations for Slavery and Native Genocide* (2013), 1, 16; Caribbean Community (CARICOM), 10–11, 21, 54, 87–88; enslavement, 13, 83–86, 233; Eurasian and European countries' slavery denials, 84–85; General History of Africa projects, 85; Martin Luther King Jr., 86–87; Sam Kutesa, 83, 85, 88; Papa Legba, 83; Abraham Lincoln, 86; Malcolm X, 87; Nelson Mandela, 87; William Murray, 1st Earl of Mansfield, 83–84; National Reparations Commissions, 87; Slave Routes project, 85; François-Dominique Toussaint Louverture (Toussaint L'Ouverture, Toussaint Bréda), 86–87; Harriet Tubman, 87; UNESCO (United Nations Educational, Scientific and Cultural Organization), 85–86; United Nations, 17, 18, 21, 83–87; Working Group of Experts on People of African Descent, 83

The University of Illinois Press
is a founding member of the
Association of University Presses.

———————————————————

Composed in 10.5/13 Adobe Minion Pro
by Lisa Connery
at the University of Illinois Press
Manufactured by Versa Press, Inc.

University of Illinois Press
1325 South Oak Street
Champaign, IL 61820-6903
www.press.uillinois.edu